Summary of Contents

Preface ix
1. Installation 1
2. Getting Started with MySQL 29
3. Getting Started with PHP 43
4. Publishing MySQL Data on the Web 67
5. Relational Database Design 85
6. A Content Management System 101
7. Content Formatting and Submission 143
8. MySQL Administration 165
9. Advanced SQL Queries 183
10. Binary Data 199
11. Cookies and Sessions in PHP 221
12. Structured PHP Programming 235
A. MySQL Syntax 277
B. MySQL Functions 301
C. MySQL Column Types 321
D. PHP Functions for Working with MySQL 331
Index 345

Build Your Own Database Driven Website Using PHP & MySQL

by Kevin Yank

Build Your Own Database Driven Website Using PHP & MySQL

by Kevin Yank

Copyright © 2004 SitePoint Pty. Ltd.

Editor: Georgina Laidlaw   **Index Editor**: Bill Johncocks
Managing Editor: Simon Mackie   **Cover Design**: Julian Carroll
Printing History:
  First Edition: August 2001
  Second Edition: February 2003
  Third Edition: October 2004

Published by SitePoint Pty. Ltd.

424 Smith Street Collingwood
VIC Australia 3066.
Web: www.sitepoint.com
Email: business@sitepoint.com

ISBN 0–9752402–1–8
Printed and bound in the United States of America

About the Author

As Technical Director for SitePoint, Kevin Yank oversees all of its technical publications—books, articles, newsletters and blogs. He has written over 50 articles for SitePoint on technologies including PHP, XML, ASP.NET, Java, JavaScript and CSS. He writes *The SitePoint Tech Times*, SitePoint's biweekly technical newsletter for Web developers, which has over 75,000 readers worldwide.

When he's not discovering new technologies, editing books, or catching up on sleep, Kevin can be found helping other up-and-coming Web developers in the SitePoint Forums.

Kevin lives in Melbourne, Australia, with several potted plants. In his spare time he enjoys flying light aircraft and learning the fine art of improvised acting. Go you big red fire engine!

About SitePoint

SitePoint specializes in publishing fun, practical, and easy-to-understand content for Web professionals. Visit http://www.sitepoint.com/ to access our books, newsletters, articles and community forums.

To my parents, Cheryl and Richard, for making all this possible.

Table of Contents

Preface ix
   Who Should Read This Book x
   What's In This Book x
   The Book's Website xiii
      The Code Archive xiii
      Updates and Errata xiii
   The SitePoint Forums xiv
   The SitePoint Newsletters xiv
   Your Feedback xiv

1. Installation 1
   Windows Installation 2
      Installing MySQL 2
      Installing PHP 6
   Linux Installation 12
      Removing Packaged Software 13
      Installing MySQL 14
      Installing PHP 17
   Mac OS X Installation 20
      Installing MySQL 20
      Installing PHP 22
      Mac OS X and Linux 22
   Post-Installation Setup Tasks 22
   If Your Web Host Provides PHP and MySQL 25
   Your First PHP Script 26
   Summary 28

2. Getting Started with MySQL 29
   An Introduction to Databases 29
   Logging On to MySQL 31
   So, What's SQL? 34
   Creating a Database 34
   Creating a Table 35
   Inserting Data into a Table 37
   Viewing Stored Data 38
   Modifying Stored Data 40
   Deleting Stored Data 41
   Summary 41

3. Getting Started with PHP 43

Introducing PHP 43
Basic Syntax and Commands 45
Variables and Operators 47
Arrays 48
User Interaction and Forms 50
Control Structures 56
Multipurpose Pages 61
Summary 66

4. Publishing MySQL Data on the Web 67

A Look Back at First Principles 67
Connecting to MySQL with PHP 69
Sending SQL Queries with PHP 71
Handling SELECT Result Sets 72
Inserting Data into the Database 75
A Challenge 80
Summary 80
"Homework" Solution 80

5. Relational Database Design 85

Giving Credit where Credit is Due 85
Rule of Thumb: Keep Things Separate 87
Dealing with Multiple Tables 90
Simple Relationships 94
Many-to-Many Relationships 96
Summary 99

6. A Content Management System 101

The Front Page 102
Managing Authors 105
Deleting Authors 107
Adding Authors 110
Editing Authors 112
Magic Quotes 115
Managing Categories 117
Managing Jokes 123
Searching for Jokes 123
Adding Jokes 129
Editing and Deleting Jokes 137
Summary 142

7. Content Formatting and Submission **143**
Out with the Old 144
Regular Expressions 145
String Replacement with Regular Expressions 148
Boldface and Italic Text 149
Paragraphs 149
Hyperlinks 150
Matching Tags 152
Splitting Text into Pages 155
Putting it all Together 157
Automatic Content Submission 162
Summary 163

8. MySQL Administration **165**
Backing up MySQL Databases 166
Database Backups using mysqldump 167
Incremental Backups using Update Logs 168
MySQL Access Control 170
Using GRANT 171
Using REVOKE 174
Access Control Tips 174
Locked Out? 177
Checking and Repairing MySQL Data Files 178
Summary 181

9. Advanced SQL Queries **183**
Sorting SELECT Query Results 183
Setting LIMITs 186
LOCKing TABLES 187
Column and Table Name Aliases 189
GROUPing SELECT Results 192
LEFT JOINs 194
Limiting Results with HAVING 197
Summary 198

10. Binary Data **199**
Semi-Dynamic Pages 199
Handling File Uploads 204
Assigning Unique File Names 206
Recording Uploaded Files in the Database 208
Binary Column Types 209
Storing Files 210
Viewing Stored Files 212

The Complete Script 215
Large File Considerations 220
    MySQL Packet Size 220
    PHP Script Timeout 220
Summary 220

11. Cookies and Sessions in PHP **221**
Cookies 221
PHP Sessions 225
A Simple Shopping Cart 228
Summary 234

12. Structured PHP Programming **235**
What is Structured Code? 235
The Need for Structured Code 236
Include Files 238
    Types of Includes 242
    Including HTML Content 244
    Locating Include Files 246
    Returning from Includes 249
Custom Functions and Function Libraries 253
    Variable Scope and Global Access 257
    Optional and Unlimited Arguments 261
Constants 263
Structure In Practice: Access Control 265
Summary 274

A. MySQL Syntax **277**
ALTER TABLE 277
ANALYZE TABLE 280
CREATE DATABASE 280
CREATE INDEX 281
CREATE TABLE 281
DELETE 283
DESCRIBE 284
DROP DATABASE 285
DROP INDEX 285
DROP TABLE 285
EXPLAIN 285
GRANT 286
INSERT 286
LOAD DATA INFILE 287
LOCK/UNLOCK TABLES 288

OPTIMIZE TABLE 289
RENAME TABLE 289
REPLACE 290
REVOKE 290
SELECT 291
    Joins 295
    Unions 297
SET 297
SHOW 298
UNLOCK TABLES 299
UPDATE 299
USE 300

B. MySQL Functions **301**
Control Flow Functions 301
Mathematical Functions 301
String Functions 305
Date and Time Functions 309
Miscellaneous Functions 315
Functions for Use with GROUP BY Clauses 318

C. MySQL Column Types **321**
Numerical Types 322
Character Types 324
Date/Time Types 327

D. PHP Functions for Working with MySQL **331**
mysql_affected_rows 331
mysql_client_encoding 331
mysql_close 332
mysql_connect 332
mysql_create_db 333
mysql_data_seek 333
mysql_db_name 333
mysql_db_query 333
mysql_drop_db 334
mysql_errno 334
mysql_error 334
mysql_escape_string 334
mysql_fetch_array 335
mysql_fetch_assoc 335
mysql_fetch_field 335
mysql_fetch_lengths 336

mysql_fetch_object 336
mysql_fetch_row 337
mysql_field_flags 337
mysql_field_len 337
mysql_field_name 337
mysql_field_seek 337
mysql_field_table 338
mysql_field_type 338
mysql_free_result 338
mysql_get_client_info 338
mysql_get_host_info 339
mysql_get_proto_info 339
mysql_get_server_info 339
mysql_info 339
mysql_insert_id 339
mysql_list_dbs 340
mysql_list_fields 340
mysql_list_processes 340
mysql_list_tables 340
mysql_num_fields 341
mysql_num_rows 341
mysql_pconnect 341
mysql_ping 341
mysql_query 342
mysql_real_escape_string 342
mysql_result 342
mysql_select_db 343
mysql_stat 343
mysql_tablename 343
mysql_thread_id 343
mysql_unbuffered_query 343
Index 345

Preface

"Content is king." Cliché, yes; but it has never been more true. Once you've mastered HTML and learned a few neat tricks in JavaScript and Dynamic HTML, you can probably design a pretty impressive-looking Website. But your next task must be to fill that fancy page layout with some real information. Any site that successfully attracts repeat visitors has to have fresh and constantly updated content. In the world of traditional site building, that means HTML files—and lots of 'em.

The problem is that, more often than not, the people who provide the content for a site are not the same people who handle its design. Frequently, the content provider doesn't even *know* HTML. How, then, is the content to get from the provider onto the Website? Not every company can afford to staff a full-time Webmaster, and most Webmasters have better things to do than copying Word files into HTML templates, anyway.

Maintenance of a content-driven site can be a real pain, too. Many sites (perhaps yours?) feel locked into a dry, outdated design because rewriting those hundreds of HTML files to reflect a new look would take forever. Server-side includes (SSIs) can help alleviate the burden a little, but you still end up with hundreds of files that need to be maintained should you wish to make a fundamental change to your site.

The solution to these headaches is database-driven site design. By achieving complete separation between your site's design and the content you want to present, you can work with each without disturbing the other. Instead of writing an HTML file for every page of your site, you need only to write a page for each *kind* of information you want to be able to present. Instead of endlessly pasting new content into your tired page layouts, create a simple content management system that allows the writers to post new content themselves without a lick of HTML!

In this book, I'll provide you with a hands-on look at what's involved in building a database-driven Website. We'll use two tools for this, both of which may be new to you: the **PHP** scripting language and the **MySQL** relational database management system. If your Web host provides PHP and MySQL support, you're in great shape. If not, we'll be looking at the setup procedures under Linux, Windows, and Mac OS X, so don't sweat it.

Who Should Read This Book

This book is aimed at intermediate and advanced Web designers looking to make the leap into server-side programming. You'll be expected to be comfortable with simple HTML, as I'll make use of it without much in the way of explanation. No knowledge of JavaScript is assumed or required, but if you *do* know JavaScript, you'll find it will make learning PHP a breeze, since the languages are quite similar.

By the end of this book, you can expect to have a grasp of what's involved in setting up and building a database-driven Website. If you follow the examples, you'll also learn the basics of PHP (a server-side scripting language that gives you easy access to a database, and a lot more) and **Structured Query Language** (**SQL**—the standard language for interacting with relational databases) as supported by **MySQL**, one of the most popular free database engines available today. Most importantly, you'll come away with everything you need to get started on your very own database-driven site!

What's In This Book

This book comprises the following 12 chapters. Read them in order from beginning to end to gain a complete understanding of the subject, or skip around if you need a refresher on a particular topic.

Chapter 1: *Installation*
Before you can start building your database-driven Web presence, you must first ensure that you have the right tools for the job. In this first chapter, I'll tell you where to obtain the two essential components you'll need: the PHP scripting language and the MySQL database management system. I'll step you through the setup procedures on Windows, Linux, and Mac OS X, and show you how to test that PHP is operational on your Web server.

Chapter 2: *Getting Started with MySQL*
Although I'm sure you'll be anxious to get started building dynamic Web pages, I'll begin with an introduction to databases in general, and the MySQL relational database management system in particular. If you've never worked with a relational database before, this should definitely be an enlightening chapter that will whet your appetite for things to come! In the process, we'll build up a simple database to be used in later chapters.

Chapter 3: *Getting Started with PHP*

Here's where the fun really starts. In this chapter, I'll introduce you to the PHP scripting language, which can easily be used to build dynamic Web pages that present up-to-the-moment information to your visitors. Readers with previous programming experience will probably be able to get away with a quick skim of this chapter, as I explain the essentials of the language from the ground up. This is a must-read chapter for beginners, however, as the rest of this book relies heavily on the basic concepts presented here.

Chapter 4: *Publishing MySQL Data on the Web*

In this chapter we bring together PHP and MySQL, which you'll have seen separately in the previous chapters, to create some of your first database-driven Web pages. We'll explore the basic techniques of using PHP to retrieve information from a database and display it on the Web in real time. I'll also show you how to use PHP to create Web-based forms for adding new entries to, and modifying existing information in, a MySQL database on-the-fly.

Chapter 5: *Relational Database Design*

Although we'll have worked with a very simple sample database in the previous chapters, most database-driven Websites require the storage of more complex forms of data than we'll have dealt with so far. Far too many database-driven Website designs are abandoned midstream, or are forced to start again from the beginning, because of mistakes made early on, during the design of the database structure. In this critical chapter, I'll teach the essential principles of good database design, emphasizing the importance of data normalization. If you don't know what that means, then this is definitely an important chapter for you to read!

Chapter 6: *A Content Management System*

In many ways the climax of the book, this chapter is the big payoff for all you frustrated site builders who are tired of updating hundreds of pages whenever you need to make a change to a site's design. I'll walk you through the code for a basic content management system that allows you to manage a database of jokes, their categories, and their authors. A system like this can be used to manage simple content on your Website; just a few modifications, and you'll have a Web administration system that will have your content providers submitting content for publication on your site in no time—all without having to know a shred of HTML!

Chapter 7: *Content Formatting and Submission*

Just because you're implementing a nice, easy tool to allow site administrators to add content to your site without their knowing HTML, doesn't mean you have to restrict that content to plain, unformatted text. In this chapter, I'll show you some neat tweaks you can make to the page that displays the contents of your database—tweaks that allow it to incorporate simple formatting such as bold or italicized text, among other things. I'll also show you a simple way safely to make a content submission form directly available to your content providers, so that they can submit new content directly into your system for publication, pending an administrator's approval.

Chapter 8: *MySQL Administration*

While MySQL is a good, simple database solution for those who don't need many frills, it does have some complexities of its own that you'll need to understand if you're going to rely on a MySQL database to store your content. In this section, I'll teach you how to perform backups of, and manage access to, your MySQL database. In addition to a couple of inside tricks (like what to do if you forget your MySQL password), I'll explain how to repair a MySQL database that has become damaged in a server crash.

Chapter 9: *Advanced SQL Queries*

In Chapter 5 we saw what was involved in modelling complex relationships between pieces of information in a relational database like MySQL. Although the theory was quite sound, putting these concepts into practice requires that you learn a few more tricks of Structured Query Language. In this chapter, I'll cover some of the more advanced features of this language to get you juggling complex data like a pro.

Chapter 10: *Binary Data*

Some of the most interesting applications of database-driven Web design include some juggling of binary files. Online file storage services like the now-defunct *iDrive* are prime examples, but even a system as simple as a personal photo gallery can benefit from storing binary files (e.g. pictures) in a database for retrieval and management on the fly. In this chapter, I'll demonstrate how to speed up your Website by creating static copies of dynamic pages as regular intervals—using PHP, of course! With these basic file-juggling skills in hand, we'll go on to develop a simple online file storage and viewing system and learn the ins and outs of working with binary data in MySQL.

Chapter 11: *Cookies and Sessions in PHP*

One of the most hyped new features in PHP 4.0 was built-in support for sessions. But what are sessions? How are they related to cookies, a long-suffering technology for preserving stored data on the Web? What makes persistent data so important in current ecommerce systems and other Web applications? This chapter answers all those questions by explaining how PHP supports both cookies and sessions, and exploring the link between the two. At the end of this chapter, we'll develop a simple shopping cart system to demonstrate their use.

Chapter 12: *Structured PHP Programming*

Techniques to better structure your code are useful in all but the simplest of PHP projects. The PHP language offers many facilities to help you do this, and in this chapter, I'll explore some of the simple techniques that exist to keep your code manageable and maintainable. You'll learn to use include files to avoid having to write the same code more than once when it's needed by many pages of your site; I'll show you how to write your own functions to extend the built-in capabilities of PHP and to streamline the code that appears within your Web pages; we'll also dabble in the art of defining constants that control aspects of your Web applications' functionality. We'll then put all these pieces together to build an access control system for your Website. Its sophisticated structure will ensure that it can be used and reused on just about any site you decide to build.

The Book's Website

Located at http://www.sitepoint.com/books/phpmysql1/, the Website supporting this book will give you access to the following facilities:

The Code Archive

As you progress through the text, you'll note a number of references to the code archive. This is a downloadable ZIP archive that contains complete code for all the examples presented in this book.

Updates and Errata

No book is perfect, and even though this is a third edition, I expect that watchful readers will be able to spot at least one or two mistakes before its end. Also, PHP and MySQL (and even the Web in general) are moving targets, constantly undergoing changes with each new release. The Errata page on the book's Website will always have the latest information about known typographical and code errors, and necessary updates for changes to PHP and MySQL.

The SitePoint Forums

While I've made every attempt to anticipate any questions you may have, and answer them in this book, there is no way that *any* book could cover everything there is to know about PHP and MySQL. If you have a question about anything in this book, the best place to go for a quick answer is http://www.sitepoint.com/forums/. Not only will you find a vibrant and knowledgeable PHP community, but you'll occasionally even find me, the author, there in my spare hours.

The SitePoint Newsletters

In addition to books like this one, I write a free, biweekly (that's every two weeks) email newsletter called *The SitePoint Tech Times*. In it, I write about the latest news, product releases, trends, tips, and techniques for all technical aspects of Web development. If nothing else, you'll get useful PHP articles and tips, but if you're interested in learning other languages, you'll find it especially useful.

SitePoint also publishes a number of other newsletters. The long-running *SitePoint Tribune* is a biweekly digest of the business and moneymaking aspects of the Web. Whether you're a freelance developer looking for tips to score that dream contract, or a marketing major striving to keep abreast of changes to the major search engines, this is the newsletter for you. *The SitePoint Design View* is a monthly compilation of the best in Web design. From new CSS layout methods to subtle PhotoShop techniques, SitePoint's chief designer shares his years of experience in its pages.

Browse the archives or sign up to any of SitePoint's free newsletters at http://www.sitepoint.com/newsletter/.

Your Feedback

If you can't find your answer through the forums, or you wish to contact me for any other reason, the best place to write is <books@sitepoint.com>. We have a well-manned email support system set up to track your inquiries, and if our support staff is unable to answer your question, they send it straight to me. Suggestions for improvement as well as notices of any mistakes you may find are especially welcome.

And now, without further ado, let's get started!

1

Installation

Over the course of this book, it will be my job to guide you as you take your first steps beyond the HTML world of client-side site design. Together, we'll explore what it takes to develop the kind of large, content-driven sites that are so successful today, but which can be a real headache to maintain if they aren't built right.

Before we get started, you need to gather together the tools you'll need for the job. In this first chapter, I'll guide you as you download and set up the two software packages you'll need: PHP and MySQL.

PHP is a server-side scripting language. You can think of it as a "plug-in" for your Web server that will allow it to do more than just send plain Web pages when browsers request them. With PHP installed, your Web server will be able to read a new kind of file (called a **PHP script**) that can do things like retrieve up-to-the-minute information from a database and insert it into a Web page before sending it to the browser that requested it. PHP is completely free to download and use.

To retrieve information from a database, you first need to *have* a database. That's where **MySQL** comes in. MySQL is a relational database management system, or RDBMS. We'll get into the exact role it plays and how it works later, but basically it's a software package that is very good at the organization and management of large amounts of information. MySQL also makes that information really easy to access with server-side scripting languages like PHP. MySQL is released under the GNU General Public License (GPL), and is thus free for most uses on all of the platforms it supports. This includes most Unix-based platforms, like Linux and even Mac OS X, as well as Windows.

If you're lucky, your current Web host may already have installed MySQL and PHP on your Web server. If that's the case, much of this chapter will not apply to you, and you can skip straight to the section called "If Your Web Host Provides PHP and MySQL" to make sure your setup is shipshape.

Everything we'll discuss in this book may be carried out on a Windows- or Unix-based[1] server. The installation procedure will differ in accordance with the type of server you have at your disposal. The next few sections deal with installation on a Windows-based Web server, installation under Linux, and installation on Mac OS X. Unless you're especially curious, you need only read the section that applies to you.

Windows Installation

Installing MySQL

As I mentioned above, MySQL may be downloaded free of charge. Simply proceed to http://dev.mysql.com/downloads/ and choose the recommended stable release (as of this writing, it is MySQL 4.0). On the MySQL 4.0 download page, under the heading Windows downloads, select and download the release that includes the installer. After downloading the file (it's about 21MB as of this writing), unzip it and run the `setup.exe` program contained therein.

Once installed, MySQL is ready to roll (barring a couple of configuration tasks that we'll look at shortly), except for one minor issue that only affects you if you're running Windows NT, 2000, XP, or Server 2003. If you use any of those operating systems, you need to create a file called `my.cnf` in the root of your `C:` drive to indicate where you have installed MySQL.

To create this file, simply open Notepad and type these three lines:

```
[mysqld]
basedir = c:/mysql/
datadir = c:/mysql/data/
```

---

[1] From this point forward, I'll refer to all Unix-style platforms supported by PHP and MySQL, such as Linux, FreeBSD, and Mac OS X, with the collective name 'Linux'.

If you installed MySQL into a directory other than C:\mysql, replace both occurrences of c:/mysql in the above with the path to which you installed. Notice the use of forward slashes (/) instead of the usual backslashes (\) in the paths. For instance, on my system I edited the file to read as follows:

```
[mysqld]
basedir = d:/Program Files/MySQL/
datadir = d:/Program Files/MySQL/data/
```

Save the file as my.cnf in the root directory of C: drive.

Notepad and File Name Extensions

Notepad is designed to edit text files, which normally have a file name extension of .txt. When you try to save a file with a different extension (e.g. my.cnf), Notepad will normally add a .txt extension to the end of the file name (my.cnf.txt) so that Windows will treat it as a text file.

To prevent this, simply put double quotes around the file name as you enter it in the Save As dialog box, as shown in Figure 1.1.

Figure 1.1. Save the File As .cnf in Notepad

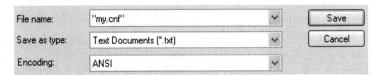

If you don't like the idea of a MySQL configuration file sitting in the root of your C: drive, instead, you can name it my.ini and put it in your Windows directory (e.g. C:\WINDOWS or C:\WINNT if Windows is installed on drive C:).

MySQL will now run on your Windows NT, 2000, XP, or Server 2003 system! If you're using Windows 95, 98, or ME, this step is not necessary—MySQL will run just fine as installed.

Working with .cnf files in Windows

It just so happens that files ending in .cnf have a special meaning to Windows, so, even if you have Windows configured to show file extensions, the my.cnf file you created will still appear as simply my with a special icon. Windows actually expects these files to contain SpeedDial links for Microsoft NetMeeting.

Assuming you don't use NetMeeting (or at least, that you don't use its SpeedDial facility) you can remove this file type from your system, enabling you to work with these files normally:

1.   Open the Windows Registry Editor (in Windows NT, 2000, XP, or Server 2003, click Start, Run..., and then type regedt32.exe to launch the editor; in Windows 9x/ME run regedit.exe instead).

2.   Navigate to the HKEY_LOCAL_MACHINE\SOFTWARE\Classes branch of the registry, where you'll find a list of all the registered file types on the system.

3.   Select the .cnf key and choose Edit, Delete from the menu to remove it.

4.   Log out and log back in, or restart Windows for the change to take effect.

If you prefer not to mess with the file types on your system, you should still be able to open the file in Notepad to edit it as needed.

Just like your Web server, MySQL is a program that should be run in the background so that it may respond to requests for information at any time. The server program may be found in the bin subfolder of the folder into which you installed MySQL. However, to complicate matters, several versions of the MySQL server are available:

mysqld.exe   This is the basic version of MySQL if you run Windows 95, 98, or ME. It includes support for all the advanced features, and includes debug code to provide additional information in the case of a crash (if your system is set up to debug programs). As a result of this code, however, the server might run a little slow, and generally I've found that MySQL is so stable that crashes aren't really a concern.

mysqld-opt.exe   This version of the server lacks a few of the advanced features of the basic server, and does not include the debug code. It's optimized to run quickly on today's processors. For beginners, the advanced features are not a big concern. You certainly won't be using them while you complete the tasks in this book. This is the version of choice for beginners running Windows 95, 98, or ME.

`mysqld-nt.exe` This version of the server is compiled and optimized like `mysqld-opt`, but is designed to run under Windows NT, 2000, XP, or Server 2003 as a service. If you're using any of those operating systems, this is probably the server for you.

`mysqld-max.exe` This version is like `mysqld-opt.exe`, but contains advanced features that support transactions. You won't need these features in this book.

`mysqld-max-nt.exe` This version's similar to `mysqld-nt.exe`, in that it will run as a Windows service, but it has the same advanced features as `mysqld-max.exe`.

All these versions were installed for you in the `bin` directory. If you're running on Win9x/ME, I recommend you stick with `mysql-opt` for now—move to `mysqld-max` if you ever need the advanced features. On WinNT/2000/XP/2003, `mysqld-nt` is my recommendation. Upgrade to `mysqld-max-nt` when you need more advanced features.

Starting MySQL is also a little different under WinNT/2000/XP/2003, but this time let's begin with the procedure for Win9x/ME. Open an MS-DOS Command Prompt,[2] proceed to the MySQL `bin` directory, and run your chosen server program:

```
C:\mysql\bin>mysqld-opt
```

Don't be surprised when you receive another command prompt. This command launches the server program so that it runs in the background, even after you close the command prompt. If you press Ctrl-Alt-Del to pull up the task list, you should see the MySQL server listed as one of the tasks that's active on your system.

---

[2]If you're unfamiliar with the workings of the Command Prompt, check out my article Kev's Command Prompt Cheat Sheet [http://www.sitepoint.com/article/846] to get familiar with how it works before you proceed further.

To ensure that the server is started whenever Windows starts, you might want to create a shortcut to the program and put it in your Startup folder. This is just like creating a shortcut to any other program on your system.

On WinNT/2000/XP/2003, you must install MySQL as a system service. Fortunately, this is very easy to do. Simply open a Command Prompt (under Accessories in the Start Menu) and run your chosen server program with the **- -install** option:

```
C:\mysql\bin>mysqld-nt --install
Service successfully installed.
```

This will install MySQL as a service that will be started the next time you reboot Windows. To start MySQL manually without having to reboot, just type this command (which can be run from any directory):

```
C:\>net start mysql
The MySQL service is starting.
The MySQL service was started successfully.
```

To verify that the MySQL server is running properly, press **Ctrl-Alt-Del** and open the Task List. If all is well, the server program should be listed on the *Processes* tab.

Installing PHP

The next step is to install PHP. At the time of this writing, PHP 5.0 has just been released, with numerous improvements over the previous version; however, PHP 4.3 has become well-established as the version of choice due to its track record of stability and performance. The procedures for installing these two versions are nearly identical. Although I'll focus primarily on installing PHP 5.0 in these pages, I'll note any significant differences if you happen to be working with PHP 4.3. All of the code in this book will work with both versions of PHP.

Download PHP for free from http://www.php.net/downloads.php. You'll want the PHP 5.x zip package under Windows Binaries; avoid the installer version if you can.

PHP was designed to run as a plug-in for existing Web server software such as Internet Information Services, Apache, Sambar or OmniHTTPD. To test dynamic Web pages with PHP, you'll need to equip your own computer with Web server software, so that PHP has something to plug into.

If you have Windows 2000, XP Professional[3], or Server 2003, then install IIS (if it's not already on your system): open Control Panel > Add/Remove Programs > Add/Remove Windows Components, and select Internet Information Services (IIS) from the list of components. If you're not lucky enough to have IIS at your disposal,[4] you can use a free, third-party Web server like Apache instead. I'll give instructions for both options in detail.

First, *whether or not you have IIS*, complete these steps:

1. Unzip the file you downloaded from the PHP Website into a directory of your choice. I recommend `C:\PHP` and will refer to this directory from this point onward, but feel free to choose another directory if you like.

2. Find the file called `php5ts.dll` in the PHP folder and copy it to the `system32` subfolder of your Windows folder (e.g. `C:\WINDOWS\system32`).

PHP 4.3

The file is called `php4ts.dll` for PHP 4.3.

3. Find the file called `php.ini-dist` in the PHP folder and copy it to your Windows folder. Once it's there, rename it `php.ini`.

4. Open the `php.ini` file in your favorite text editor (use WordPad if Notepad doesn't display the file properly). It's a large file with a lot of confusing options, but look for a line that begins with `extension_dir`, and set it so that it points to the `ext` subfolder of your PHP folder:

```
extension_dir = "C:\PHP\ext"
```

A little further down, you'll see a bunch of lines beginning with `;extension=`. These are optional extensions, disabled by default. We want to enable the MySQL extension so that PHP can communicate with MySQL. To do this, remove the semicolon from the start of the `php_mysql.dll` line:

```
extension=php_mysql.dll
```

---

[3]Windows XP Home Edition does not come with IIS.
[4]A feature-limited edition of IIS called "Personal Web Server" (PWS) was distributed on the Windows 98 Second Edition CD, and was available for earlier editions of Windows as well. While, technically, PHP can run on PWS, this Web server is somewhat unstable and has a great many known security holes. For these reasons, I highly recommend using Apache if an up-to-date version of IIS is not available for your Windows operating system.

Even further down, look for a line that starts with `session.save_path` and set it to your Windows TEMP folder:

```
session.save_path = "C:\WINDOWS\Temp"
```

Save the changes you made and close your text editor.

Now, if *you have IIS*, follow these instructions:

1. In the Windows Control Panel, open Administrative Tools > Internet Information Services.

2. In the tree view, expand the entry labelled local computer, then under Web Sites look for Default Web Site (unless you have virtual hosts set up, in which case, choose the site to which you want to add PHP support). Right-click on the site and choose Properties.

3. Click the ISAPI Filters tab, and click Add.... In the Filter Name field, type PHP, and in the Executable field, browse for the file called `php5isapi.dll` in the PHP folder. Click OK.

PHP 4.3

For PHP 4.3, the file is called `php4isapi.dll`, and is located in the `sapi` subfolder of your PHP folder.

Can't click OK?

In older versions of Windows, the OK button may remain disabled even after you have used the Browse... button to fill in the Executable field. Simply make a small change to the value of the field using the keyboard and then reverse it to enable the button.

4. Click the Home Directory tab, and click the Configuration... button. On the Mappings tab, click Add. Again choose your `php5isapi.dll` file as the executable (note that the file type filter in the dialog is set to show `.exe` files only by default) and type `.php` in the extension box (including the `.`). Leave everything else unchanged and click OK. If you want your Web server to treat other file extensions as PHP files (`.php3`, `.php4`, and `.phtml` are common choices), repeat this step for each extension. Click OK to close the Application Configuration window.

5. Click the Documents tab, and click the Add... button. Type `index.php` as the Default Document Name and click OK. This will ensure that a file called `index.php` will be displayed as the default document in a given folder on your site. You may also want to add entries for `index.php3` and `index.phtml`.

6. Click OK to close the Web Site Properties window. Close the Internet Information Services window.

7. Again, in the Control Panel under Administrative Tools, open Services. Look for the World Wide Web Publishing service near the bottom of the list. Right-click on it and choose Restart to restart IIS with the new configuration options. Close the Services window.

8. You're done! PHP is installed!

If *you don't have IIS*, you'll first need to install some other Web server. For our purposes, I'll assume you have downloaded and installed Apache server from http://httpd.apache.org/; however, PHP can also be installed on Sambar Server[5], OmniHTTPD[6], and others. I recommend Apache 1.3 for now, but if you want to use Apache 2.0, be sure to read the following sidebar.

---

[5] http://www.sambar.com/
[6] http://www.omnicron.ca/httpd/

PHP and Apache 2.0 in Windows

As of this writing, the PHP team continues to insist that support for PHP on Apache 2.0 is *experimental only*. There are a number of bugs that arise within PHP when it is run on an Apache 2.0 server and, on Windows especially, installation can be problematic. That said, many people (myself included!) are running PHP on Apache 2.0 quite successfully, and the bugs that do exist probably won't affect you if you're just setting up a low-traffic testing server.

The instructions below apply to both Apache 1.3 and Apache 2.0; however, it is possible that after configuring Apache 2.0 to use PHP, the server will fail to start. It is also possible that it will start, but that it will fail to process PHP scripts. In both cases, an error message should appear when you start Apache and/or in the Apache error log file.

This problem is caused by the fact that Apache 2.0 is a server still very much under development. With each minor release they put out, they tend to break compatibility with all server plug-in modules (such as PHP) that were compiled to work with the previous version. On Linux, this isn't such a big deal because people tend to compile PHP for themselves, so they simply recompile PHP at the same time they're compiling the new release of Apache and PHP adapts accordingly. Unfortunately, on Windows, where people are used to simply downloading precompiled files, the situation is different.

The `php4apache2.dll` file that is distributed with PHP will only work on versions of Apache 2.0 up to the one that was current at the time that version of PHP was released. So if you run into problems, the version of PHP you're using is probably older than the version of Apache you're using. This problem can often be fixed by downloading the very latest version of PHP; however, every time a new release of Apache 2.0 comes out, the current release of PHP will be incompatible until they get around to updating it.

Should you ever install a later version of Apache and break compatibility with the latest PHP build, you should be able to download a 'work-in-progress' version of PHP and grab only the files you need (those responsible for the PHP-Apache interface). Information about doing this can be found in the PHP bug database[7].

Once you've downloaded and installed Apache according to the instructions included with it, open http://localhost/ in your Web browser, to make sure it works properly. If you don't see a Web page explaining that Apache was successfully installed, then either you haven't yet run Apache, or your installation is faulty. Check the documentation and make sure Apache is running properly before you install PHP.

If you've made sure Apache is up and running, you can add PHP support:

---

[7] http://bugs.php.net/bug.php?id=17826

1. On your Start Menu, choose Programs > Apache HTTP Server > Configure Apache Server > Edit the Apache httpd.conf Configuration File. This will open the `httpd.conf` file (choose Notepad if you don't have a text editor configured to edit `.conf` files).

2. All of the options in this long and intimidating configuration file should have been set up correctly by the Apache install program. All you need to do is add the following lines to the very bottom of the file:

```
LoadModule php5_module c:/php/php5apache.dll
AddModule mod_php5.c
AddType application/x-httpd-php .php
AddType application/x-httpd-php-source .phps
```

Make sure the `LoadModule` line points to the appropriate file in the PHP installation directory on your system, and note the use of forward slashes (/) instead of backslashes (\).

Apache 2.0

If you're using Apache 2.0 or later, the `LoadModule` line needs to point to `php5apache2.dll` instead of `php5apache.dll`, and you must remove the `AddModule` line entirely.

PHP 4.3

For PHP 4.3, the file in the `LoadModule` line is called `php4apache.dll` (`php4apache2.dll` for Apache 2.0) and is located in the `sapi` sub-folder of your PHP folder.

3. Next, look for the line that begins with `DirectoryIndex`. This line tells Apache which file names to use when it looks for the default page for a given directory. You'll see the usual `index.html` and so forth, but you need to add `index.php` to that list if it's not there already:

```
DirectoryIndex index.html ... index.php
```

4. Save your changes and close Notepad.

5. Restart Apache by restarting the Apache service in Control Panel > Administrative Tools > Services. If all is well, Apache will start up again without complaint.

6. You're done! PHP is installed!

With MySQL and PHP installed, you're ready to proceed to the section called "Post-Installation Setup Tasks".

Linux Installation

This section covers the procedure for installing PHP and MySQL under most current distributions of Linux. These instructions were tested under Fedora Core 2; however, they should work on other distributions such as Debian, SUSE, and Mandrake without much trouble. The steps involved will be very similar, if not identical.

As a user of one of the handful of Linux distributions available, you may be tempted to download and install **packaged distributions** of PHP and MySQL. Debian users will be used to installing software using the `apt-get` utility, while distributions like Fedora Core tend to rely on RPM packages. These prepackaged versions of software are really easy to install; unfortunately, they also limit the software configuration options available to you. If you already have MySQL and PHP installed in packaged form, feel free to proceed with those versions, and skip forward to the section called "Post-Installation Setup Tasks". If you encounter any problems, you can always return here to uninstall the packaged versions and reinstall PHP and MySQL by hand.

This section will assume that you have the Apache Web server installed on your machine already. If you don't, chances are that your distribution offers an easy way to install it (I have no objection to your using the packaged distributions of Apache). I recommend Apache 1.3 over Apache 2.0, as support for Apache 2.0 in PHP is still experimental, but I'll provide instructions for both versions here.

Building Apache yourself

If you want to compile and install Apache by hand, the necessary downloads and ample installation instructions may be found at the Apache Website[9]. To support the PHP installation instructions provided below, you will have to build Apache with shared module support. When you configure your copy of Apache prior to compiling it, make sure you include the `--enable-module=so` option.

---

[9] http://httpd.apache.org/

Removing Packaged Software

Since many Linux distributions will automatically install PHP and MySQL for you, your first step should be to remove any old packaged versions of PHP and MySQL from your system. If one exists, use your distribution's graphical software manager to remove all packages with php or mysql in their names.

If your distribution doesn't have a graphical software manager, or if you didn't install a graphical user interface for your server, you can remove these packages from the command prompt. You'll need to be logged in as the root user to issue the commands to do this. Note that in the following commands, shell# represents the shell prompt, and shouldn't be typed in.

In Fedora Core, RedHat, or Mandrake, you can use the rpm command-line utility:

```
shell#rpm -e mysql
shell#rpm -e php
```

In Debian, you can use apt-get to remove the relevant packages:

```
shell#apt-get remove mysql-server
shell#apt-get remove mysql-client
shell#apt-get remove php4
shell#apt-get remove php5
```

If any of these commands tell you that the package in question is not installed, don't worry about it unless you know for a fact that it is. In such cases, it will be necessary for you to remove the offending item by hand. Seek help from an experienced user if you don't know how.

If the command(s) for removing PHP completed successfully (i.e. no error message was displayed), then you have just removed PHP from your Web server, and you should check that you haven't broken it in the process. To make sure Apache is still in working order, you should restart it without the PHP plug-in:

```
shell#apachectl graceful
```

If Apache fails to start up, you'll need to have a look through its configuration file, which is usually called httpd.conf and may be found in /etc/apache or /etc/httpd. Look for leftover commands that may be trying to load the PHP plug-in that you have just removed from the system. The Apache error log files may be of assistance in tracking these down if you can't find them. When you're finished, try restarting Apache again.

With everything neat and tidy, you're ready to download and install MySQL and PHP.

Installing MySQL

MySQL is freely available for Linux from http://dev.mysql.com/downloads/. Download the recommended stable release (4.0 as of this writing). You should grab the Standard version under Linux (x86, libc6) in the Linux downloads section.

Once you've downloaded the program (it was about 15MB as of this writing), you should make sure you're logged in as root before proceeding with the installation, unless you want to install MySQL only in your own home directory. To begin, move to /usr/local (unless you want to install MySQL elsewhere for some reason) and unpack the downloaded file to create the MySQL directory (replace *version* with the full version of your MySQL download to match the downloaded file name on your system):

```
shell#cd /usr/local
shell#tar xfz mysql-version.tar.gz
```

Next, create a symbolic link to the mysql-*version* directory with the name mysql to make accessing the directory easier, then enter the directory:

```
shell#ln -s mysql-version mysql
shell#cd mysql
```

While you can run the server as the root user, or even as yourself (if, for example, you installed the server in your own home directory), the best idea is to set up on the system a special user whose sole purpose is to run the MySQL server. This will remove any possibility of someone using the MySQL server as a way to break into the rest of your system. To create a special MySQL user, you'll need to log in as root and type the following commands:

```
shell#groupadd mysql
shell#useradd -g mysql mysql
```

MySQL is now installed, but before it can do anything useful, its database files need to be installed, too. In the new mysql directory, type the following command:

```
shell#scripts/mysql_install_db --user=mysql
```

By default, MySQL stores all database information in the data subdirectory of the directory to which it was installed. We want to ensure that nobody can access that directory except our new MySQL user. Assuming you installed MySQL to the /usr/local/mysql directory, you can use these commands:

```
shell#cd /usr/local/mysql
shell#chown -R root .
shell#chown -R mysql data
shell#chgrp -R mysql .
```

Now everything's set for you to launch the MySQL server for the first time. From the MySQL directory, type the following command:

```
shell#bin/mysqld_safe --user=mysql &
```

safe_mysqld

Prior to MySQL 4.0, the mysqld_safe script was called safe_mysqld. If you happen to be installing an old version of MySQL, you'll have to use that file name instead.

If you see the message mysql daemon ended, then the MySQL server was prevented from starting. The error message should have been written to a file called *hostname*.err (where *hostname* is your machine's host name) in MySQL's data directory. You'll usually find that this happens because another MySQL server is already running on your computer.

If the MySQL server was launched without complaint, the server will run (just like your Web or FTP server) until your computer is shut down. To test that the server is running properly, type the following command:

```
shell#bin/mysqladmin -u root status
```

A little blurb with some statistics about the MySQL server should be displayed. If you receive an error message, something has gone wrong. Again, check the *hostname*.err file to see if the MySQL server output an error message while starting up. If you retrace your steps to make sure you followed the process described above, and this doesn't solve the problem, a post to the SitePoint Forums[11] will help you pin it down in no time.

If you want your MySQL server to run automatically whenever the system is running (just like your Web server probably does), you'll have to set it up to do so. In the support-files subdirectory of the MySQL directory, you'll find a

---

[11] http://www.sitepoint.com/forums/

script called `mysql.server` that can be added to your system startup routines to do this. Let me show you how.

First of all, assuming you've set up a special MySQL user to run the MySQL server, you'll need to tell the MySQL server to start as that user by default. To do this, create in your system's `/etc` directory a file called `my.cnf` that contains these two lines:

```
[mysqld]
user=mysql
```

Now, when you run `safe_mysqld` or `mysql.server` to start the MySQL server, it will launch as user `mysql` automatically. You can test this by stopping MySQL, then running `mysql.server` with the `start` argument:

```
shell#bin/mysqladmin -u root shutdown
shell#support-files/mysql.server start
```

Request the server's status using `mysqladmin` as before, to make sure it's running correctly.

All that's left to do is to set up your system to run `mysql.server` automatically at startup (to launch the server) and at shutdown (to terminate the server). This is a highly operating system-dependant task. If you're not sure how to do it, you'd be best to ask someone who is. The following commands, however, will do the trick for most versions of Linux:

```
shell#cp /usr/local/mysql/support-files/mysql.server /etc/init.d/
shell#cd /etc/rc2.d
shell#ln -s ../init.d/mysql.server S99mysql
shell#cd /etc/rc3.d
shell#ln -s ../init.d/mysql.server S99mysql
shell#cd /etc/rc5.d
shell#ln -s ../init.d/mysql.server S99mysql
shell#cd /etc/rc0.d
shell#ln -s ../init.d/mysql.server K01mysql
```

That's it! To test that this works, reboot your system and request the status of the server as before.

One final thing you might like to do for the sake of convenience is to place the MySQL client programs, which you'll use to administer your MySQL server later on, in the system path. To this end, you can place symbolic links to `mysql`, `mysqladmin`, and `mysqldump` in your `/usr/local/bin` directory:

```
shell#ln -s /usr/local/mysql/bin/mysql /usr/local/bin/mysql
shell#ln -s /usr/local/mysql/bin/mysqladmin
/usr/local/bin/mysqladmin
shell#ln -s /usr/local/mysql/bin/mysqldump
/usr/local/bin/mysqldump
```

Installing PHP

As mentioned above, PHP is not really a program in and of itself. Instead, it's a plug-in module for your Web server (probably Apache). There are actually three ways to install the PHP plug-in for Apache:

❑ As a CGI program that Apache runs every time it needs to process a PHP-enhanced Web page

❑ As an Apache module compiled right into the Apache program

❑ As an Apache module loaded by Apache each time it starts up

The first option is the easiest to install and set up, but it requires Apache to launch PHP as a program on your computer every time a PHP page is requested. This activity can really slow down the response time of your Web server, especially if more than one request needs to be processed at a time.

The second and third options are almost identical in terms of performance, but since you're likely to have Apache installed already, you'd probably prefer to avoid having to download, recompile, and reinstall it from scratch. For this reason, we'll use the third option.

To start, download the PHP Complete Source Code package from http://www.php.net/downloads.php. At the time of this writing, PHP 4 has become well-established as the version of choice; however, the newly released PHP 5 is gaining ground quickly. I'll be covering the installation of PHP 5.0 here, but the same steps should work just as well with PHP 4.

The file you downloaded should be called php-*version*.tar.gz. To begin, we'll extract the files it contains (the shell% prompt is included to represent that you can run these steps without being logged in as root):

```
shell%tar xfz php-version.tar.gz
shell%cd php-version
```

To install PHP as a loadable Apache module, you'll need the Apache `apxs` program. This comes with most versions of Apache (both versions 1.3 and 2.0), but if you're using the copy that was installed with your distribution of Linux, you may need to install the "Apache development" package to access Apache `apxs`. You should be able to install this package by the means provided by your software distribution. For example, on Debian Linux, you can use `apt-get` to install it as follows (you'll have to log in as `root` first):

```
shell#apt-get install apache-dev
```

By default, Fedora Core, RedHat, and Mandrake will install the program as `/usr/sbin/apxs`, so if you see this file, you know it's installed. If you've installed Apache by hand, it will probably be `/usr/local/apache/bin/apxs`.

For the rest of the install procedure, you'll need to be logged in as the root user so you can make changes to the Apache configuration files.

The next step is to configure the PHP installation program by telling it which options you want to enable, and where it should find the programs it needs to know about (such as Apache and MySQL). Unless you know exactly what you're doing, simply type the command like this (all on one line):

```
shell#./configure --prefix=/usr/local/php
  --with-apxs=/usr/sbin/apxs
  --with-mysql=/usr/local/mysql
  --enable-magic-quotes
```

Replace `/usr/sbin/apxs` and `/usr/local/mysql` with the location of your `apxs` program and the base directory of your MySQL installation, respectively.

IMPORTANT

Apache 2.0

If you're using Apache 2.0 or later, you need to type `--with-apxs2=...` instead of `--with-apxs=...` to enable support for Apache 2.0. As of this writing, this support is still experimental and is not recommended for production sites. As a result of the ongoing work on this front, you may need to download the latest pre-release (unstable) version of PHP to get it working with the latest release of Apache 2.0, but it's worth trying the stable release version first.

For full instructions on how to download the latest pre-release version of PHP, see http://www.php.net/anoncvs.php.

Again, check for any error messages and install any files it identifies as missing. On Mandrake 8.0, for example, it complained that the `lex` command wasn't found. I searched for "lex" in the Mandrake package list and it came up with flex, which it described as a program for matching patterns of text used in many programs' build processes. Once that was installed, the configuration process went without a hitch. After you watch several screens of tests scroll by, you'll be returned to the command prompt. The following two commands will compile and then install PHP. Take a coffee break: this will take some time.

```
shell#make
shell#make install
```

Upon completion of make install, PHP is installed in /usr/local/php (unless you specified a different directory with the --prefix option of the configure script above), with one important exception—its configuration file, php.ini. PHP comes with two sample php.ini files called php.ini-dist and php.ini-recommended. Copy these files from your installation work directory to the /usr/local/php/lib directory, then make a copy of the php.ini-dist file and call it php.ini:

```
shell#cp php.ini* /usr/local/php/lib/
shell#cd /usr/local/php/lib
shell#cp php.ini-dist php.ini
```

You may now delete the directory from which you compiled PHP—it's no longer needed.

We'll worry about fine-tuning php.ini shortly. For now, we need to tweak Apache's configuration to make it more PHP-friendly. Open your Apache httpd.conf configuration file (usually under /etc/apache/ or /etc/httpd/ if you're using your Linux distribution's copy of Apache) in your favorite text editor.

Next, look for the line that begins with DirectoryIndex. In certain distributions, this may be in a separate file called commonhttpd.conf. This line tells Apache which file names to use when it looks for the default page for a given directory. You'll see the usual index.html, but you need to add index.php to the list if it's not there already:

```
DirectoryIndex index.html index.php
```

Finally, go right to the bottom of the file (again, this should go in commonhttpd.conf if you have such a file) and add these lines to tell Apache which file extensions should be seen as PHP files:

```
AddType application/x-httpd-php .php
AddType application/x-httpd-php-source .phps
```

That should do it! Save your changes and restart your Apache server. If all things go according to plan, Apache should start up without any error messages. If you run into any trouble, the helpful folks in the SitePoint Forums[14] (myself included) will be happy to help.

Mac OS X Installation

As of version 10.2 (Jaguar), Mac OS X distinguishes itself by being the only consumer OS to install both Apache and PHP as components of every standard installation. That said, the version of PHP provided is a little out-of-date, and you'll need to install the MySQL database as well.

In this section, I'll briefly cover what's involved in setting up up-to-date versions of PHP and MySQL on Mac OS X. Before doing that, however, I'll ask you to make sure that the Apache Web server built into your Mac OS X installation is enabled.

1. Click to pull down the Apple menu.

2. Choose System Preferences from the menu.

3. Select Sharing from the System Preferences panel.

4. If the Sharing preference panel says Web Sharing Off, click the Start button to launch the Apache Web server.

5. Exit the System Preferences program.

With this procedure complete, Apache will automatically be run at startup on your system from now on. You're now ready to enhance this server by installing PHP and MySQL!

Installing MySQL

Apple maintains a fairly comprehensive guide to installing MySQL on Mac OS X on its Mac OS X Internet Developer site[15] if you want to get your hands dirty and compile MySQL yourself. It is much easier, however, to obtain the precompiled binary version directly from the MySQL Website, and follow the installation instructions in the MySQL manual. In this section, I'll attempt to

[14] http://www.sitepoint.com/forums/
[15] http://developer.apple.com/internet/macosx/osdb.html

boil down this information to the essentials to help you get started as quickly as possible.

First of all, if you happen to be running Mac OS X Server, MySQL is already installed for you. You can run `Applications/Utilities/MySQL Manager` to access it. More likely, however, you are using the client version of Mac OS X.

To install MySQL on the client version of Mac OS X, begin by going to http://dev.mysql.com/downloads/ and selecting the latest production release of MySQL (4.0 as of this writing). Scroll down to the Mac OS X downloads section, then select and download the Installer package version for your operating system. You'll have a choice of the Standard, Max, and Debug releases; choose the Standard release unless you have a special reason for choosing one of the others.

Once you've downloaded the `mysql-standard-version-apple-darwinversion-powerpc.dmg` file, double-click it to mount the disk image if your browser hasn't already done this for you. Inside it, you'll find the installer in `.pkg` format, as well as a `MySQLStartupItem.pkg` file. Double-click the installer, which will guide you through the installation of MySQL.

Once MySQL is installed, you can launch the MySQL server by opening a Terminal window and typing this command:

```
shell%sudo /usr/local/mysql/bin/mysqld_safe
```

Enter the administrator password if prompted. Once MySQL is running, you can switch it to background execution by typing **Ctrl-Z** to suspend it, and typing this command:

```
shell%bg
```

You can then close the Terminal window and MySQL will continue to run as a server on your system.

Presumably, you'll want your system automatically to launch the MySQL server at startup so that you don't have to repeat the above process whenever you restart your system. To do this, simply double-click the `MySQLStartupItem.pkg` file and follow the instructions.

When you're done, you can safely drag the mounted drive for the MySQL installation package to the trash, then delete the `.dmg` file.

Installing PHP

As with MySQL, a Mac OS X version of PHP is not available from the official Website, but from a third party. Again, Apple also maintains a Web page detailing the installation procedure[17], although in this case it is somewhat out of date. A better source of information is http://www.entropy.ch/software/macosx/php/, where you can download an installer package in the form of a disk image.

The latest version of PHP available for Mac OS X 10.2 is PHP 4.3.4. More recent versions of PHP (up to 5.0.1 as of this writing) are available for Mac OS X 10.3 or later only. Select the version that is right for your system and download it.

If your browser doesn't do it for you, mount the disk image by double-clicking the Entropy-PHP-*version*.dmg file, then double-click the installer .pkg file it contains. Simply follow the instructions, and PHP will be installed on your server. That's all there is to it!

Mac OS X and Linux

Because Mac OS X is based on the BSD operating system, much of its internals work just like any other Unix-like OS (e.g. Linux). From this point forward, owners of Mac OS X servers can follow the instructions provided for Unix/Linux systems unless otherwise indicated. No separate instructions are provided for Mac OS X unless they differ from those for other Unix-like systems.

Post-Installation Setup Tasks

No matter which operating system you're running, once PHP is installed and the MySQL server is in operation, the very first thing you need to do is assign a **root password** for MySQL. MySQL allows authorized users only to view and manipulate the information stored in its databases, so you'll need to tell MySQL who is an authorized user, and who isn't. When MySQL is first installed, it's configured with a user named root that has access to do pretty much anything without even entering a password. Your first task should be to assign a password to the root user so that unauthorized users can't tamper with your databases.

[17] http://developer.apple.com/internet/macosx/php.html

IMPORTANT

Why should I bother?

It's important to realize that MySQL, just like a Web server or an FTP server, can be accessed from any computer on the same network. If you're working on a computer connected to the Internet, then, depending on your security measures, that means anyone in the world could try to connect to your MySQL server! The need to pick a hard-to-guess password should be immediately obvious!

To set a root password for MySQL, open a command prompt (or Terminal window) and type the following command in the `bin` directory of your MySQL installation:

```
mysql -u root mysql
```

This command connects you to your newly-installed MySQL server as the `root` user, and chooses the `mysql` database. After a few lines of introductory text, you should see the MySQL command prompt (`mysql>`). To assign a password to the `root` user, type the following two commands (pressing **Enter** after each one):

```
mysql>UPDATE mysql.user SET Password=PASSWORD("new password")
    ->WHERE User="root";
Query OK, 2 rows affected (0.12 sec)
Rows matched: 2  Changed: 2  Warnings: 0
mysql>FLUSH PRIVILEGES;
Query OK, 0 rows affected (0.24 sec)
```

Be sure to replace *new password* with the password you want to assign to your `root` user.

With that done, disconnect from MySQL with the `quit` command:

```
mysql>quit
Bye
```

Now, to try out your new password, request that the MySQL server tell you its current status at the system command prompt:

```
mysqladmin -u root -p status
```

Enter your new password when prompted. You should see a brief message that provides information about the server and its current status. The `-u root` argument tells the program that you want to be identified as the MySQL user called `root`. The `-p` argument tells the program to prompt you for your password before it tries to connect. The `status` argument just tells it that you're interested in viewing the system status.

If at any time you want to shut down the MySQL server, you can use the command below. Notice the same `-u root` and `-p` arguments as before:

```
mysqladmin -u root -p shutdown
```

With your MySQL database system safe from intrusion, all that's left is to configure PHP. To do this, we'll use a text file called `php.ini`. If you installed PHP under Windows, you should already have copied `php.ini` into your Windows directory. If you installed PHP under Linux using the instructions above, you should already have copied `php.ini` into the PHP `lib` folder (`/usr/local/php/lib`), or wherever you chose to put it. The Mac OS X installation program will have placed the file in `/usr/local/php/lib` for you automatically.

Open `php.ini` in your favorite text editor and have a glance through it. Most of the settings are fairly well explained, and most of the default settings are fine for our purposes. Just check to make sure that your settings match these:

```
register_globals = Off
magic_quotes_gpc = On⁵
extension_dir = the directory where you installed PHP⁶
```

Save the changes to `php.ini`, and then restart your Web server. To restart Apache under Linux (or Mac OS X), log in as `root` and type this command:

```
shell#apachectl graceful
```

You're done! Now, you just need to test to make sure everything's working (see the section called "Your First PHP Script").

---

[5] PHP experts may tell you that you'll achieve better performance with it set to Off, but that setting exposes you to hackers attempting SQL injection attacks on your Website if you are not very careful to write scripts that protect themselves from such malicious behavior. Until you fully understand PHP and the types of security issues that scripts must combat, leave this setting On.

[6] Usually c:\php on Windows, and /usr/local/php on Linux.

If Your Web Host Provides PHP and MySQL

If the host that provides you with Web space has already installed and set up MySQL and PHP for you, and you just want to learn how to use them, there really isn't a lot you need to do. Now would be a good time to get in touch with your host and request any information you may need to access these services.

Specifically, you'll need a user name and password to access the MySQL server they've set up for you. They'll probably also have provided an empty database for your use, which prevents you from interfering with the databases of other users who share the same MySQL server, and you'll want to know the name of your database.

There are two ways you can access the MySQL server directly. Firstly, you can use telnet or secure shell (SSH) to log in to the host. You can then use the MySQL client programs (`mysql`, `mysqladmin`, `mysqldump`) installed there to interact with the MySQL server directly. The second method is to install those client programs onto your own computer, and have them connect to your host's MySQL server. Your Web host may support one, both, or neither of these methods, so you'll need to ask.

If your host allows you to log in by telnet or SSH to do your work, you'll need a user name and password for the login, in addition to those you'll use to access the MySQL server (they can be different). Be sure to ask for both sets of information.

If they support direct access to the MySQL server, you'll want to download a program that lets you connect to, and interact with, the server. This book assumes you've downloaded from http://www.mysql.com/ a binary distribution of MySQL that includes the three client programs (`mysql`, `mysqladmin`, and `mysqldump`). Free packages are available for Windows, Linux and other operating systems. Installation basically consists of finding the three programs and putting them in a convenient place. The rest of the package, which includes the MySQL server, can be freely discarded. If you prefer a more graphical interface, download something like MySQL Control Center[20]. I'd recommend getting comfortable with the basic client programs first, though, as the commands you use with them

---

[20] http://www.mysql.com/products/mysqlcc/

will be similar to those you'll include in your PHP scripts to access MySQL databases.

Many less expensive Web hosts support neither telnet/SSH access, nor direct access to their MySQL servers. Instead, they normally provide a management console that allows you to browse and edit your database through your Web browser (though some actually expect you to install one yourself, which I'll cover briefly in Chapter 2). Although this is a fairly convenient and not overly restrictive solution, it doesn't help you learn. Instead, I'd recommend you install a MySQL server on your own system for experimentation, especially in the next chapter. Once you're comfortable working with your learning server, you can start using the server provided by your Web host with the Web-based management console. See the previous sections for instructions on installing MySQL under Windows, Linux, and Mac OS X.

Your First PHP Script

It would be unfair of me to help you get everything installed and not even give you a taste of what a PHP-driven Web page looks like until Chapter 3, so here's a little something to whet your appetite.

Open your favorite text or HTML editor and create a new file called **today.php**. Windows users should note that, to save a file with a .php extension in Notepad, you'll need to either select *All Files* as the file type, or surround the file name with quotes in the Save As dialogue; otherwise, Notepad will helpfully save the file as **today.php.txt**, which won't work (see the note earlier in this chapter for more information). Mac OS users are advised not to use TextEdit to edit .php files, as it saves them in Rich Text Format with an invisible .rtf file name extension. Learn to use the **vi** editor in a Terminal window or obtain an editor that can save .php files as plain text.

Whichever editor you use, type this into the file:

File: **today.php**

```
<!DOCTYPE html PUBLIC "-//W3C//DTD XHTML 1.0 Strict//EN"
    "http://www.w3.org/TR/xhtml1/DTD/xhtml1-strict.dtd">
<html xmlns="http://www.w3.org/1999/xhtml">
<head>
<title>Today's Date</title>
<meta http-equiv="content-type"
    content="text/html; charset=iso-8859-1" />
</head>
```

```
<body>
<p>Today's Date (according to this Web server) is
<?php

echo date('l, F dS Y.');

?></p>
</body>
</html>
```

If you prefer, you can download this file, which, along with the rest of the code in this book, is contained in the code archive. See the Preface for details on how to download the archive.

Save the file, and place it on your Website as you would any regular HTML file, then view it in your browser. Note that if you view the file on your own machine, you *cannot* use the File > Open... feature of your browser, because your Web server must intervene to interpret the PHP code in the file. Instead, you must move the file into the **root document folder** of your Web server software (e.g. `C:\inetpub\wwwroot\` in IIS, or `C:\Program Files\Apache Group\Apache\htdocs\` in Apache for Windows), then load it into your browser by typing http://localhost/today.php. This process allows the Web server to run the PHP code in the file and replace it with the date before it's sent to the Web browser. Figure 1.2 shows what the output should look like.

Figure 1.2. See your first PHP script in action!

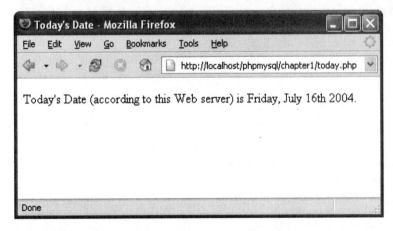

Pretty neat, huh? If you use the View Source feature in your browser, all you'll see is a regular HTML file with the date in it. The PHP code (everything between

<?php and ?> in the code above) was interpreted by the Web server and converted to normal text before it was sent to your browser. The beauty of PHP, and other server-side scripting languages, is that the Web browser doesn't have to know anything about it — the Web server does all the work!

Don't worry too much about the exact code I used in this example. Before too long you'll know it like the back of your hand.

If you don't see the date, then something is wrong with the PHP support on your Web server. Use View Source in your browser to look at the code of the page. You'll probably see the PHP code there in the page. Since the browser doesn't understand PHP, it just sees <?php ... ?> as one long, invalid HTML tag, which it ignores. Make sure that PHP support has been properly installed on your Web server, either in accordance with the instructions provided in previous sections of this chapter, or by your Web host.

Summary

You should now have everything you need to install MySQL and PHP on your Web Server. If the little example above didn't work (for example, if the raw PHP code appeared instead of the date), something went wrong with your setup procedure. Drop by the SitePoint Forums[22] and we'll be glad to help you figure out the problem!

In Chapter 2, you'll learn the basics of relational databases and get started working with MySQL. If you've never even touched a database before, I promise you it'll be a real eye-opener!

---

[22] http://www.sitepoint.com/forums/

2

Getting Started with MySQL

In Chapter 1, we installed and set up two software programs: PHP and MySQL. In this chapter, we'll learn how to work with MySQL databases using Structured Query Language (SQL).

An Introduction to Databases

As I've already explained, PHP is a server-side scripting language that lets you insert into your Web pages instructions that your Web server software (be it Apache, IIS, or whatever) will execute before it sends those pages to browsers that request them. In a brief example, I showed how it was possible to insert the current date into a Web page every time it was requested.

Now, that's all well and good, but things really get interesting when a database is added to the mix. A database server (in our case, MySQL) is a program that can store large amounts of information in an organized format that's easily accessible through scripting languages like PHP. For example, you could tell PHP to look in the database for a list of jokes that you'd like to appear on your Website.

In this example, the jokes would be stored entirely in the database. The advantages of this approach would be twofold. First, instead of having to write an HTML file for each of your jokes, you could write a single PHP file that was designed to fetch any joke from the database and display it. Second, adding a joke to your Website would be a simple matter of inserting the joke into the database. The PHP code would take care of the rest, automatically displaying the new joke along with the others when it fetched the list from the database.

Let's run with this example as we look at how data is stored in a database. A database is composed of one or more **tables**, each of which contains a list of *things*. For our joke database, we'd probably start with a table called `joke` that would contain a list of jokes. Each table in a database has one or more **columns**, or **fields**. Each column holds a certain piece of information about each item in the table. In our example, our `joke` table might have one column for the text of the jokes, and another for the dates on which the jokes were added to the database. Each joke stored in this way would then be said to be a **row** in the table. These rows and columns form a table that looks like Figure 2.1.

Figure 2.1. The structure of a typical database table includes rows and columns.

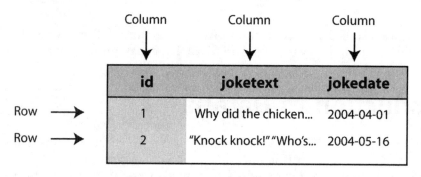

Notice that, in addition to columns for the joke text (`joketext`) and the date of the joke (`jokedate`), I included a column named `id`. As a matter of good design, a database table should always provide a means by which we can identify each of its rows uniquely. Since it's possible that a single joke could be entered more than once on the same date, the `joketext` and `jokedate` columns can't be relied upon to tell all the jokes apart. The function of the `id` column, therefore, is to assign a unique number to each joke so that we have an easy way to refer to them and to keep track of which joke is which. Such database design issues will be covered in greater depth in Chapter 5.

So, to review, the above is a three-column table with two rows, or entries. Each row in the table contains three fields, one for each column in the table: the joke's

ID, its text, and the date of the joke. With this basic terminology under our belts, we're ready to get started with MySQL.

Logging On to MySQL

The standard interface for working with MySQL databases is to connect to the MySQL server software (which you set up in Chapter 1) and type commands one at a time. To make this connection to the server, you'll need the MySQL client program. If you installed the MySQL server software yourself, either under Windows or some brand of UNIX, this program will have been installed in the same location as the server program. Under Linux, for example, the program is called `mysql` and is located by default in the `/usr/local/mysql/bin` directory. Under Windows, the program is called `mysql.exe` and is located by default in the `C:\mysql\bin` directory.

If you didn't set up the MySQL server yourself (if, for example, you're working on your Web host's MySQL server), there are two ways to connect to the MySQL server. The first is to use Telnet or a Secure Shell (SSH) connection to log into your Web host's server, then run `mysql` from there. The second is to download the MySQL client software from http://www.mysql.com/ (available free for Windows and Linux), install it on your own computer, and use it to connect to the MySQL server over the Internet. Both methods work well, and your Web host may support one, the other, or both—you'll need to ask.

Tip

No shell? No direct connection? No problem!

Many Web hosts do not allow direct access to their MySQL servers over the Internet for security reasons. If your host has adopted this policy (you'll have to ask them if you're not sure), installing the MySQL client software on your own computer won't do you any good. Instead, you'll need to install a Web-based MySQL administration script onto your site. phpMyAdmin[2] is the most popular script available; indeed, many Web hosts will configure your account with a copy of phpMyAdmin.

While Web-based MySQL administration systems provide a convenient, graphical interface for working with your MySQL databases, it is still important to learn the basics of MySQL's command-line interface. The commands you use in this interface are the very same commands you'll have to include in your PHP code later in this book. I therefore recommend going back to Chapter 1 and installing MySQL on your own computer so you can complete

---

[2] http://www.phpmyadmin.net/

the exercises in this chapter before you get comfortable with your Web-based administration interface.

Whichever method and operating system you use, you'll end up at a command prompt, ready to run the MySQL client program and connect to your MySQL server. Here's what you should type:

```
mysql -h hostname -u username -p
```

You need to replace *hostname* with the host name or IP address of the computer on which the MySQL server is running. If the client program is run on the same computer as the server, you would use `-h localhost` or `-h 127.0.0.1`, but in this special case you can actually leave off this part of the command entirely. *username* should be your MySQL user name. If you installed the MySQL server yourself, this will just be `root`. If you're using your Web host's MySQL server, this should be the MySQL user name the host assigned you.

The `-p` argument tells the program to prompt you for your password, which it should do as soon as you enter the command above. If you set up the MySQL server yourself, this password is the root password you chose in Chapter 1. If you're using your Web host's MySQL server, this should be the MySQL password the host gave you.

If you typed everything correctly, the MySQL client program will introduce itself and dump you on the MySQL command prompt:

```
mysql>
```

The MySQL server can actually keep track of more than one database. This allows a Web host to set up a single MySQL server for use by several of its subscribers, for example. So, your next step should be to choose a database with which to work. First, let's retrieve a list of databases on the current server. Type this command (don't forget the semicolon!) and press Enter.

```
mysql>SHOW DATABASES;
```

MySQL will show you a list of the databases on the server. If you're working on a brand new server (i.e. if you installed the server yourself in Chapter 1), the list should look like this:

```
+----------+
| Database |
+----------+
| mysql    |
| test     |
```

```
+----------+
2 rows in set (0.11 sec)
```

The MySQL server uses the first database, named `mysql`, to keep track of users, their passwords, and what they're allowed to do. We'll steer clear of this database for now, though we will revisit it in Chapter 8, when we discuss MySQL Administration. The second database, named `test`, is a sample database. You can actually get rid of this database. I won't be referring to it in this book, and we'll create our own example database momentarily. Deleting something in MySQL is called "dropping" it, and the command for doing so is appropriately named:

```
mysql>DROP DATABASE test;
```

If you type this command and press Enter, MySQL will obediently delete the database, displaying "Query OK" in confirmation. Notice that you're not prompted with any kind of "Are you sure?" message. You have to be very careful to type your commands correctly in MySQL because, as this example shows, you can obliterate your entire database—along with all the information it contains—with a single command!

Before we go any further, let's learn a couple of things about the MySQL command prompt. As you may have noticed, all commands in MySQL are terminated by a semicolon (;). If you forget the semicolon, MySQL will think you haven't finished typing your command, and will let you continue to type on another line:

```
mysql>SHOW
    ->DATABASES;
```

MySQL shows that it's waiting for you to type more of your command by changing the prompt from `mysql>` to `->`. This handy functionality allows you to spread long commands over several lines.

If you get halfway through a command and realize that you made a mistake early on, you may want to cancel the current command entirely and start over from scratch. To do this, type \c and press Enter:

```
mysql>DROP DATABASE\c
mysql>
```

MySQL will ignore completely the command you had begun to type and will return to the prompt to await another command.

Finally, if at any time you want to exit the MySQL client program, just type quit or exit (either will work). This is the only command that doesn't need a semi-colon, but you can use one if you want to.

```
mysql>quit
Bye
```

So, What's SQL?

The set of commands we'll use to direct MySQL throughout the rest of this book is part of a standard called **Structured Query Language**, or **SQL** (pronounced either "sequel" or "ess-cue-ell"—take your pick). Commands in SQL are also referred to as **queries** (I'll use these two terms interchangeably).

SQL is the standard language for interacting with most databases, so, even if you move from MySQL to a database like Microsoft SQL Server in the future, you'll find that most of the commands are identical. It's important that you understand the distinction between SQL and MySQL. MySQL is the database server software that you're using. SQL is the language that you use to interact with that database.

Creating a Database

Those who are working on their Web host's MySQL server are likely already to have been assigned a database with which to work. Sit tight; we'll get back to you in a moment. If you're running a MySQL server that you installed yourself, however, you'll need to create your own database. It's just as easy to create a database as it is to delete one:

```
mysql>CREATE DATABASE ijdb;
```

I chose to name the database ijdb, for Internet Joke Database, because that fits with the example we're using. Feel free to give the database any name you like, though. Those of you working on your Web host's MySQL server will probably have no choice in what to name your database, as it will probably already have been created for you.

Now that we have a database, we need to tell MySQL that we want to use it. Again, the command isn't difficult to remember:

```
mysql>USE ijdb;
```

You're now ready to use your database. Since a database is empty until you add some tables to it, our first order of business will be to create a table that will hold our jokes.

Creating a Table

The SQL commands we've encountered so far have been reasonably simple, but as tables are so flexible, it takes a more complicated command to create them. The basic form of the command is as follows:

```
mysql>CREATE TABLE table_name (
    ->  column_1_name column_1_type column_1_details,
    ->  column_2_name column_2_type column_2_details,
    ->  ...
    ->);
```

Let's return to our example joke table. Recall that it had three columns: id (a number), joketext (the text of the joke), and jokedate (the date on which the joke was entered). The command to create this table is as follows:

```
mysql>CREATE TABLE joke (
    ->  id INT NOT NULL AUTO_INCREMENT PRIMARY KEY,
    ->  joketext TEXT,
    ->  jokedate DATE NOT NULL
    ->);
```

It looks pretty scary, huh? Let's break it down:

❑ The first line is fairly simple; it says that we want to create a new table named joke.

❑ The second line says that we want a column called id that will contain an integer (INT), that is, a whole number. The rest of this line deals with special details for the column. First, this column is not allowed to be left blank (NOT NULL). Next, if we don't specify any value in particular when we add a new entry to the table, we want MySQL to pick a value that is one more than the highest value in the table so far (AUTO_INCREMENT). Finally, this column is to act as a unique identifier for the entries in the table, so all values in this column must be unique (PRIMARY KEY).

❑ The third line is super-simple; it says that we want a column called joketext, which will contain text (TEXT).

❏ The fourth line defines our last column, called `jokedate`, which will contain data of type `DATE`, and which cannot be left blank (`NOT NULL`).

Note that, while you're free to type your SQL commands in upper– or lowercase, a MySQL server running on a UNIX-based system will be case-sensitive when it comes to database and table names, as these correspond to directories and files in the MySQL data directory. Otherwise, MySQL is completely case-insensitive, but for one exception: table, column, and other names must be spelled exactly the same when they're used more than once in the same command.

Note also that we assigned a specific type of data to each column we created. `id` will contain integers, `joketext` will contain text, and `jokedate` will contain dates. MySQL requires you to specify in advance a data type for each column. Not only does this help keep your data organized, but it allows you to compare the values within a column in powerful ways, as we'll see later. For a complete list of supported MySQL data types, see Appendix C.

Now, if you typed the above command correctly, MySQL will respond with `Query OK`, and your first table will be created. If you made a typing mistake, MySQL will tell you there was a problem with the query you typed, and will try to indicate where it had trouble understanding what you meant.

For such a complicated command, `Query OK` is a pretty boring response. Let's have a look at your new table to make sure it was created properly. Type the following command:

```
mysql>SHOW TABLES;
```

The response should look like this:

```
+----------------+
| Tables in ijdb |
+----------------+
| joke           |
+----------------+
1 row in set
```

This is a list of all the tables in our database (which I named `ijdb` above). The list contains only one table: the `joke` table we just created. So far, everything seems fine. Let's take a closer look at the `joke` table itself:

```
mysql>DESCRIBE joke;
+-----------+----------+------+-----+------------+----------------+
| Field     | Type     | Null | Key | Default    | Extra          |
```

```
+-----------+----------+------+-----+------------+----------------+
| id        | int(11)  |      | PRI | NULL       | auto_increment |
| joketext  | text     | YES  |     | NULL       |                |
| jokedate  | date     |      |     | 0000-00-00 |                |
+-----------+----------+------+-----+------------+----------------+
3 rows in set
```

As you can see, there are three columns (or fields) in this table, which appear as the three rows in this table of results. The details are somewhat cryptic, but if you look at them closely, you should be able to figure out what they mean. Don't worry about it too much, though. We've got better things to do, like adding some jokes to our table!

We need to look at just one more thing before we get to that, though: deleting a table. This task is as frighteningly easy as deleting a database. In fact, the command is almost identical:

```
mysql>DROP TABLE tableName;
```

Inserting Data into a Table

Our database is created and our table is built; all that's left is to put some actual jokes into the database. The command that inserts data into a database is called, appropriately enough, INSERT. This command takes two basic forms:

```
mysql>INSERT INTO table_name SET
    -> columnName1 = value1,
    -> columnName2 = value2,
    -> ...
    ->;
```

```
mysql>INSERT INTO table_name
    -> (columnName1, columnName2, ...)
    -> VALUES (value1, value2, ...);
```

So, to add a joke to our table, we can use either of these commands:

```
mysql>INSERT INTO joke SET
    ->joketext = "Why did the chicken cross the road? To get to
    "> the other side!",
    ->jokedate = "2004-04-01";
```

```
mysql>INSERT INTO joke
    ->(joketext, jokedate) VALUES (
    ->"Why did the chicken cross the road? To get to the other
```

```
"> side!",
->"2004-04-01"
->);
```

Note that in the second form of the INSERT command, the order in which you list the columns must match the order in which you list the values. Otherwise, the order of the columns doesn't matter, as long as you provide values for all required fields. Now that you know how to add entries to a table, let's see how we can view those entries.

Viewing Stored Data

The command we use to view data stored in database tables, SELECT, is the most complicated command in the SQL language. The reason for this complexity is that the chief strength of a database is its flexibility in data retrieval and presentation. At this early point in our experience with databases we need only fairly simple lists of results, so we'll just consider the simpler forms of the SELECT command here. This command will list everything that's stored in the joke table:

```
mysql>SELECT * FROM joke;
```

Read aloud, this command says "select everything from joke." If you try this command, your results will resemble the following:

```
+----+----------------------------------------------
-------------+-----------+
| id | joketext
          | jokedate  |
+----+----------------------------------------------
-------------+-----------+
|  1 | Why did the chicken cross the road? To get to the
other side! | 2004-04-01 |
+----+----------------------------------------------
-------------+-----------+
1 row in set (0.05 sec)
```

The results look a little disorganized because the text in the joketext column is so long that the table can't fit on the screen properly. For this reason, you might want to tell MySQL to leave out the joketext column. The command for doing this is as follows:

```
mysql>SELECT id, jokedate FROM joke;
```

This time, instead of telling it to "select everything," we told it precisely which columns we wanted to see. The results look like this:

```
+----+------------+
| id | jokedate   |
+----+------------+
| 1  | 2004-04-01 |
+----+------------+
1 row in set (0.00 sec)
```

Not bad, but we'd like to see at least *some* of the joke text, wouldn't we? As well as being able to name specific columns that we want the SELECT command to show us, we can use functions to modify each column's display. One function, called LEFT, lets us tell MySQL to display a column's contents up to a specified maximum number of characters. For example, let's say we wanted to see only the first 20 characters of the joketext column. Here's the command we'd use:

```
mysql>SELECT ID, LEFT(joketext, 20), jokedate FROM joke;
+----+----------------------+------------+
| id | LEFT(joketext, 20)   | jokedate   |
+----+----------------------+------------+
| 1  | Why did the chicken  | 2004-04-01 |
+----+----------------------+------------+
1 row in set (0.05 sec)
```

See how that worked? Another useful function is COUNT, which lets us count the number of results returned. If, for example, we wanted to find out how many jokes were stored in our table, we could use the following command:

```
mysql>SELECT COUNT(*) FROM joke;
+----------+
| COUNT(*) |
+----------+
| 1        |
+----------+
1 row in set (0.06 sec)
```

As you can see, we have just one joke in our table and, so far, all the examples have fetched all the entries in our table. However, we can limit our results to include only those database entries that have the specific attributes we want. We set these restrictions by adding what's called a **WHERE clause** to the SELECT command. Consider this example:

```
mysql>SELECT COUNT(*) FROM joke WHERE jokedate >= "2004-01-01";
```

This query will count the number of jokes that have dates greater than or equal to January 1, 2004. In the case of dates, "greater than or equal to" means "on or after." Another variation on this theme lets you search for entries that contain a certain piece of text. Check out this query:

```
mysql>SELECT joketext FROM joke WHERE joketext LIKE "%chicken%";
```

The above query displays the text of all jokes that contain the word "chicken" in their joketext column. The LIKE keyword tells MySQL that the named column must match the given pattern. In this case, the pattern we've used is "%chicken%". The % signs indicate that the word "chicken" may be preceded and/or followed by any string of text.

Additional conditions may also be combined in the WHERE clause to further restrict results. For example, to display knock-knock jokes from April 2004 only, we could use the following query:

```
mysql>SELECT joketext FROM joke WHERE
    ->joketext LIKE "%knock%" AND
    ->jokedate >= "2004-04-01" AND
    ->jokedate < "2004-05-01";
```

Enter a few more jokes into the table and experiment with SELECT statements. A good familiarity with the SELECT statement will come in handy later in this book.

You can do a lot with the SELECT statement. We'll look at some of its more advanced features later, when we need them.

Modifying Stored Data

Having entered your data into a database table, you might like to change it. Whether you want to correct a spelling mistake, or change the date attached to a joke, such alterations are made using the UPDATE command. This command contains elements of the INSERT command that set column values, and elements of the SELECT command that pick out entries for modification. The general form of the UPDATE command is as follows:

```
mysql>UPDATE table_name SET
    ->  col_name = new_value, ...
    ->WHERE conditions;
```

So, for example, if we wanted to change the date on the joke we entered above, we'd use the following command:

```
mysql>UPDATE joke SET jokedate="1994-04-01" WHERE id=1;
```

Here's where that `id` column comes in handy: it allows us to easily single out a joke for changes. The `WHERE` clause used here works just as it did in the `SELECT` command. This next command, for example, changes the date of all entries that contain the word "chicken:"

```
mysql>UPDATE joke SET jokedate="1994-04-01"
    ->WHERE joketext LIKE "%chicken%";
```

Deleting Stored Data

The deletion of entries in SQL is dangerously easy, which, if you haven't noticed yet, is a recurring theme. Here's the command syntax:

```
mysql>DELETE FROM table_name WHERE conditions;
```

To delete all chicken jokes from your table, you'd use the following query:

```
mysql>DELETE FROM joke WHERE joketext LIKE "%chicken%";
```

One thing to note is that the `WHERE` clause is actually optional. You should be very careful, however, if you leave it out, as the `DELETE` command will then apply to all entries in the table. This command will empty the `joke` table in one fell swoop:

```
mysql>DELETE FROM joke;
```

Scary, huh?

Summary

There's a lot more to the MySQL database system and the SQL language than the few basic commands we've discussed here, but these commands are by far the most commonly used. To date, we've only worked with a single table, but to realize the true power of a relational database, we'll also need to learn how to use multiple tables together to represent potentially complex relationships between database entities.

We'll cover all this and more in Chapter 5, where we'll discuss database design principles and look at some more advanced examples. For now, though, we've accomplished our objective, and you can comfortably interact with MySQL using the command line interface. In Chapter 3, the fun continues as we delve into the PHP server-side scripting language, and use it to create dynamic Web pages. If you like, you can practice with MySQL a little before you move on by creating a decent-sized `joke` table. This knowledge will come in handy in Chapter 4.

3

Getting Started with PHP

In Chapter 2, we learned how to use the MySQL database engine to store a list of jokes in a simple database (composed of a single table named joke). To do so, we used the MySQL command-line client to enter SQL commands (queries). In this chapter, we'll introduce the PHP server-side scripting language. In addition to the basic features we'll explore here, this language has full support for communication with MySQL databases.

Introducing PHP

As we've discussed previously, PHP is a server-side scripting language. This concept is not obvious, especially if you're used to designing pages with just HTML and JavaScript. A server-side scripting language is similar to JavaScript in that it allows you to embed little programs (scripts) into the HTML of a Web page. When executed, such scripts allow you to control what appears in the browser window more flexibly than straight HTML.

The key difference between JavaScript and PHP is simple. JavaScript is interpreted by the Web browser once the Web page that contains the script has been downloaded. Conversely, server-side scripting languages such as PHP are interpreted by the Web server before the page is even sent to the browser. And, once it's interpreted, the results of the script replace the PHP code in the Web page itself—all the browser sees is a standard HTML file. The script is processed entirely by the server, hence the designation: server-side scripting language.

Let's look back at the `today.php` example presented in Chapter 1:

File: **today.php**

```
<!DOCTYPE html PUBLIC "-//W3C//DTD XHTML 1.0 Strict//EN"
    "http://www.w3.org/TR/xhtml1/DTD/xhtml1-strict.dtd">
<html xmlns="http://www.w3.org/1999/xhtml">
<head>
<title>Today's Date</title>
<meta http-equiv="content-type"
    content="text/html; charset=iso-8859-1" />
</head>
<body>
<p>Today's Date (according to this Web server) is
<?php

echo date('l, F dS Y.');

?></p>
</body>
</html>
```

Most of this is plain HTML; however, the line between `<?php` and `?>` is written in PHP. `<?php` means "begin PHP code," and `?>` means "end PHP code." The Web server is asked to interpret everything between these two delimiters, and to convert it to regular HTML code before it sends the Web page to the requesting browser. The browser is presented with something like this:

```
<!DOCTYPE html PUBLIC "-//W3C//DTD XHTML 1.0 Strict//EN"
    "http://www.w3.org/TR/xhtml1/DTD/xhtml1-strict.dtd">
<html xmlns="http://www.w3.org/1999/xhtml">
<head>
<title>Today's Date</title>
<meta http-equiv="content-type"
    content="text/html; charset=iso-8859-1" />
</head>
<body>
<p>Today's Date (according to this Web server) is
Sunday, May 16th 2004.</p>
</body>
</html>
```

Notice that all signs of the PHP code have disappeared. In its place, the output of the script has appeared, and it looks just like standard HTML. This example demonstrates several advantages of server-side scripting:

No browser compatibility issues
> PHP scripts are interpreted by the Web server alone, so you don't have to worry about whether the language you're using is supported by visitors' browsers.

Access to server-side resources
> In the above example, we placed the date, according to the Web server, into the Web page. If we had inserted the date using JavaScript, we would only be able to display the date according to the computer on which the Web browser was running. Now, while this isn't an especially impressive example of the exploitation of server-side resources, we could just as easily have inserted some other information that would be available only to a script running on the Web server. An example might be information stored in a MySQL database that runs on the Web server computer.

Reduced load on the client
> JavaScript can slow significantly the display of a Web page on slower computers, as the browser must run the script before it can display the Web page. With server-side scripting, this burden is passed to the Web server machine.

Basic Syntax and Commands

PHP syntax will be very familiar to anyone with an understanding of C, C++, C#, Java, JavaScript, Perl, or any other C-derived language. A PHP script consists of a series of commands, or **statements**. Each statement is an instruction that must be followed the Web server before it can proceed to the next. PHP statements, like those in the above-mentioned languages, are always terminated by a semicolon (;).

This is a typical PHP statement:

```
echo 'This is a <b>test</b>!';
```

This is an `echo` statement, which is used to send output to the browser. An `echo` statement simply takes the text it's given, and places it into the page's HTML code at the current location.

In this case, we have supplied a string of text to be output: 'This is a **<b>test</b>**!'. Notice that the string of text contains HTML tags (<b> and </b>), which is perfectly acceptable. So, if we take this statement and put it into a complete PHP script (echo.php in the code archive), here's the code we get:

File: **echo.php**

```
<!DOCTYPE html PUBLIC "-//W3C//DTD XHTML 1.0 Strict//EN"
    "http://www.w3.org/TR/xhtml1/DTD/xhtml1-strict.dtd">
<html xmlns="http://www.w3.org/1999/xhtml">
<head>
<title>Simple PHP Example</title>
<meta http-equiv="content-type"
    content="text/html; charset=iso-8859-1" />
</head>
<body>
<p><?php echo 'This is a <b>test</b>!'; ?></p>
</body>
</html>
```

If you place this file on your Web server, a browser that views the page will see this:

```
<!DOCTYPE html PUBLIC "-//W3C//DTD XHTML 1.0 Strict//EN"
    "http://www.w3.org/TR/xhtml1/DTD/xhtml1-strict.dtd">
<html xmlns="http://www.w3.org/1999/xhtml">
<head>
<title>Simple PHP Example</title>
<meta http-equiv="content-type"
    content="text/html; charset=iso-8859-1" />
</head>
<body>
<p>This is a <b>test</b>!</p>
</body>
</html>
```

Our today.php example contained a slightly more complex echo statement:

File: **today.php (excerpt)**

```
echo date('l, F dS Y.');
```

Instead of giving echo a simple string of text to output, this statement invokes a **built-in function** called date and passes *it* a string of text: 'l, F ds Y.'. Built-in functions can be thought of as things that PHP knows how to do without our needing to spell out the details. PHP has many built-in functions that let us do everything from sending email, to working with information stored in various types of databases. In this case, the `date` function produces a text representation of the current date, using the string it is given to determine the format.

You may wonder why we need to surround the string of text with both parentheses (`()`) and single quotes (`' '`). Quotes are used to mark the beginning and end of strings of text in PHP, so their presence is fully justified. The parentheses serve two purposes. First, they indicate that `date` is a function that you want to call. Second, they mark the beginning and end of a list of **parameters** that you wish to provide, in order to tell the function what to do. In the case of the `date` function, you need to provide a string of text that describes the format in which you want the date to appear.[1] Later on, we'll look at functions that take more than one parameter, and we'll separate those parameters with commas. We'll also consider functions that take no parameters at all. These functions will still need the parentheses, though we won't type anything between them.

Variables and Operators

Variables in PHP are identical to variables in most other programming languages. For the uninitiated, a variable can be thought of as a name that's given to an imaginary box into which any value may be placed. The following statement creates a variable called `$testvariable` (all variable names in PHP begin with a dollar sign) and assigns it a value of **3**:

```
$testvariable = 3;
```

PHP is a **loosely typed** language. This means that a single variable may contain any type of data, be it a number, a string of text, or some other kind of value, and may change types over its lifetime. So the following statement, if it appears after the statement above, assigns a new value to our existing `$testvariable`. In the process, the variable changes type: where it used to contain a number, it now contains a string of text:

```
$testvariable = "Three";
```

The equals sign we used in the last two statements is called the **assignment operator**, as it is used to assign values to variables. Other operators may be used to perform various mathematical operations on values:

```
$testvariable = 1 + 1;   // Assigns a value of 2
$testvariable = 1 - 1;   // Assigns a value of 0
```

---

[1]A full reference is available in the online documentation for the `date` function [http://www.php.net/date].

```
$testvariable = 2 * 2;   // Assigns a value of 4
$testvariable = 2 / 2;   // Assigns a value of 1
```

Each of the lines above ends with a **comment**. Comments are a way to describe what your code is doing—they insert explanatory text into your code, and tell the PHP interpreter to ignore it. Comments begin with // and they finish at the end of the same line. You might be familiar with the /* */ style of comment used in other languages—these work in PHP as well. I'll be using comments throughout the rest of this book to help explain the code I present.

Now, let's get back to the four statements above. The operators we used are called the **arithmetic operators**, and allow you to add, subtract, multiply, and divide numbers. Among others, there is an operator that sticks strings of text together, called the **concatenation operator**:

```
$testvariable = "Hi " . "there!";
                     // Assigns a value of "Hi there!"
```

Variables may be used almost anywhere that you use an actual value. Consider these examples:

```
$var1 = 'PHP';           // Assigns a value of 'PHP' to $var1
$var2 = 5;               // Assigns a value of 5 to $var2
$var3 = $var2 + 1;       // Assigns a value of 6 to $var3
$var2 = $var1;           // Assigns a value of 'PHP' to $var2
echo $var1;              // Outputs 'PHP'
echo $var2;              // Outputs 'PHP'
echo $var3;              // Outputs '6'
echo $var1 . ' rules!';  // Outputs 'PHP rules!'
echo "$var1 rules!";     // Outputs 'PHP rules!'
echo '$var1 rules!';     // Outputs '$var1 rules!'
```

Notice the last two lines in particular. You can include the name of a variable right inside a text string, and have the value inserted in its place if you surround the string with double quotes instead of single quotes. This process of converting variable names to their values is known as **variable interpolation**. However, as the last line demonstrates, a string surrounded with single quotes will not interpolate the variable names it contains.

Arrays

An **array** is a special kind of variable that contains multiple values. If you think of a variable as a box that contains a value, then an array can be thought of as a box with compartments, where each compartment is able to store an individual value.

The simplest way to create an array in PHP is to use the built-in `array` function:

```
$myarray = array('one', 2, '3');
```

This code creates an array called `$myarray` that contains three values: `'one'`, `2`, and `'three'`. Just like an ordinary variable, each space in an array can contain any type of value. In this case, the first and third spaces contain strings, while the second contains a number.

To get at a value stored in an array, you need to know its **index**. Typically, arrays use numbers, starting with zero, as indices to point to the values they contain. That is, the first value (or element) of an array has index 0, the second has index 1, the third has index 2, and so on. In general, therefore, the index of the nth element of an array is $n-1$. Once you know the index of the value you're interested in, you can get that value by placing that index in square brackets after the array variable name:

```
echo $myarray[0];      // Outputs 'one'
echo $myarray[1];      // Outputs '2'
echo $myarray[2];      // Outputs '3'
```

You can also use the index in square brackets to create new elements, or assign new values to existing array elements:

```
$myarray[1] = 'two';   // Assign a new value
$myarray[3] = 'four';  // Create a new element
```

You can add elements to the end of an array using the assignment operator as usual, but leaving empty the square brackets that follow the variable name:

```
$myarray[] = 'the fifth element';
echo $myarray[4];      // Outputs 'the fifth element'
```

Array indices don't always have to be numbers; that's just the most common choice. You can also use strings as indices to create what is called an **associative array**. This type of array is called associative because it associates values with meaningful indices. In this example, we associate a date with each of three names:

```
$birthdays['Kevin'] = '1978-04-12';
$birthdays['Stephanie'] = '1980-05-16';
$birthdays['David'] = '1983-09-09';
```

The `array` function also lets you create associative arrays, if you prefer that method. Here's how we'd use it to create the `$birthdays` array:

```
$birthdays = array('Kevin' => '1978-04-12', 'Stephanie' =>
    '1980-05-16', 'David' => '1983-09-09');
```

Now, if we want to know Kevin's birthday, we look it up using the name as the index:

```
echo 'My birthday is: ' . $birthdays['Kevin'];
```

This type of array is especially important when it comes to user interaction in PHP, as we'll see in the next section. I'll demonstrate other uses of arrays throughout this book.

User Interaction and Forms

The ability to interact with users who view a Web page is essential for many applications of PHP. Veterans of JavaScript tend to think in terms of event handlers, which let you react directly to the actions of the user—for example, the movement of the cursor over a link on the page. Server-side scripting languages such as PHP have a more limited scope when it comes to user interaction. As PHP code is activated when a page is requested from the server, user interaction can occur only in a back-and-forth fashion: the user sends requests to the server, and the server replies with dynamically generated pages.

The key to creating interactivity with PHP is to understand the techniques we can use to send information about a user's interaction along with his or her request for a new Web page. PHP makes this fairly easy, as we'll now see.

The simplest method we can use to send information along with a page request uses the **URL query string**. If you've ever seen a URL in which a question mark followed the file name, you've witnessed this technique in use. Let's look at an easy example. Create a regular HTML file called `welcome1.html` (no `.php` file extension is required, since there will be no PHP code in this file) and insert this link:

File: **welcome.html (excerpt)**

```
<a href="welcome1.php?name=Kevin">Hi, I'm Kevin!</a>
```

This is a link to a file called `welcome1.php`, but as well as linking to the file, we're also passing a variable along with the page request. The variable is passed as part of the query string, which is the portion of the URL that follows the question mark. The variable is called name and its value is Kevin. To restate, we have created a link that loads welcome1.php, and informs the PHP code contained in the file that name equals Kevin.

To really understand the results of this process, we need to look at welcome1.php. Create it as a new HTML file, but, this time, note the .php extension—this tells the Web server that it can expect to interpret some PHP code in the file. In the body of this new file, type the following:

File: **welcome1.php** (excerpt)

```php
<?php
$name = $_GET['name'];
echo "Welcome to our Website, $name!";
?>
```

Now, if you use the link in the first file to load this second file, you'll see that the page says "Welcome to our Website, Kevin!" This is illustrated in Figure 3.1.

Figure 3.1. Greet users with a personalized welcome message.

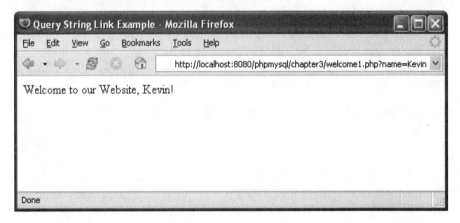

PHP creates automatically an array variable called $_GET that contains any values passed in the query string. $_GET is an associative array, so the value of the name variable passed in the query string can be accessed as $_GET['name']. Our script assigns this value to an ordinary PHP variable ($name), then displays it as part of a text string using an echo statement.

`register_globals` before PHP 4.2

In versions of PHP prior to 4.2, the `register_globals` setting in `php.ini` was set to On by default. This setting tells PHP to create ordinary variables for all the values supplied in the request automatically. In the previous example, the `$name = $_GET['name'];` line would be completely unnecessary if the `register_globals` setting were set to On, since PHP would do it automatically. Although the convenience of this feature was one aspect that helped to make PHP such a popular language in the first place, novice developers could easily leave security holes in sensitive scripts with it enabled.

For a full discussion of the issues surrounding `register_globals`, see my article *Write Secure Scripts with PHP 4.2!*[2] at sitepoint.com.

You can pass more than one value in the query string. Let's look at a slightly more complex version of the same example. Change the link in the HTML file to read as follows:

File: **welcome2.html** (excerpt)

```
<a href="welcome2.php?firstname=Kevin&amp;lastname=Yank">Hi,
I'm Kevin Yank!</a>
```

This time, we'll pass two variables: `firstname` and `lastname`. The variables are separated in the query string by an ampersand (&, which is encoded as `&amp;` as it is a special character in HTML). You can pass even more variables by separating each *name=value* pair from the next with an ampersand.

As before, we can use the two variable values in our `welcome2.php` file:

File: **welcome2.php** (excerpt)

```
<?php
$firstname = $_GET['firstname'];
$lastname = $_GET['lastname'];
echo "Welcome to my Website, $firstname $lastname!";
?>
```

The result is shown in Figure 3.2.

---

[2] http://www.sitepoint.com/article.php/758

Figure 3.2. Create an even more personalized welcome message.

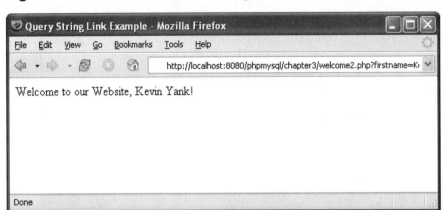

This is all well and good, but we still have yet to achieve our goal of true user interaction, where the user can enter arbitrary information and have it processed by PHP. To continue with our example of a personalized welcome message, we'd like to allow the user to type his or her name and have it appear in the message. To allow the user to type in a value, we'll need to use an HTML form.

Here's the code:

File: **welcome3.html** (excerpt)

```
<form action="welcome3.php" method="get">
<label>First Name: <input type="text" name="firstname" />
  </label><br />
<label>Last Name: <input type="text" name="lastname" />
  </label><br />
<input type="submit" value="GO" />
</form>
```

Self-closing tags

Don't be alarmed at the slashes that appear in some of these tags (e.g. **
). The XHTML standard for coding Web pages calls for slashes to be used in any tag that does not have a closing tag, which includes **input and **br** tags, among others. Current browsers do not require you to use the slashes, of course, but for the sake of standards-compliance, the HTML code in this book will observe this recommendation.

The form this code produces is shown in Figure 3.3.

Figure 3.3. Make your own welcome message.

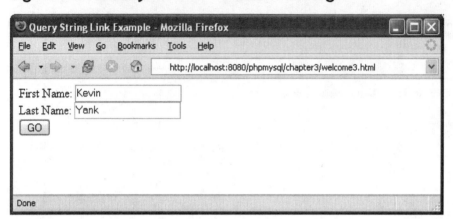

This form has the exact same effect as the second link we looked at (with firstname=Kevin&lastname=Yank in the query string), except that you can now enter whatever names you like. When you click the submit button (which is labelled GO), the browser will load welcome3.php and add the variables and their values to the query string for you automatically. It retrieves the names of the variables from the name attributes of the input type="text" tags, and obtains the values from the information the user typed into the text fields.

The method attribute of the form tag is used to tell the browser how to send the variables and their values along with the request. A value of get (as used above) causes them to be passed in the query string (and appear in PHP's $_GET array), but there is an alternative. It's not always desirable—or even technically feasible—to have the values appear in the query string. What if we included a textarea tag in the form, to let the user enter a large amount of text? A URL whose query string contained several paragraphs of text would be ridiculously long, and would possibly exceed the maximum length for a URL in today's browsers. The alternative is for the browser to pass the information invisibly, behind the scenes. The code for this looks exactly the same, but where we set the form method to get in the last example, here we set it to post:

File: **welcome4.html (excerpt)**

```
<form action="welcome4.php" method="post">
<label>First Name:
  <input type="text" name="firstname" /></label><br />
<label>Last Name:
  <input type="text" name="lastname" /></label><br />
```

```
<input type="submit" value="GO" />
</form>
```

As we're no longer sending the variables as part of the query string, they no longer appear in PHP's $_GET array. Instead, they are placed in another array reserved especially for 'posted' form variables: $_POST. We must therefore modify wel-come4.php to retrieve the values from this new array:

File: **welcome4.php (excerpt)**

```
<?php
$firstname = $_POST['firstname'];
$lastname = $_POST['lastname'];
echo "Welcome to my Website, $firstname $lastname!";
?>
```

Figure 3.4 shows what the resulting page looks like once this new form is submitted.

Figure 3.4. This personalized welcome is achieved without a query string.

The form is functionally identical to the previous one; the only difference is that the URL of the page that's loaded when the user clicks the GO button will not have a query string. On the one hand, this lets you include large values, or sensitive values (like passwords), in the data that's submitted by the form, without their appearing in the query string. On the other hand, if the user bookmarks the page that results from the form's submission, that bookmark will be useless, as it doesn't contain the submitted values. This, incidentally, is the main reason that search engines use the query string to submit search terms. If you bookmark a search results page on Google[3] or AltaVista[4], you can use that bookmark to perform the same search again later, because the search terms are contained in the URL.

Sometimes, you want access to a variable without having to worry about whether it was sent as part of the query string or a form post. In cases like these, the special $_REQUEST array comes in handy. It contains all the variables that appear in both $_GET and $_POST. With this variable, we can modify our form processing script one more time so that it can receive the first and last names of the user from either source:

File: **welcome5.php (excerpt)**

```php
<?php
$firstname = $_REQUEST['firstname'];
$lastname = $_REQUEST['lastname'];
echo "Welcome to my Website, $firstname $lastname!";
?>
```

That covers the basics of using forms to produce rudimentary user interaction with PHP. I'll cover more advanced issues and techniques in later examples.

Control Structures

All the examples of PHP code we've seen so far have been either simple, one-statement scripts that output a string of text to the Web page, or series of statements that were to be executed one after the other in order. If you've ever written programs in other languages (JavaScript, C, or BASIC) you already know that practical programs are rarely so simple.

PHP, just like any other programming language, provides facilities that allow us to affect the **flow of control** in a script. That is, the language contains special statements that permit you to deviate from the one-after-another execution order that has dominated our examples so far. Such statements are called **control structures**. Don't get it? Don't worry! A few examples will illustrate perfectly.

The most basic, and most often-used, control structure is the **if-else statement**. Here's what it looks like:

```php
if (condition) {
  // Statement(s) to be executed if
```

---

[3] http://www.google.com/
[4] http://www.altavista.com/

```
    // condition is true.
} else {
    // (Optional) Statement(s) to be
    // executed if condition is false.
}
```

This control structure lets us tell PHP to execute one set of statements or another, depending on whether some condition is true or false. If you'll indulge my vanity for a moment, here's an example that shows a twist on the personalized welcome page example we created earlier:

File: **welcome6.php (excerpt)**

```
$name = $_REQUEST['name'];
if ($name == 'Kevin') {
    echo 'Welcome, oh glorious leader!';
} else {
    echo "Welcome to our Website, $name!";
}
```

Now, if the name variable passed to the page has a value of Kevin, a special message will be displayed. Otherwise, the normal message will be displayed and will contain the name that the user entered. The result in the former case is shown in Figure 3.5.

Figure 3.5. It's good to be the king.

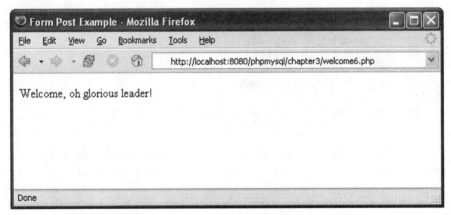

As indicated in the code structure above, the **else clause** (that part of the if-else statement that says what to do if the condition is false) is optional. Let's say you wanted to display the special message above only if the appropriate name was entered; otherwise, you didn't want to display any message. Here's how the code would look:

```
$name = $_REQUEST['name'];
if ($name == 'Kevin') {
  echo 'Welcome, oh glorious leader!';
}
```

The == used in the condition above is the PHP **equal-to operator** that's used to compare two values to see whether they're equal.

IMPORTANT

Double Trouble

Remember to type the double-equals, because if you were to use a single equals sign you'd be using the assignment operator discussed above. So, instead of comparing the variable to the designated value, instead, you'd assign a new value to the variable—an operation that evaluates as true as long as the new value isn't zero, false, or an empty string. This would not only cause the condition always to be true, but would also change the value in the variable you're checking, which could cause all sorts of problems later in the script.

Conditions can be more complex than a single comparison for equality. Recall that our form examples above would receive a first and last name. If we wanted to display a special message only for a particular person, we'd have to check the values of *both* names:

File: **welcome7.php (excerpt)**

```
$firstname = $_REQUEST['firstname'];
$lastname = $_REQUEST['lastname'];
if ($firstname == 'Kevin' and $lastname == 'Yank') {
  echo 'Welcome, oh glorious leader!';
} else {
  echo "Welcome to my Website, $firstname $lastname!";
}
```

This condition will be true if and only if `$firstname` has a value of `Kevin` and `$lastname` has a value of Yank. The word and in the above condition makes the whole condition true only if both of the comparisons evaluate to true. Another such operator is `or`, which makes the whole condition true if one or both of two simple conditions are true. If you're more familiar with the JavaScript or C forms of these operators (`&&` and `||` for and and or respectively), that's fine—they work in PHP as well.

Figure 3.6 shows that getting only one of the names right in this example doesn't cut the mustard.

Figure 3.6. Frankly, my dear...

We'll look at more complicated conditions as the need arises. For the time being, a general familiarity with the if-else statement is sufficient.

Another often-used PHP control structure is the **while loop**. Where the if-else statement allowed us to choose whether or not to execute a set of statements depending on some condition, the while loop allows us to use a condition to determine how many times we'll execute a set of statements repeatedly. Here's what a while loop looks like:

```
while (condition) {
  // statement(s) to execute over
  // and over as long as condition
  // remains true
}
```

The while loop works very similarly to an if-else statement without an else clause. The difference arises when the condition is true and the statement(s) are executed. Instead of continuing the execution with the statement that follows the closing brace (}), the condition is checked again. If the condition is still true, then the statement(s) are executed a second time, and a third, and will continue to be executed as long as the condition remains true. The first time the condition evaluates false (whether it's the first time it's checked, or the one-hundred-and-first), execution jumps immediately to the statement that follows the while loop, after the closing brace.

Loops like these come in handy whenever you're working with long lists of things (such as jokes stored in a database... hint, hint!), but for now we'll illustrate with a trivial example: counting to ten.

File: **count10.php (excerpt)**

```
$count = 1;
while ($count <= 10) {
  echo "$count ";
  ++$count;
}
```

It looks a bit frightening, I know, but let me talk you through it line by line. The first line creates a variable called $count and assigns it a value of 1. The second line is the start of a while loop, the condition for which is that the value of $count is less than or equal (<=) to 10. The third and fourth lines make up the body of the while loop, and will be executed over and over, as long as that condition holds true. The third line simply outputs the value of $count, followed by a space. The fourth line adds one to the value of $count (++$count is a short cut for $count = $count + 1—both will work).

So here's what happens when this piece of code is executed. The first time the condition is checked, the value of $count is 1, so the condition is definitely true. The value of $count (1) is output, and $count is given a new value of 2. The condition is still true the second time it is checked, so the value (2) is output and a new value (3) is assigned. This process continues, outputting the values 3, 4, 5, 6, 7, 8, 9, and 10. Finally, $count is given a value of 11, and the condition is false, which ends the loop. The net result of the code is shown in Figure 3.7.

Figure 3.7. PHP demonstrates kindergarten-level math skills.

The condition in this example used a new operator: <= (**less than or equal**). Other numerical comparison operators of this type include >= (**greater than or equal**), < (**less than**), > (**greater than**), and != (**not equal**). That last one also works when comparing text strings, by the way.

Another type of loop that is designed specifically to handle examples like that above, in which we're counting through a series of values until some condition is met, is called a **for loop**. Here's what it looks like:

```
for (initialize; condition; update) {
  // statement(s) to execute over
  // and over as long as condition
  // remains true after each update
}
```

The *initialize* statement is executed once at the start of the loop; the *condition* statement is checked each time through the loop, before the statements in the body are executed; the *update* statement is executed each time through the loop, but after the statements in the body.

Here's what the "counting to 10" example looks like when implemented with a for loop:

File: **count10-for.php** (excerpt)

```
for ($count = 1; $count <= 10; ++$count) {
  echo "$count ";
}
```

As you can see, the statements that initialize and increment the $count variable join the condition on the first line of the for loop. Although, at first glance, the code seems a little more difficult to read, putting all the code that deals with controlling the loop in the same place actually makes it easier to understand once you're used to the syntax. Many of the examples in this book will use for loops, so you'll have plenty of opportunity to practice reading them.

Multipurpose Pages

Let's say you wanted to construct your site so that it showed the visitor's name at the top of every page. With our custom welcome message example above, we're halfway there already. Here are the problems we'll need to overcome to extend the example:

❑ We need the name on every page of the site, not just one.

❏ We have no control over which page of our site users will view first.

The first problem isn't too hard to overcome. Once we have the user's name in a variable on one page, we can pass it with any request to another page by adding the name to the query string of all links:[2]

```
<a href="newpage.php?name=<?php echo urlencode($_GET['name']);?>">
A link</a>
```

Notice that we've embedded PHP code right in the middle of an HTML tag. This is perfectly legal, and will work just fine.

You're familiar with `echo` statements, but the `urlencode` function is probably new to you. This function takes special characters in the string (for example, spaces) and converts them into the special codes they need to be in order to appear in the query string. For example, if the `$name` variable had a value of 'Kevin Yank', then, as spaces are not allowed in the query string, the output of `urlencode` (and thus, the string output by `echo`) would be 'Kevin+Yank'. PHP would then convert it back automatically when it created the `$_GET` variable in `newpage.php`.

Okay, so the user's name will be passed with every link in our site. Now all we need is to get that name in the first place. In our welcome message example, we had a special HTML page containing a form that prompted the user for his or her name. The problem with this (identified by the second point above) is that we couldn't—nor would we wish to—force the user to enter our Website by that page every time he or she visited our site.

The solution is to have every page of our site check to see if a name has been specified, and prompt the user for a name if necessary.[3] This means that every page of our site will either display its content, or prompt the user to enter a name, depending on whether the `$name` variable is found to have a value. If you think this is beginning to sound like a good place for an `if-else` statement, you're a quick study!

We'll refer to pages that can decide whether to display one thing or another as **multipurpose pages**. The code of a multipurpose page looks something like this:

```
<!DOCTYPE html PUBLIC "-//W3C//DTD XHTML 1.0 Strict//EN"
    "http://www.w3.org/TR/xhtml1/DTD/xhtml1-strict.dtd">
```

---

[2] If this sounds like a lot of work to you, it is. Don't worry; we'll learn much more practical methods for sharing variables between pages in Chapter 11.

[3] Again, if you're dreading the thought of adding PHP code to prompt the user for a name to every page of your site, don't fret; we'll cover a more practical way to do this later.

```
<html xmlns="http://www.w3.org/1999/xhtml">
<head>
<title>Multipurpose Page Outline</title>
<meta http-equiv="content-type"
    content="text/html; charset=iso-8859-1" />
</head>
<body>

<?php if (condition) { ?>

<!-- HTML content to display if condition is true -->

<?php } else { ?>

<!-- HTML content to display if condition is false -->

<?php } ?>

</body>
</html>
```

This code may confuse you at first, but, in fact, this is just a normal `if-else` statement with HTML code sections that depend on the condition, instead of PHP statements. This example illustrates one of the big selling points of PHP: that you can switch in and out of "PHP mode" whenever you like. If you think of `<?php` as the command to switch into "PHP mode", and `?>` as the command to go back into "normal HTML mode," the above example should make perfect sense.

There's an alternate form of the `if-else` statement that can make your code more readable in situations like this. Here's the outline for a multipurpose page using the alternate `if-else` form:

```
<!DOCTYPE html PUBLIC "-//W3C//DTD XHTML 1.0 Strict//EN"
    "http://www.w3.org/TR/xhtml1/DTD/xhtml1-strict.dtd">
<html xmlns="http://www.w3.org/1999/xhtml">
<head>
<title>Multipurpose Page Outline</title>
<meta http-equiv="content-type"
    content="text/html; charset=iso-8859-1" />
</head>
<body>

<?php if (condition): ?>
```

```
<!-- HTML content to display if condition is true -->

<?php else: ?>

<!-- HTML content to display if condition is false -->

<?php endif; ?>

</body>
</html>
```

Okay, now that we have all the tools we need in hand, let's look at a sample page of our site:

File: **samplepage.php**

```
<!DOCTYPE html PUBLIC "-//W3C//DTD XHTML 1.0 Strict//EN"
    "http://www.w3.org/TR/xhtml1/DTD/xhtml1-strict.dtd">
<html xmlns="http://www.w3.org/1999/xhtml">
<head>
<title>Sample Page</title>
<meta http-equiv="content-type"
    content="text/html; charset=iso-8859-1" />
</head>
<body>

<?php if (!isset($_GET['name'])): ?>

  <!-- No name has been provided, so we
      prompt the user for one.          -->

  <form action="<?php echo $_SERVER['PHP_SELF']; ?>" method="get">
  <label>Please enter your name:
    <input type="text" name="name" /></label>
  <input type="submit" value="GO" />
  </form>

<?php else: ?>

  <p>Your name: <?php echo $_GET['name']; ?></p>

  <p>This paragraph contains a
    <a href="newpage.php?name=<?php echo urlencode($_GET['name']);
    ?>">link</a> that passes the name variable on to the next
    document.</p>

<?php endif; ?>
```

```
</body>
</html>
```

There are two new tricks in the above code, but overall you should be fairly comfortable with the way it works. First of all, we're using a new function called isset in the condition. This function returns (outputs) a value of true if the variable it is given has been assigned a value (i.e. if a name has been provided in this example), and false if the variable does not exist (i.e. if a name has not yet been provided). The exclamation mark (also known as the **negation operator**, or the **not operator**), which appears before the name of the function, reverses the returned value from true to false, or vice-versa. Thus, the form is displayed when the $_GET['name'] variable is not set.

The second new trick is the use of the variable $_SERVER['PHP_SELF'] to specify the action attribute of the <form> tag. Like $_GET, $_POST, and $_REQUEST, $_SERVER is an array variable that is automatically created by PHP. $_SERVER contains a whole bunch of information supplied by your Web server. In particular, $_SERVER['PHP_SELF'] will always be set to the URL of the current page. This gives us an easy way to create a form that, when submitted, will load the very same page, but this time with the $name variable specified.

Figure 3.8. Kicking butt and taking names.

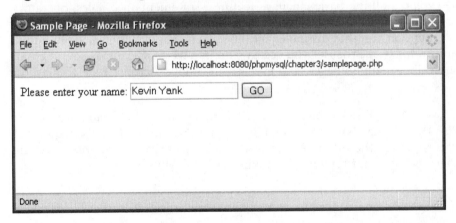

If we structure all the pages on our site in this way, visitors will be prompted for their name by the first page they attempt to view, whichever page this happens to be, as shown in Figure 3.8. Once they enter their names and click GO, they'll be presented with the exact page they requested. As shown in the status bar of

Figure 3.9, the entered name is then passed in the query string of every link from that point onward, ensuring that the user is prompted only once.

Figure 3.9. We know who you are.

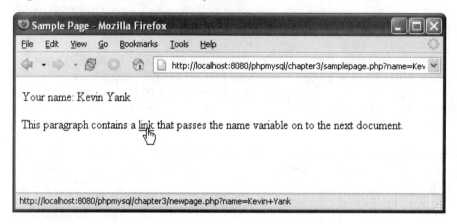

Summary

In this chapter, we've seen the PHP server-side scripting language in action as we've explored all the basic language features: statements, variables, operators, and control structures. The sample applications we've seen have been reasonably simple, but don't let that dissuade you. The real power of PHP is in its hundreds of built-in functions that let you access data in a MySQL database, send email, dynamically generate images, and even create Adobe Acrobat PDF files on the fly.

In Chapter 4, we'll delve into the MySQL functions in PHP, and see how to publish the joke database we created in Chapter 2 to the Web. This chapter will set the scene for the ultimate goal of this book—creating a complete content management system for your Website in PHP and MySQL.

Publishing MySQL Data on the Web

This is it—the stuff you signed up for! In this chapter, you'll learn how to take information stored in a database and display it on a Web page for all to see. So far, you've installed and learned the basics of MySQL, a relational database engine, and PHP, a server-side scripting language. Now you'll see how to use these two new tools together to create a true database-driven Website!

A Look Back at First Principles

Before we leap forward, it's worth a brief look back to remind you of our ultimate goal. We have two powerful tools at our disposal: the PHP scripting language, and the MySQL database engine. It's important to understand how these will fit together.

The whole idea of a database-driven Website is to allow the content of the site to reside in a database, and for that content to be pulled from the database dynamically to create Web pages for people to view with a regular Web browser. So, on one end of the system you have a visitor to your site who uses a Web browser to request a page, and expects to receive a standard HTML document. On the other end you have the content of your site, which sits in one or more tables in a MySQL database that understands only how to respond to SQL queries (commands).

Figure 4.1. PHP retrieves MySQL data to produce Web pages.

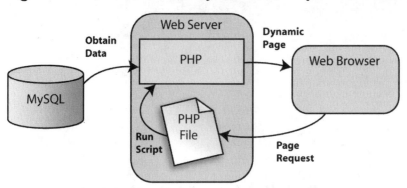

As shown in Figure 4.1, the PHP scripting language is the go-between that speaks both languages. It processes the page request and fetches the data from the MySQL database, then spits it out dynamically as the nicely-formatted HTML page that the browser expects. With PHP, you can write the presentation aspects of your site (the fancy graphics and page layouts) as "templates" in regular HTML. At the points at which content belongs in those templates, you use some PHP code to connect to the MySQL database and—using SQL queries just like those you used to create a table of jokes in Chapter 2—retrieve and display some content in its place.

Just so it's clear and fresh in your mind, this is what will happen when someone visits a page on your database-driven Website:

1. The visitor's Web browser requests the Web page using a standard URL.

2. The Web server software (Apache, IIS, or whatever) recognizes that the re-quested file is a PHP script, so the server interprets the file using its PHP plug-in before responding to the page request.

3. Certain PHP commands (which you have yet to learn) connect to the MySQL database and request the content that belongs in the Web page.

4. The MySQL database responds by sending the requested content to the PHP script.

5. The PHP script stores the content into one or more PHP variables, then uses the now-familiar `echo` statement to output the content as part of the Web page.

6.   The PHP plug-in finishes up by handing a copy of the HTML it has created to the Web server.

7.   The Web server sends the HTML to the Web browser as it would a plain HTML file, except that instead of coming directly from an HTML file, the page is the output provided by the PHP plug-in.

Connecting to MySQL with PHP

Before you can get content out of your MySQL database for inclusion in a Web page, you must know how to establish a connection to MySQL from inside a PHP script. Back in Chapter 2, you used a program called `mysql` that allowed you to make such a connection from the command prompt. PHP has no need of any special program, however; support for connecting to MySQL is built right into the language. The built-in function `mysql_connect` establishes the connection:

```
mysql_connect(address, username, password)
```

Here, *address* is the IP address or host name of the computer on which the MySQL server software is running (`'localhost'` if it's running on the same computer as the Web server software), and *username* and *password* are the same MySQL user name and password you used to connect to the MySQL server in Chapter 2.

You may remember that functions in PHP usually return (output) a value when they're called. Don't worry if this doesn't ring any bells for you—it's a detail that I glossed over when I first discussed functions in Chapter 3. In addition to doing something useful when they are called, most functions output a value; that value may be stored in a variable for later use. The `mysql_connect` function shown above, for example, returns a number that identifies the connection that has been established. Since we intend to make use of the connection, we should hold onto this value. Here's an example of how we might connect to our MySQL server.

```
$dbcnx = mysql_connect('localhost', 'root', 'mypasswd');
```

As described above, the values of the three function parameters may differ for your MySQL server. What's important to see here is that the value returned by `mysql_connect` (which we'll call a **connection identifier**) is stored in a variable named `$dbcnx`.

As the MySQL server is a completely separate piece of software, we must consider the possibility that the server may be unavailable or inaccessible due to a network outage, or because the user name/password combination you provided is not accepted by the server. In such cases, the `mysql_connect` function doesn't return a connection identifier, as no connection is established; instead, it returns false. This allows us to react to such failures using an `if` statement:

```
$dbcnx = @mysql_connect('localhost', 'root', 'mypasswd');
if (!$dbcnx) {
  echo '<p>Unable to connect to the ' .
      'database server at this time.</p>' );
  exit();
}
```

There are three new tricks in the above code fragment. First, we have placed an @ symbol in front of the `mysql_connect` function. Many functions, including `mysql_connect`, automatically display ugly error messages when they fail. Placing the @ symbol (also known as the **error suppression operator**) in front of the function name tells the function to fail silently, and allows us to display our own, friendlier error message.

Next, we put an exclamation mark (!) in front of the `$dbcnx` variable in the condition of the `if` statement. The exclamation mark is the PHP **negation operator**, which basically flips a false value to true, or a true value to false. Thus, if the connection fails and `mysql_connect` returns false, `!$dbcnx` will evaluate to true, and cause the statements in the body of our `if` statement to be executed. Alternatively, if a connection was made, the connection identifier stored in `$dbcnx` will evaluate to true (any number other than zero is considered "true" in PHP), so `!$dbcnx` will evaluate to false, and the statements in the `if` statement will not be executed.

The last new trick is the `exit` function, which is the first example that we've encountered of a function that can be called with no parameters. When called this way, all this function does is cause PHP to stop reading the page at this point. This is a good response to a failed database connection because in most cases the page will be unable to display any useful information without that connection.

As in Chapter 2, once a connection is established, the next step is to select the database with which you want to work. Let's say we want to work with the joke database we created in Chapter 2. The database we created was called `ijdb`. Selecting that database in PHP is just a matter of another function call:

```
mysql_select_db('ijdb', $dbcnx);
```

Notice we use the `$dbcnx` variable that contains the database connection identifier to tell the function which database connection to use. This parameter is actually optional. When it's omitted, the function will automatically use the link identifier for the last connection opened. This function returns true when it's successful and false if an error occurs. Once again, it's prudent to use an `if` statement to handle errors:

```
if (!@mysql_select_db('ijdb')) {
  exit('<p>Unable to locate the joke ' .
     'database at this time.</p>');
}
```

Note that this time, instead of assigning the result of the function to a variable and then checking if the variable is true or false, I have simply used the function call itself as the condition. This may look a little strange, but it's a very commonly used shortcut. To check whether the condition is true or false, PHP executes the function and then checks its return value—exactly what we need to happen.

Another short cut I've used here is to call `exit` with a string parameter. When called with a parameter, `exit` works just like an `echo` statement, except that the script exits after the string is output. So, calling `exit` this way is equivalent to an `echo` statement followed by a call to `exit` with no parameters, which is what we used for `mysql_connect` above.

With a connection established and a database selected, we're ready to begin using the data stored in the database.

Sending SQL Queries with PHP

In Chapter 2, we connected to the MySQL database server using a program called `mysql` that allowed us to type SQL queries (commands) and view the results of those queries immediately. In PHP, a similar mechanism exists: the `mysql_query` function.

```
mysql_query(query[, connection_id])
```

Here *query* is a string that contains the SQL command we want to execute. As with `mysql_select_db`, the connection identifier parameter is optional.

What this function returns will depend on the type of query being sent. For most SQL commands, `mysql_query` returns either true or false to indicate success or failure respectively. Consider the following example, which attempts to create the `joke` table we created in Chapter 2:

```
$sql = 'CREATE TABLE joke (
        id INT NOT NULL AUTO_INCREMENT PRIMARY KEY,
        joketext TEXT,
        jokedate DATE NOT NULL
    )';
if (@mysql_query($sql)) {
  echo '<p>joke table successfully created!</p>';
} else {
  exit('<p>Error creating joke table: ' .
      mysql_error() . '</p>');
}
```

Again, we use the @ trick to suppress any error messages produced by `mysql_query`, and instead print out a friendlier error message of our own. The `mysql_error` function used here returns a string of text that describes the last error message that was sent by the MySQL server.

For `DELETE`, `INSERT`, and `UPDATE` queries (which serve to modify stored data), MySQL also keeps track of the number of table rows (entries) that were affected by the query. Consider the SQL command below, which we used in Chapter 2 to set the dates of all jokes that contained the word "chicken":

```
$sql = "UPDATE joke SET jokedate='1994-04-01'
    WHERE joketext LIKE '%chicken%'";
```

When we execute this query, we can use the `mysql_affected_rows` function to view the number of rows that were affected by this update:

```
if (@mysql_query($sql)) {
  echo '<p>Update affected ' . mysql_affected_rows() .
      ' rows.</p>';
} else {
  exit('<p>Error performing update: ' . mysql_error() .
      '</p>');
}
```

`SELECT` queries are treated a little differently, as they can retrieve a lot of data, and PHP must provide ways to handle that information.

Handling SELECT Result Sets

For most SQL queries, the `mysql_query` function returns either true (success) or false (failure). For `SELECT` queries, this just isn't enough. You'll recall that `SELECT` queries are used to view stored data in the database. In addition to indicating whether the query succeeded or failed, PHP must also receive the results of the query. Thus, when it processes a SELECT query, mysql_query returns a number that identifies a **result set**, which contains a list of all the rows (entries) returned from the query. False is still returned if the query fails for any reason.

```php
$result = @mysql_query('SELECT JokeText FROM Jokes');
if (!$result) {
  exit('<p>Error performing query: ' . mysql_error() .
    '</p>');
}
```

Provided that no error was encountered in processing the query, the above code will place a number into the variable $result. This number corresponds to a result set that contains the text of all the jokes stored in the joke table. As there's no practical limit on the number of jokes in the database, that result set can be pretty big.

We mentioned before that the while loop is a useful control structure for dealing with large amounts of data. Here's an outline of the code that will process the rows in a result set one at a time:

```php
while ($row = mysql_fetch_array($result)) {
  // process the row...
}
```

The condition for the while loop probably doesn't resemble the conditions you're used to, so let me explain how it works. Consider the condition as a statement all by itself:

```php
$row = mysql_fetch_array($result);
```

The mysql_fetch_array function accepts a result set number as a parameter (stored in the $result variable in this case), and returns the next row in the result set as an array (see Chapter 3 for a discussion of arrays). When there are no more rows in the result set, mysql_fetch_array instead returns false.

Now, the above statement assigns a value to the $row variable, but, at the same time, the whole statement itself takes on that same value. This is what lets you use the statement as a condition in the while loop. Since a while loop will keep looping until its condition evaluates to false, this loop will occur as many times as there are rows in the result set, with $row taking on the value of the next row each time the loop executes. All that's left to figure out is how to get the values out of the $row variable each time the loop runs.

Rows of a result set returned by `mysql_fetch_array` are represented as associative arrays. The indices are named after the table columns in the result set. If $row is a row in our result set, then $row['joketext'] is the value in the `joketext` column of that row. So here's what our `while` loop should look like if we want to print the text of all the jokes in our database:

```
while ($row = mysql_fetch_array($result)) {
  echo '<p>' . $row['joketext'] . '</p>';
}
```

To summarize, here's the complete code of a PHP Web page that will connect to our database, fetch the text of all the jokes in the database, and display them in HTML paragraphs:

File: **jokelist.php**

```
<!DOCTYPE html PUBLIC "-//W3C//DTD XHTML 1.0 Strict//EN"
    "http://www.w3.org/TR/xhtml1/DTD/xhtml1-strict.dtd">
<html xmlns="http://www.w3.org/1999/xhtml">
<head>
<title>Our List of Jokes</title>
<meta http-equiv="content-type"
    content="text/html; charset=iso-8859-1" />
</head>
<body>
<?php

// Connect to the database server
$dbcnx = @mysql_connect('localhost', 'root', 'mypasswd');
if (!$dbcnx) {
  exit('<p>Unable to connect to the ' .
      'database server at this time.</p>');
}

// Select the jokes database
if (!@mysql_select_db('ijdb')) {
  exit('<p>Unable to locate the joke ' .
      'database at this time.</p>');
}

?>
<p>Here are all the jokes in our database:</p>
<blockquote>
<?php

// Request the text of all the jokes
```

```
$result = @mysql_query('SELECT joketext FROM joke');
if (!$result) {
  exit('<p>Error performing query: ' . mysql_error() . '</p>');
}

// Display the text of each joke in a paragraph
while ($row = mysql_fetch_array($result)) {
  echo '<p>' . $row['joketext'] . '</p>';
}

?>
</blockquote>
</body>
</html>
```

Figure 4.2 shows what this page looks like once you've added a couple of jokes to the database.

Figure 4.2. All my best material—in one place!

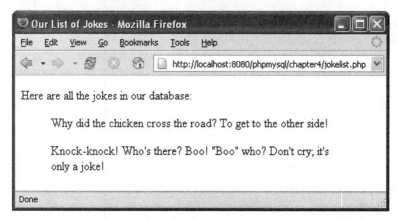

Inserting Data into the Database

In this section, we'll see how we can use the tools at our disposal to allow site visitors to add their own jokes to the database. If you enjoy a challenge, you might want to try to figure this out on your own before you read any further. There is *little* new material in this section, but it's mostly just a sample application that incorporates everything we've learned so far.

If you want to let visitors to your site type in new jokes, you'll obviously need a form. Here's the code for a form that will fit the bill:

File: **jokes.php** (excerpt)

```
<form action="<?php echo $_SERVER['PHP_SELF']; ?>" method="post">
<label>Type your joke here:<br />
<textarea name="joketext" rows="10" cols="40">
</textarea></label><br />
<input type="submit" value="SUBMIT" />
</form>
```

Figure 4.3 shows what this form looks like in a browser.

Figure 4.3. Another nugget of comic genius is added to the database.

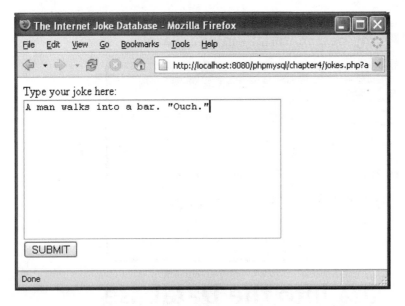

As we've seen before, when submitted, this form will load the very same page (because we used the $_SERVER['PHP_SELF'] variable for the form's action attribute) with one difference: a variable will be attached to the request. The variable, joketext, will contain the text of the joke as typed into the text area, and will appear in the $_POST and $_REQUEST arrays created by PHP.

To insert the submitted joke into the database, we use `mysql_query` to run an INSERT query, using the value stored in `$_POST['joketext']` to fill in the joke-text column in the query:

File: **jokes.php (excerpt)**

```
if (isset($_POST['joketext'])) {
  $joketext = $_POST['joketext'];
  $sql = "INSERT INTO joke SET
      joketext='$joketext',
      jokedate=CURDATE()";
  if (@mysql_query($sql)) {
    echo '<p>Your joke has been added.</p>';
  } else {
    echo '<p>Error adding submitted joke: ' .
      mysql_error() . '</p>';
  }
}
```

The one new trick in this example is shown in bold. The MySQL function `CURDATE()` is used here to assign the current date as the value of the `jokedate` column. MySQL actually has dozens of these functions, but we'll introduce them only as required. For a complete MySQL function reference, refer to Appendix B.

We now have the code that will allow a user to type a joke and add it to our database. All that remains is to slot it into our existing joke viewing page in a useful fashion. As most users will only want to view jokes, we don't want to mar our page with a big, ugly form unless the user expresses an interest in adding a new joke. For this reason, our application is well suited for implementation as a multipurpose page. Here's the full code:

File: **jokes.php**

```
<!DOCTYPE html PUBLIC "-//W3C//DTD XHTML 1.0 Strict//EN"
    "http://www.w3.org/TR/xhtml1/DTD/xhtml1-strict.dtd">
<html xmlns="http://www.w3.org/1999/xhtml">
<head>
<title>The Internet Joke Database</title>
<meta http-equiv="content-type"
    content="text/html; charset=iso-8859-1" />
</head>
<body>

<?php if (isset($_GET['addjoke'])): // User wants to add a joke
?>

<form action="<?php echo $_SERVER['PHP_SELF']; ?>" method="post">
```

```
<label>Type your joke here:<br />
<textarea name="joketext" rows="10" cols="40">
</textarea></label><br />
<input type="submit" value="SUBMIT" />
</form>

<?php else: // Default page display

  // Connect to the database server
  $dbcnx = @mysql_connect('localhost', 'root', 'mypasswd');
  if (!$dbcnx) {
    exit('<p>Unable to connect to the ' .
        'database server at this time.</p>');
  }

  // Select the jokes database
  if (!@mysql_select_db('ijdb')) {
    exit('<p>Unable to locate the joke ' .
        'database at this time.</p>');
  }

  // If a joke has been submitted,
  // add it to the database.
  if (isset($_POST['joketext'])) {
    $joketext = $_POST['joketext'];
    $sql = "INSERT INTO joke SET
        joketext='$joketext',
        jokedate=CURDATE()";
    if (@mysql_query($sql)) {
      echo '<p>Your joke has been added.</p>';
    } else {
      echo '<p>Error adding submitted joke: ' .
          mysql_error() . '</p>';
    }
  }

  echo '<p>Here are all the jokes in our database:</p>';

  // Request the text of all the jokes
  $result = @mysql_query('SELECT joketext FROM joke');
  if (!$result) {
    exit('<p>Error performing query: ' .
        mysql_error() . '</p>');
  }

  // Display the text of each joke in a paragraph
```

```
  while ($row = mysql_fetch_array($result)) {
    echo '<p>' . $row['joketext'] . '</p>';
  }

  // When clicked, this link will load this page
  // with the joke submission form displayed.
  echo '<p><a href="' . $_SERVER['PHP_SELF'] .
      '?addjoke=1">Add a Joke!</a></p>';

endif;
?>
</body>
</html>
```

Load this up and add a new joke or two to the database via your browser. The resulting page should look like Figure 4.4.

Figure 4.4. Look, Ma! No SQL!

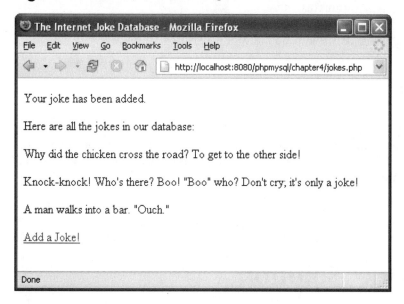

There we go! With a single file that contains a little PHP code, we're able to view existing jokes in, and add new jokes to, our MySQL database.

A Challenge

As "homework", see if you can figure out how to place next to each joke on the page a link labelled Delete this joke that, when clicked, will remove that joke from the database and display the updated joke list. Here are a few hints to get you started:

❑ You'll still be able to do it all in a single multipurpose page.

❑ You'll need to use the SQL DELETE command, which we learned about in Chapter 2.

❑ This is the tough one: to delete a particular joke, you'll need to be able to identify it uniquely. The id column in the joke table was designed to serve this purpose. You're going to have to pass the ID of the joke to be deleted with the request to delete a joke. The query string of the Delete this joke link is a perfect place to put this value.

If you think you have the answer, or if you'd just like to see the solution, turn the page. Good luck!

Summary

In this chapter, you learned some new PHP functions that allow you to interface with a MySQL database server. Using these functions, you built your first database-driven Website, which published the ijdb database online, and allowed visitors to add jokes to it.

In Chapter 5, we go back to the MySQL command line. We'll learn how to use relational database principles and advanced SQL queries to represent more complex types of information, and give our visitors credit for the jokes they add!

"Homework" Solution

Here's the solution to the "homework" challenge posed above. These changes were required to insert a Delete this joke link next to each joke:

❑ Previously, we passed an addjoke variable with our Add a Joke! link at the bottom of the page to signal that our script should display the joke entry form, instead of the usual list of jokes. In a similar fashion, we pass a deletejoke variable with our Delete this joke link to indicate our desire to have a joke deleted.

❏ For each joke, we fetch the `id` column from the database, along with the `joketext` column, so that we know which ID is associated with each joke in the database.

❏ We set the value of the `$_GET['deletejoke']` variable to the ID of the joke that we're deleting. To do this, we insert the ID value fetched from the database into the HTML code for the Delete this joke link of each joke.

❏ Using an `if` statement, we watch to see if `$_GET['deletejoke']` is set to a particular value (through the `isset` function) when the page loads. If it is, we use the value to which it is set (the ID of the joke to be deleted) in an SQL `DELETE` statement that deletes the joke in question.

Here's the complete code. If you have any questions, don't hesitate to post them in the SitePoint Forums[1]!

File: **challenge.php**

```
<!DOCTYPE html PUBLIC "-//W3C//DTD XHTML 1.0 Strict//EN"
    "http://www.w3.org/TR/xhtml1/DTD/xhtml1-strict.dtd">
<html xmlns="http://www.w3.org/1999/xhtml">
<head>
<title>The Internet Joke Database</title>
<meta http-equiv="content-type"
    content="text/html; charset=iso-8859-1" />
</head>
<body>
<?php if (isset($_GET['addjoke'])): // User wants to add a joke
?>

<form action="<?php echo $_SERVER['PHP_SELF']; ?>" method="post">
<label>Type your joke here:<br />
<textarea name="joketext" rows="10" cols="40">
</textarea></label><br />
<input type="submit" value="SUBMIT" />
</form>

<?php else: // Default page display

  // Connect to the database server
  $dbcnx = @mysql_connect('localhost', 'root', 'mypasswd');
```

[1] http://www.sitepoint.com/forums/

```php
if (!$dbcnx) {
  exit('<p>Unable to connect to the ' .
      'database server at this time.</p>');
}

// Select the jokes database
if (!@mysql_select_db('ijdb')) {
  exit('<p>Unable to locate the joke ' .
      'database at this time.</p>');
}

// If a joke has been submitted,
// add it to the database.
if (isset($_POST['joketext'])) {
  $joketext = $_POST['joketext'];
  $sql = "INSERT INTO joke SET
      joketext='$joketext',
      jokedate=CURDATE()";
  if (@mysql_query($sql)) {
    echo '<p>Your joke has been added.</p>';
  } else {
    echo '<p>Error adding submitted joke: ' .
        mysql_error() . '</p>';
  }
}

// If a joke has been deleted,
// remove it from the database.
if (isset($_GET['deletejoke'])) {
  $jokeid = $_GET['deletejoke'];
  $sql = "DELETE FROM joke
      WHERE id=$jokeid";
  if (@mysql_query($sql)) {
    echo '<p>The joke has been deleted.</p>';
  } else {
    echo '<p>Error deleting joke: ' .
        mysql_error() . '</p>';
  }
}

echo '<p> Here are all the jokes in our database: </p>';

// Request the ID and text of all the jokes
$result = @mysql_query('SELECT id, joketext FROM joke');
if (!$result) {
  exit('<p>Error performing query: ' .
```

```
          mysql_error() . '</p>');
   }

   // Display the text of each joke in a paragraph
   // with a "Delete this joke" link next to each.
   while ($row = mysql_fetch_array($result)) {
     $jokeid = $row['id'];
     $joketext = $row['joketext'];
     echo '<p>' . $joketext .
          ' <a href="' . $_SERVER['PHP_SELF'] .
          '?deletejoke=' . $jokeid . '">' .
          'Delete this joke</a></p>';
   }

   // When clicked, this link will load this page
   // with the joke submission form displayed.
   echo '<p><a href="' . $_SERVER['PHP_SELF'] .
        '?addjoke=1">Add a Joke!</a></p>';

endif;
?>
</body>
</html>
```

5

Relational Database Design

Since Chapter 2, we've worked with a very simple database of jokes, which is composed of a single table named, appropriately enough, `joke`. While this database has served us well as an introduction to MySQL databases, there's more to relational database design than this simple example illustrates. In this chapter, we'll expand on our example, and learn a few new features of MySQL, in an effort to realize and appreciate what relational databases have to offer.

Be forewarned that many topics will be covered only in an informal, hands-on (i.e. non-rigorous) sort of way. As any computer science major will tell you, database design is a serious area of research, with tested and mathematically provable principles that, while useful, are beyond the scope of this text. If you want more information, stop by http://www.datamodel.org/ for a list of good books, as well as several useful resources on the subject. In particular, check out *Rules of Data Normalization* in the Data Modelling section of the site.

Giving Credit where Credit is Due

To start things off, let's recall the structure of our `joke` table. It contains three columns: `id`, `joketext`, and `jokedate`. Together, these columns allow us to identify jokes (`id`), and keep track of their text (`joketext`) and the date they were entered (`jokedate`). The SQL code that creates this table and inserts a couple of entries is provided as `jokes1.sql` in the code archive.

Now, let's say we wanted to track another piece of information about our jokes: the names of the people who submitted them. It would seem natural to want to add a new column to our `joke` table for this. The SQL `ALTER TABLE` command (which we haven't seen before) lets us do exactly that. Log into your MySQL server using the `mysql` command-line program as in Chapter 2, select your database (`ijdb` if you used the name suggested in that chapter), then type this command:

```
mysql>ALTER TABLE joke ADD COLUMN
    ->authorname VARCHAR(255);
```

This code adds a column called `authorname` to your table. The type declared is a variable-length character string of up to 255 characters—plenty of space for even very esoteric names. Let's also add a column for the authors' email addresses:

```
mysql>ALTER TABLE joke ADD COLUMN
    ->authoremail VARCHAR(255);
```

For more information about the `ALTER TABLE` command, see Appendix A. Just to make sure the two columns were added properly, we should ask MySQL to describe the table to us:

```
mysql>DESCRIBE joke;
+-------------+--------------+------+-----+------------+-- -
| Field       | Type         | Null | Key | Default    |
+-------------+--------------+------+-----+------------+-- -
| id          | int(11)      |      | PRI | NULL       |
| joketext    | text         | YES  |     | NULL       |
| jokedate    | date         |      |     | 0000-00-00 |
| authorname  | varchar(255) | YES  |     | NULL       |
| authoremail | varchar(255) | YES  |     | NULL       |
+-------------+--------------+------+-----+------------+-- -
5 rows in set (0.01 sec)
```

Looks good, right? Obviously, we would need to make changes to the HTML and PHP form code we created in Chapter 4 that allowed us to add new jokes to the database. Using `UPDATE` queries, we could now add author details to all the jokes in the table. But before we get carried away with these changes, we need to stop and consider whether this new table design was the right choice here. In this case, it turns out that it wasn't.

Rule of Thumb: Keep Things Separate

As your knowledge of database-driven Websites continues to grow, you may decide that a personal joke list isn't enough. In fact, you might begin to receive more submitted jokes than you have original jokes of your own. Let's say you decide to launch a Website where people from all over the world can share jokes with each other. You've heard of the Internet Movie Database (IMDB)? You decide to open the Internet Joke Database (IJDB)! To add the author's name and email address to each joke certainly makes a lot of sense, but the method we used above leads to several potential problems:

❑ What if a frequent contributor to your site named Joan Smith changed her email address? She might begin to submit new jokes using the new address, but her old address would still be attached to all the jokes she'd submitted in the past. Looking at your database, you might simply think there were two different people named Joan Smith who submit jokes. If she were especially thoughtful, she might inform you of the change of address, and you might try to update all the old jokes with the new address, but if you missed just one joke, your database would still contain incorrect information. Database design experts refer to this sort of problem as an **update anomaly**.

❑ It would be natural for you to rely on your database to provide a list of all the people who have ever submitted jokes to your site. In fact, you could easily obtain a mailing list using the following query:

```
mysql>SELECT DISTINCT authorname, authoremail
    ->FROM joke;
```

The word `DISTINCT` in the above query tells MySQL not to output duplicate result rows. For example, if Joan Smith submitted 20 jokes to your site, her name and email address would appear 20 times in the list, instead of just once, if you failed to use the `DISTINCT` option.

If, for some reason, you decided to remove all the jokes that a particular author had submitted to your site, you'd remove any record of this person from the database in the process, and you'd no longer be able to email him or her with information about your site! As your mailing list might be a major source of income for your site, you wouldn't want to go throwing away an author's email address just because you didn't like the jokes that person had submitted to your site. Database design experts call this a **delete anomaly**.

❏ You have no guarantee that Joan Smith would not enter her name as "Joan Smith" one day, as "J. Smith" the next, and as "Smith, Joan" on yet another occasion. This would make keeping track of a particular author exceedingly difficult, especially if Joan Smith also had several email addresses she liked to use.

These problems—and more—can be dealt with very quickly. Instead of storing the information for the authors in the joke table, let's create an entirely new table for our list of authors. Since we used a column called id in the joke table to identify each of our jokes with a unique number, we'll use an identically-named column in our new table to identify our authors. We can then use those author IDs in our joke table to associate authors with their jokes. The complete database layout is shown in Figure 5.1.

Figure 5.1. The authorid field associates each row in joke with a row in author.

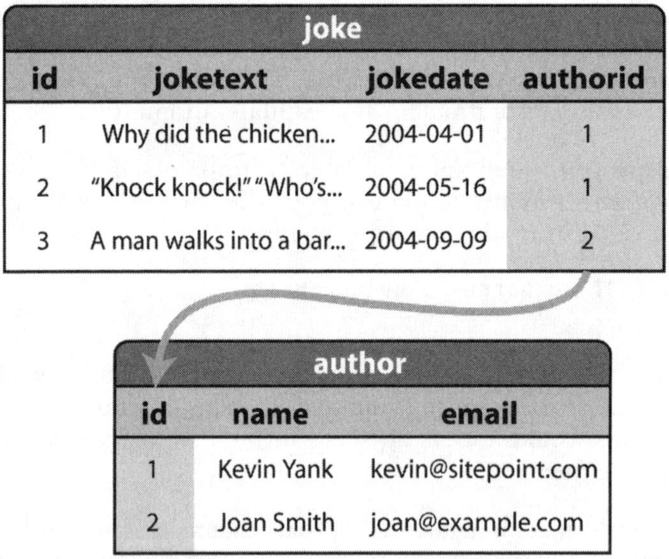

joke			
id	**joketext**	**jokedate**	**authorid**
1	Why did the chicken...	2004-04-01	1
2	"Knock knock!" "Who's...	2004-05-16	1
3	A man walks into a bar...	2004-09-09	2

author		
id	**name**	**email**
1	Kevin Yank	kevin@sitepoint.com
2	Joan Smith	joan@example.com

What the above two tables show are three jokes and two authors. The authorid column of the joke table provides a relationship between the two tables, indicating that Kevin Yank submitted jokes 1 and 2 and Joan Smith submitted joke 3. Notice also that, since each author now only appears once in the database, and appears independently of the jokes he or she has submitted, we've avoided all the problems outlined above.

The most important characteristic of this database design, however, is that, since we're storing information about two types of "things" (jokes and authors), it's most appropriate to have two tables. This is a rule of thumb that you should always keep in mind when designing a database: *each type of entity (or "thing") that you want to be able to store information about should be given its own table.*

To set up the above database from scratch is fairly simple (involving just two CREATE TABLE queries), but since we'd like to make these changes in a nondestructive manner (i.e. without losing any of our precious knock-knock jokes), we'll use the ALTER command again. First, we get rid of the author-related columns in the joke table:

```
mysql>ALTER TABLE joke DROP COLUMN authorname;
Query OK, 0 rows affected (0.00 sec)
Records: 0  Duplicates: 0  Warnings: 0

mysql>ALTER TABLE joke DROP COLUMN authoremail;
Query OK, 0 rows affected (0.00 sec)
Records: 0  Duplicates: 0  Warnings: 0
```

Now, we create our new table:

```
mysql>CREATE TABLE author (
    ->   id INT NOT NULL AUTO_INCREMENT PRIMARY KEY,
    ->   name VARCHAR(255),
    ->   email VARCHAR(255)
    ->);
```

Finally, we add the authorid column to our joke table:

```
mysql>ALTER TABLE joke ADD COLUMN authorid INT;
```

If you prefer, the CREATE TABLE commands that will create the two tables from scratch are provided in 2tables.sql in the code archive.

All that's left is to add some authors to the new table, and assign authors to all the existing jokes in the database by filling in the authorid column.[1] Go ahead and do this now if you like—it should give you some practice with INSERT and UPDATE queries.

---

[1]For now, you'll have to do this manually. But don't worry, in Chapter 6 we'll see how PHP automatically can insert entries with the correct IDs, reflecting the relationships between them.

Dealing with Multiple Tables

With your data now separated into two tables, it may seem that you're complic-ating the process of data retrieval. Consider, for example, our original goal: to display a list of jokes with the name and email address of the author next to each joke. In the single-table solution, you could get all the information you needed to produce such a list using a single SELECT statement in your PHP code:

```php
$jokelist = mysql_query(
    "SELECT joketext, authorname, authoremail FROM jokes");

while ($joke = mysql_fetch_array($jokelist)) {
  $joketext = $joke['joketext'];
  $name = $joke['authorname'];
  $email = $joke['authoremail'];

  // Display the joke with author information
  echo "<p>$joketext<br />" .
      "(by <a href='mailto:$email'>$name</a>)</p>";
}
```

In the new system, this would, at first, no longer seem possible. As the details about the author of each joke aren't stored in the joke table, you might think that you'd have to fetch those details separately for each joke you wanted to display. The code to perform this task would look like this:

```php
// Get the list of jokes
$jokelist = mysql_query("SELECT joketext, authorid FROM joke");

while ($joke = mysql_fetch_array($jokelist)) {

  // Get the text and authorid for the joke
  $joketext = $joke['joketext'];
  $authorid = $joke['authorid'];

  // Get the author details for the joke
  $authordetails = mysql_query(
      "SELECT name, email FROM author WHERE id=$authorid");
  $author = mysql_fetch_array($authordetails);
  $name = $author['name'];
  $email = $author['email'];

  // Display the joke with author information
  echo "<p>$joketext<br />" .
```

```
          "(by <a href='mailto:$email'>$name</a>)</p>";
}
```

It's pretty messy, and it involves a query to the database for every single joke that's displayed, which could slow down the display of your page considerably. With all this taken into account, it would seem that the "old way" was actually the better solution, despite its weaknesses. Fortunately, relational databases like MySQL are designed to make it easy to work with data stored in multiple tables! Using a new form of the SELECT statement, called a **join**, you can have the best of both worlds. Joins allow you to treat related data in multiple tables as if they were stored in a single table. Here's what the syntax of a simple join looks like:

```
mysql>SELECT columns FROM tables
    ->WHERE condition(s) for data to be related;
```

In your case, the columns you're interested in are joketext in the joke table, and name and email in the author table. The condition for an entry in the joke table to be related to an entry in the author table is that the value of the authorid column in the joke table is equal to the value of the id column in the author table. Here's an example of a join (the first two queries simply show you what's contained in the two tables—they aren't necessary):

```
mysql>SELECT LEFT(joketext, 20), authorid FROM joke;
+----------------------+----------+
| LEFT(joketext, 20)   | authorid |
+----------------------+----------+
| Why did the chicken  |        1 |
| Knock knock. Who's t |        1 |
| A man walks into a b |        2 |
+----------------------+----------+
3 rows in set (0.00 sec)

mysql>SELECT * FROM author;
+----+-------------+----------------------+
| id | name        | email                |
+----+-------------+----------------------+
|  1 | Kevin Yank  | kevin@sitepoint.com  |
|  2 | Joan Smith  | joan@example.com     |
+----+-------------+----------------------+
2 rows in set (0.00 sec)

mysql>SELECT LEFT(joketext, 20), name, email
    ->FROM joke, author WHERE authorid = author.id;
+----------------------+-------------+----------------------+
| LEFT(joketext, 20)   | name        | email                |
```

```
+--------------------------+-------------+-----------------------+
| Why did the chicken      | Kevin Yank  | kevin@sitepoint.com   |
| Knock-knock! Who's t     | Kevin Yank  | kevin@sitepoint.com   |
| A man walks into a b     | Joan Smith  | joan@example.com      |
+--------------------------+-------------+-----------------------+
3 rows in set (0.00 sec)
```

See? The results of the third SELECT, which is a join, group the values stored in the two tables into a single table of results, with related data correctly appearing together. Even though the data is stored in two tables, you can still get all the information you need to produce the joke list on your Web page with a single database query. Note in the query that, since there are columns named id in both tables, you must specify the name of the table when you refer to the id column in the author table (author.id). If you don't specify the table name, MySQL won't know which id you're referring to, and will produce this error:

```
mysql>SELECT LEFT(joketext, 20), name, email
    ->FROM joke, author WHERE authorid = id;
ERROR 1052: Column: 'id' in where clause is ambiguous
```

Now that you know how to access the data stored in your two tables efficiently, you can rewrite the code for your joke list to take advantage of joins:

File: **jokelist2.php (excerpt)**

```php
$jokelist = @mysql_query(
    'SELECT joketext, name, email
    FROM joke, author WHERE authorid=author.id');
if (!$jokelist) {
  exit('<p>Error performing query: ' . mysql_error() . '</p>');
}

while ($joke = mysql_fetch_array($jokelist)) {
  $joketext = $joke['joketext'];
  $name = $joke['name'];
  $email = $joke['email'];

  // Display the joke with author information
  echo "<p>$joketext<br />" .
    "(by <a href='mailto:$email'>$name</a>)</p>";
}
```

The resulting display is shown in Figure 5.2.

Figure 5.2. I wrote all the best ones myself.

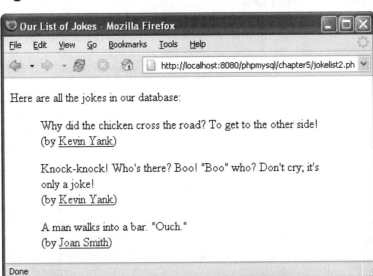

The more you work with databases, the more you'll come to realize just how powerful is the ability to combine data contained in separate tables into a single table of results. Consider, for example, the following query, which displays a list of all jokes written by Joan Smith:

```
mysql>SELECT joketext FROM joke, author WHERE
    ->name="Joan Smith" AND authorid=author.id;
+----------------------------------+
| joketext                         |
+----------------------------------+
| A man walks into a bar. "Ouch."  |
+----------------------------------+
1 row in set (0.02 sec)
```

The results that are output from the above query come only from the joke table, but the query uses a join to let it search for jokes based on a value stored in the author table. There will be plenty more examples of clever queries like this throughout the book, but this example alone illustrates that the practical applications of joins are many and varied and, in almost all cases, can save you a lot of work!

Simple Relationships

The best type of database layout for a given situation is usually dictated by the type of relationship that exists between the pieces of data that it needs to store. In this section, I'll examine the typical relationship types, and explain how best to represent them in a relational database.

In the case of a simple **one-to-one relationship**, a single table is all you'll need. An example of a one-to-one relationship that you've seen so far is the email address of each author in our joke database. Since there will be one email address for each author, and one author for each email address, there is no reason to split the addresses into a separate table.

A **many-to-one relationship** is a little more complicated, but you've already seen one of these as well. Each joke in our database is associated with just one author, but many jokes may have been written by that one author. This joke-author relationship is many-to-one. I've already covered the problems that result from storing the information associated with a joke's author in the same table as the joke itself. In brief, it can result in many copies of the same data, which are difficult to keep synchronized, and waste space. If we split the data into two tables, and use an ID column to link the two together, which will make joins possible as shown above, all these problems disappear.

A **one-to-many relationship** is simply a many-to-one relationship seen from the opposite direction. Since the joke-author relationship is many-to-one, the author-joke relationship is one-to-many (there is one author, potentially, for many jokes). This is easy to see in theory, but when you're coming at a problem from the opposite direction, it's not so obvious. In the case of jokes and authors, we started with a library of jokes (the many) and then wanted to assign an author to each of them (the one). Let's now look at a hypothetical design problem where we start with the one and want to add the many.

Say we wanted to allow each of the authors in our database (the one) to have multiple email addresses (the many). When someone inexperienced in database design approaches a one-to-many relationship like this one, his or her first thought is often to try to store multiple values in a single database field, as shown in Figure 5.3.

Figure 5.3. Never overload a table field to store multiple values, as is done here.

author		
id	**name**	**email**
1	Kevin Yank	kevin@sitepoint.com, thatguy@kevinyank.com
2	Joan Smith	joan@example.com, jsmith@example.net

While this would work, to retrieve a single email address from the database, we'd need to break up the string by searching for commas (or whatever special character you chose to use as a separator)—a not-so-simple and potentially time-consuming operation. Try to imagine the PHP code necessary to remove one particular email address from one particular author! In addition, you'd need to allow for much longer values in the `email` column, which could result in wasted disk space, because the majority of authors would have just one email address.

Now take a step back, and realize this one-to-many relationship is just the same as the many-to-one relationship we faced between jokes and authors. The solution, therefore, is also the same: split the "things" (in this case, email addresses) into their own table. The resulting database structure is shown in Figure 5.4.

Figure 5.4. The `authorid` field associates each row of `email` with one row of `author`.

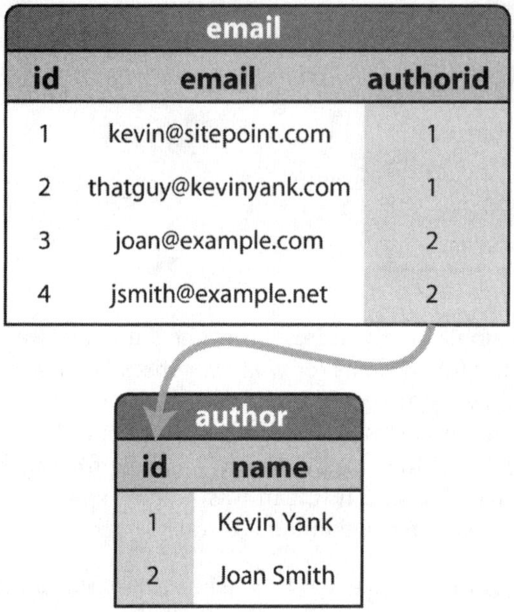

email		
id	**email**	**authorid**
1	kevin@sitepoint.com	1
2	thatguy@kevinyank.com	1
3	joan@example.com	2
4	jsmith@example.net	2

author	
id	**name**
1	Kevin Yank
2	Joan Smith

Using a join with this structure, we can easily list the email addresses associated with a particular author:

```
mysql>SELECT email FROM author, email WHERE
    ->name="Kevin Yank" AND authorid=author.id;
+-----------------------+
| email                 |
+-----------------------+
| kevin@sitepoint.com   |
| thatguy@kevinyank.com |
+-----------------------+
2 rows in set (0.00 sec)
```

Many-to-Many Relationships

Okay, you've now got a steadily-growing database of jokes published on your Website. It's growing so quickly, in fact, that the number of jokes has become unmanageable! People who visit your site are faced with a mammoth page that contains hundreds of jokes listed without any structure whatsoever. Something has to change.

You decide to place your jokes into categories such as "Knock-Knock Jokes," "Crossing the Road Jokes," "Lawyer Jokes," and "Political Jokes." Remembering our rule of thumb from earlier, you identify joke categories as a different type of "thing", and create a new table for them:

```
mysql>CREATE TABLE category (
    ->   id INT NOT NULL AUTO_INCREMENT PRIMARY KEY,
    ->   name VARCHAR(255)
    ->);
Query OK, 0 rows affected (0.00 sec)
```

Now you come to the daunting task of assigning categories to your jokes. It occurs to you that a "political" joke might also be a "crossing the road" joke, and a "knock-knock" joke might also be a "lawyer" joke. A single joke might belong to many categories, and each category will contain many jokes. This is a **many-to-many** relationship.

Once again, many inexperienced developers begin to think of ways to store several values in a single column, because the obvious solution is to add a `category` column to the `joke` table and use it to list the IDs of those categories to which each joke belongs. A second rule of thumb would be useful here: *if you need to store multiple values in a single field, your design is probably flawed.*

The correct way to represent a many-to-many relationship is to use a **lookup table**. This is a table that contains no actual data, but which lists pairs of entries that are related. Figure 5.5 shows what the database design would look like for our joke categories.

Figure 5.5. The `jokecategory` table associates pairs of rows from the `joke` and `category` tables.

joke		jokecategory		category	
id	joketext	jokeid	categoryid	id	name
1	Why did the chicken...	1	2	1	Knock-knock
2	"Knock knock!" "Who's...	2	1	2	Cross the road
3	A man walks into a bar...	3	4	3	Lawyers
4	How many lawyers...	4	3	4	Walk the bar
		4	5	5	Light bulb

The `jokecategory` table associates joke IDs (`jokeid`) with category IDs (`categoryid`). In this example, we can see that the joke that starts with "How many lawyers..." belongs to both the "Lawyers" and "Light bulb" categories.

A lookup table is created in much the same way as is any other table. The difference lies in the choice of the primary key. Every table we've created so far has had a column named `id` that was designated to be the PRIMARY KEY when the table was created. Designating a column as a primary key tells MySQL not to allow two entries in that column to have the same value. It also speeds up join operations based on that column.

In the case of a lookup table, there is no single column that we want to force to have unique values. Each joke ID may appear more than once, as a joke may belong to more than one category, and each category ID may appear more than once, as a category may contain many jokes. What we don't want to allow is the same *pair* of values to appear in the table twice. And, since the sole purpose of this table is to facilitate joins, the speed benefits offered by a primary key would come in very handy. For this reason, we usually create lookup tables with a multi-column primary key as follows:

```
mysql>CREATE TABLE jokecategory (
    ->    jokeid INT NOT NULL,
    ->    categoryid INT NOT NULL,
```

```
    ->   PRIMARY KEY(jokeid, categoryid)
    ->);
```

This creates the table in which the `jokeid` and `categoryid` columns together form the primary key. This enforces the uniqueness that is appropriate to a lookup table, preventing a particular joke from being assigned to a particular category more than once, and speeds up joins that make use of this table.

Now that your lookup table is in place, and contains category assignments, you can use joins to create several interesting and very practical queries. This query lists all jokes in the "Knock-knock" category:

```
mysql>SELECT joketext
    ->FROM joke, category, jokecategory
    ->WHERE name="Knock-knock" AND
    ->categoryid=category.id AND jokeid=joke.id;
```

The following query lists the categories that contain jokes beginning with "How many lawyers...":

```
mysql>SELECT name
    ->FROM joke, category, jokecategory
    ->WHERE joketext LIKE "How many lawyers%"
    ->AND categoryid=category.id AND jokeid=joke.id;
```

And this query, which also makes use of our `author` table to form a join of *four tables*, lists the names of all authors who have written knock-knock jokes:

```
mysql>SELECT author.name
    ->FROM joke, author, category, jokelookup
    ->WHERE category.name="Knock-knock"
    ->AND categoryid=category.id AND jokeid=joke.id
    ->AND authorid=author.id;
```

Summary

In this chapter, I explained the fundamentals of good database design, and we learned how MySQL and, for that matter, all relational database management systems provide support for the representation of different types of relationships between entities. From your meager understanding of one-to-one relationships, you should now have expanded your knowledge to include many-to-one, one-to-many, and many-to-many relationships.

In the process, you learned a few new features of common SQL commands. In particular, you learned how to use a `SELECT` query to join data spread between multiple tables into a single set of results. In Chapter 6, you'll use all the knowledge you have gained so far, plus a few new tricks, to build a basic content management system in PHP. The aim of such a system is to provide a customized, secure, Web-based interface that manages the contents of the database, instead of requiring you to type everything by hand on the MySQL command line.

6

A Content Management System

So far, we've seen several examples of database-driven Web pages that display information that's culled from a MySQL database when the page is requested. Until now, however, we haven't seen a solution that would be very much more manageable than raw HTML files if it were scaled up to encompass a Website as large and complex as, say, sitepoint.com. Sure, our Internet Joke Database was nice, but when it came to managing categories and authors, we'd always have to return to the MySQL command line and try to remember complicated `SELECT` and `INSERT` statements, as well as table and column names, to accomplish the most menial of tasks.

To make the leap from a Web page that displays information stored in a database to a completely database-driven Website, we need to add a **content management system (CMS)**. Such a system usually takes the form of a series of Web pages, access to which is restricted to users who are authorized to make changes to the Website. These pages provide a database administration interface that allows a user to view and change the information that's stored in the database without bothering with the mundane details of SQL syntax.

The beginnings of a CMS were seen at the end of Chapter 4, where we allowed site visitors to add jokes to, and (if you worked through the challenge) delete jokes from, the database using a Web-based form and a Delete this joke link, respectively. While impressive, these are not features that you'd normally include in the interface presented to casual site visitors. For example, you don't want someone to be able to add offensive material to your Website without your knowledge. And you *definitely* don't want just anyone to be able to delete jokes from your site.

By relegating those "dangerous" features to the restricted-access site administration pages, you avoid the risk of exposing your data to the average user, and you maintain the power to manage the contents of your database without having to memorize SQL queries. In this chapter, we'll expand on the capabilities of our joke management system to take advantage of the enhancements we made to our database in Chapter 5. Specifically, we'll allow a site administrator to manage authors and categories, and assign these to appropriate jokes.

As we've seen, these administration pages must be protected by an appropriate access restriction scheme. One way to do this would be to configure your Web server to protect the relevant PHP files by prompting users for valid user names and passwords. On Apache servers, you can do this with an .htaccess file that lists authorized users. Consult your Web server's documentation or ask your Web host for information on how to restrict access to Web pages.

Another method protects the administration pages with PHP itself. This option is generally more flexible, but takes a bit more work to set up. We'll see how it's done in Chapter 12.

The Front Page

At the end of Chapter 5, your database contained tables for three types of entities: jokes, authors, and joke categories. This database layout is represented in Figure 6.1. Note that we're sticking with our original assumption that we'll have one email address per author.

Figure 6.1. The structure of the finished `ijdb` database contains three entities.

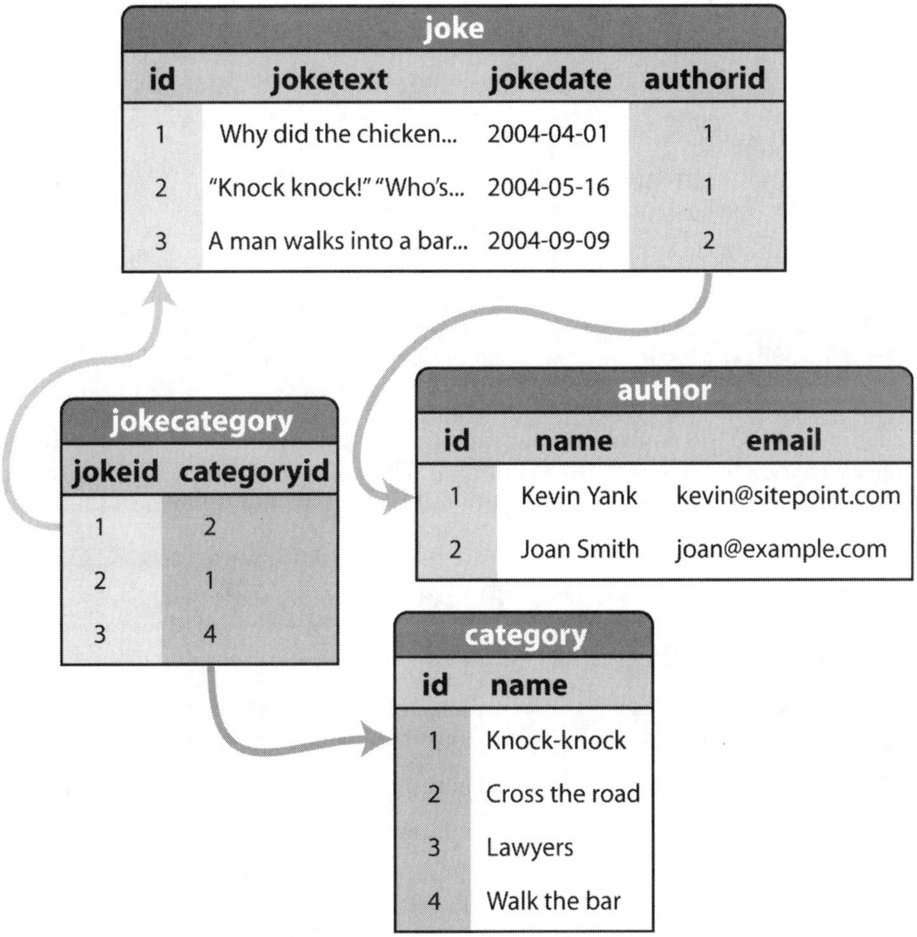

joke			
id	**joketext**	**jokedate**	**authorid**
1	Why did the chicken...	2004-04-01	1
2	"Knock knock!" "Who's...	2004-05-16	1
3	A man walks into a bar...	2004-09-09	2

jokecategory	
jokeid	**categoryid**
1	2
2	1
3	4

author		
id	**name**	**email**
1	Kevin Yank	kevin@sitepoint.com
2	Joan Smith	joan@example.com

category	
id	**name**
1	Knock-knock
2	Cross the road
3	Lawyers
4	Walk the bar

If you need to recreate this table structure, here are the SQL queries to do so:

File: **joketables.sql**

```
CREATE TABLE joke (
 id INT NOT NULL AUTO_INCREMENT PRIMARY KEY,
 joketext TEXT,
 jokedate DATE NOT NULL,
 authorid INT
);
```

```
CREATE TABLE author (
 id INT NOT NULL AUTO_INCREMENT PRIMARY KEY,
 name VARCHAR(255),
 email VARCHAR(255)
);

CREATE TABLE jokecategory (
 jokeid INT NOT NULL,
 categoryid INT NOT NULL,
 PRIMARY KEY (jokeid, categoryid)
);

CREATE TABLE category (
 id INT NOT NULL AUTO_INCREMENT PRIMARY KEY,
 name VARCHAR(255)
);
```

The front page of the content management system, therefore, will contain links to pages that manage these three entities. The following simple HTML code produces the index page shown in Figure 6.2.

File: **index.html**

```
<!DOCTYPE html PUBLIC "-//W3C//DTD XHTML 1.0 Strict//EN"
    "http://www.w3.org/TR/xhtml1/DTD/xhtml1-strict.dtd">
<html xmlns="http://www.w3.org/1999/xhtml">
<head>
<title>Joke CMS</title>
<meta http-equiv="content-type"
    content="text/html; charset=iso-8859-1" />
</head>
<body>
<h1>Joke Management System</h1>
<ul>
  <li><a href="jokes.php">Manage Jokes</a></li>
  <li><a href="authors.php">Manage Authors</a></li>
  <li><a href="cats.php">Manage Joke Categories</a></li>
</ul>
</body>
</html>
```

Figure 6.2. The Joke CMS index page offers three links.

Managing Authors

Let's begin with `authors.php`, the file that allows administrators to add new authors, and delete and edit existing ones. If you're comfortable with the idea of multipurpose pages, you may want to place the code for all of this into the single file, `authors.php`. Since the code for this file would be fairly long, I'll use separate files in my examples to break it up a little.

The first thing we'll present to an administrator who needs to manage authors is a list of all authors currently stored in the database. Code-wise, this is the same as listing the jokes in the database. As we'll want to allow administrators to delete and edit existing authors, you should include links for these features next to each author's name. Just like the Delete this joke links in the challenge at the end of Chapter 4, these links will have the ID of the author attached to them, so that the target document knows which author's details the user wishes to edit or delete. Finally, we'll provide an Add new author link that leads to a form similar in operation to the Add a joke link we created in Chapter 4.

File: **authors.php**

```
<!DOCTYPE html PUBLIC "-//W3C//DTD XHTML 1.0 Strict//EN"
    "http://www.w3.org/TR/xhtml1/DTD/xhtml1-strict.dtd">
<html xmlns="http://www.w3.org/1999/xhtml">
<html>
<head>
```

```
<title>Joke CMS: Manage Authors</title>
<meta http-equiv="content-type"
    content="text/html; charset=iso-8859-1" />
</head>
<body>
<h1>Manage Authors</h1>
<ul>
<?php

$dbcnx = @mysql_connect('localhost', 'root', 'mypasswd');
if (!$dbcnx) {
  exit('<p>Unable to connect to the ' .
      'database server at this time.</p>');
}

if (!@mysql_select_db('ijdb')) {
  exit('<p>Unable to locate the joke ' .
      'database at this time.</p>');
}

$authors = @mysql_query('SELECT id, name FROM author');
if (!$authors) {
  exit('<p>Error retrieving authors from database!<br />'.
      'Error: ' . mysql_error() . '</p>');
}

while ($author = mysql_fetch_array($authors)) {
  $id = $author['id'];
  $name = htmlspecialchars($author['name']);
  echo "<li>$name ".
      "<a href='editauthor.php?id=$id'>Edit</a> ".
      "<a href='deleteauthor.php?id=$id'>Delete</a></li>";
}

?>
</ul>
<p><a href="newauthor.php">Add new author</a></p>
<p><a href="index.html">Return to front page</a></p>
</body>
</html>
```

The htmlspecialchars function used within the while loop in the code above may be a little worrisome to you. For the moment, you can simply ignore it. I'll explain exactly what it does in the section called "Editing Authors".

The interface produced by this script is shown in Figure 6.3.

Figure 6.3. The maintenance of author details begins with the Manage Authors interface.

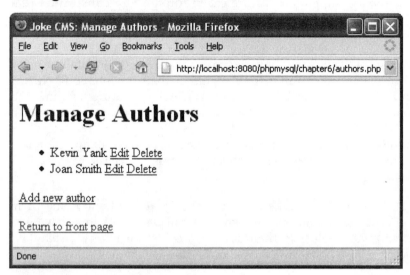

Deleting Authors

`deleteauthor.php` will allow us to remove an author from the database, given that author's ID. As we have seen before, this is frighteningly easy to do, but there is added complexity here. Remember that our `joke` table has an `authorid` column that indicates the author responsible for any given joke. When we remove an author from the database, we must also get rid of any references to that author in other tables. If we didn't, our database might contain jokes associated with nonexistent authors.

We have three possible ways to handle this situation:

☐ Don't allow users to delete authors that are associated with jokes in the database.

☐ When we delete an author, also delete any jokes attributed to the author.

☐ When we delete an author, set the `authorid` of any jokes attributed to the author to NULL, to indicate that they have no author.

When we take measures like these to preserve the relationships in our database, we are said to be protecting the database's **referential integrity**. MySQL, like most database servers, supports a feature called **foreign key constraints** that can do this automatically. By setting up these constraints, you can instruct MySQL to take any of the steps listed above, in order to keep your data properly related.

To take advantage of this feature, however, you must create your database using the more advanced **InnoDB table format**, rather than the simple **MyISAM table format** that MySQL creates by default. While more feature-rich, InnoDB tables work more slowly because of the added overhead of those features. In simple applications like this, the best result is usually achieved by letting the application code (in this case, the PHP script) take care of maintaining referential integrity. For more information on foreign key constraints, see the MySQL Reference Manual[1].

Since most authors would not like us to use their jokes without giving them credit, we'll choose the second option above. This also saves us from having to handle jokes with NULL values in their authorid column when we display our library of jokes.

File: **deleteauthor.php**

```
<!DOCTYPE html PUBLIC "-//W3C//DTD XHTML 1.0 Strict//EN"
    "http://www.w3.org/TR/xhtml1/DTD/xhtml1-strict.dtd">
<html xmlns="http://www.w3.org/1999/xhtml">
<head>
<title>Joke CMS: Delete Author</title>
<meta http-equiv="content-type"
    content="text/html; charset=iso-8859-1" />
</head>
<body>
<?php

$dbcnx = @mysql_connect('localhost', 'root', 'mypasswd');
if (!$dbcnx) {
  exit('<p>Unable to connect to the ' .
      'database server at this time.</p>');
}

if (!@mysql_select_db('ijdb')) {
  exit('<p>Unable to locate the joke ' .
      'database at this time.</p>');
}
```

[1] http://dev.mysql.com/doc/mysql/en/ANSI_diff_Foreign_Keys.html

```
// Delete all jokes belonging to the author
// along with the entry for the author.
$id = $_GET['id'];
$ok1 = @mysql_query("DELETE FROM joke WHERE authorid='$id'");
$ok2 = @mysql_query("DELETE FROM author WHERE id='$id'");
if ($ok1 and $ok2) {
  echo '<p>Author deleted successfully!</p>';
} else {
  echo '<p>Error deleting author from database!<br />'.
     'Error: ' . mysql_error() . '</p>';
}

?>
<p><a href="authors.php">Return to authors list</a></p>
</body>
</html>
```

Just like that, we can delete an author—and all his or her jokes—with a single click, as shown in Figure 6.4.

Figure 6.4. Be careful where you click!

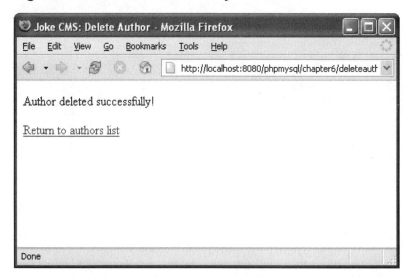

As an exercise, you may want to try adding a confirmation prompt to this page, which must be accepted before the system goes ahead and deletes the author.

Simply make this a multipurpose page, with the default view displaying the prompt.

Adding Authors

Next comes newauthor.php, which allows administrators to add new authors to the database. This is just like adding new jokes, which we tackled in Chapter 4, so I won't waste time explaining the code here.

File: **newauthor.php**

```
<!DOCTYPE html PUBLIC "-//W3C//DTD XHTML 1.0 Strict//EN"
    "http://www.w3.org/TR/xhtml1/DTD/xhtml1-strict.dtd">
<html xmlns="http://www.w3.org/1999/xhtml">
<head>
<title>Joke CMS: Add New Author</title>
<meta http-equiv="content-type"
    content="text/html; charset=iso-8859-1" />
</head>
<body>
<?php if (isset($_POST['name'])):

  // A new author has been entered
  // using the form below.

  $dbcnx = @mysql_connect('localhost', 'root', 'mypasswd');
  if (!$dbcnx) {
    exit('<p>Unable to connect to the ' .
        'database server at this time.</p>');
  }

  if (!@mysql_select_db('ijdb')) {
    exit('<p>Unable to locate the joke ' .
        'database at this time.</p>');
  }

  $name = $_POST['name'];
  $email = $_POST['email'];
  $sql = "INSERT INTO author SET
      name='$name',
      email='$email'";
  if (@mysql_query($sql)) {
    echo '<p>New author added</p>';
  } else {
    echo '<p>Error adding new author: ' .
```

```
            mysql_error() . '</p>';
  }

?>

<p><a href="<?php echo $_SERVER['PHP_SELF']; ?>">Add another
  author</a></p>
<p><a href="authors.php">Return to authors list</a></p>

<?php else: // Allow the user to enter a new author ?>

<form action="<?php echo $_SERVER['PHP_SELF']; ?>" method="post">
<p>Enter the new author:</p>
<label>Name: <input type="text" name="name" /></label><br />
<label>Email: <input type="text" name="email" /></label><br />
<input type="submit" value="SUBMIT" />
</form>

<?php endif; ?>

</body>
</html>
```

We now have a simple form that can be used to create new authors in the database, as shown in Figure 6.5.

Figure 6.5. I'll bet she's funny...

Editing Authors

All that's left is `editauthor.php`, which must provide an interface through which we can edit existing authors' details. This page will actually be very similar to `newauthor.php`, except that the form fields will initially contain the values stored in the database, and an `UPDATE` query will be used instead of an `INSERT` query when the form is submitted.

One minor complication comes into play here. To initialize the form fields with the values stored in the database, this page needs to retrieve these values and store them in PHP variables (say, `$name` and `$email`). It will use the `$id` variable passed from `authors.php` to do this. The code for our form should then look like this:

```
<form action="<?php echo $_SERVER['PHP_SELF']; ?>" method="post">
<p>Edit the author:</p>
<label>Name: <input type="text" name="name"
    value="<?php echo $name; ?>" /></label><br />
<label>Email: <input type="text" name="email"
    value="<?php echo $email; ?>" /></label><br />
<input type="hidden" name="id" value="<?php echo $id; ?>" />
<input type="submit" value="SUBMIT" /></p>
</form>
```

As an aside, notice the hidden form field; we use this to pass the author's ID along with the updated values when the form is submitted.

But consider what would happen if the author's name were `"The Jokester"` (*with* the quotes). The input tag produced by the PHP script would look like this:

```
<input type="text" name="name" value=""The Jokester"" />
```

Obviously, this is invalid HTML. We need to replace the quotes in the name with their HTML **character entity** equivalents. Specifically, any double quotes in the name should be converted to the character code `&quot;` as follows:

```
<input type="text" name="name" value="&quot;The Jokester&quot;" />
```

PHP provides a function called `htmlspecialchars` that converts special HTML characters such as <, > and quotes (among others) into their respective character codes automatically. Consider the following basic example:

```
$text = htmlspecialchars('<HTML> can be dangerous!');
echo $text; // output: &lt;HTML&gt; can be dangerous!
```

To avoid problems with quotes and angled brackets in your text strings, you should use this function whenever you output a non-HTML text string—especially when you output variables that, as they're retrieved from a database, or are submitted by users, can have unpredictable values.

```php
// Convert special characters for safe use
// as HTML attributes.
$name = htmlspecialchars($name);
$email = htmlspecialchars($email);
```

With this issue in mind, we can create an author editing page.

File: **editauthor.php**

```php
<!DOCTYPE html PUBLIC "-//W3C//DTD XHTML 1.0 Strict//EN"
    "http://www.w3.org/TR/xhtml1/DTD/xhtml1-strict.dtd">
<html xmlns="http://www.w3.org/1999/xhtml">
<head>
<title>Joke CMS: Edit Author</title>
<meta http-equiv="content-type"
    content="text/html; charset=iso-8859-1" />
</head>
<body>
<?php

$dbcnx = @mysql_connect('localhost', 'root', 'mypasswd');
if (!$dbcnx) {
  exit('<p>Unable to connect to the ' .
      'database server at this time.</p>');
}

if (!@mysql_select_db('ijdb')) {
  exit('<p>Unable to locate the joke ' .
      'database at this time.</p>');
}

if (isset($_POST['name'])):
  // The author's details have been updated.

  $name = $_POST['name'];
  $email = $_POST['email'];
  $id = $_POST['id'];
  $sql = "UPDATE author SET
          name='$name',
          email='$email'
          WHERE id='$id'";
  if (@mysql_query($sql)) {
```

```php
    echo '<p>Author details updated.</p>';
  } else {
    echo '<p>Error updating author details: ' .
        mysql_error() . '</p>';
  }

?>

<p><a href="authors.php">Return to authors list</a></p>

<?php
else: // Allow the user to edit the author

  $id = $_GET['id'];
  $author = @mysql_query(
      "SELECT name, email FROM author WHERE id='$id'");
  if (!$author) {
    exit('<p>Error fetching author details: ' .
        mysql_error() . '</p>');
  }

  $author = mysql_fetch_array($author);

  $name = $author['name'];
  $email = $author['email'];

  // Convert special characters for safe use
  // as HTML attributes.
  $name = htmlspecialchars($name);
  $email = htmlspecialchars($email);

?>

<form action="<?php echo $_SERVER['PHP_SELF']; ?>" method="post">
<p>Edit the author:</p>
<label>Name: <input type="text" name="name"
    value="<?php echo $name; ?>" /></label><br />
<label>Email: <input type="text" name="email"
    value="<?php echo $email; ?>" /></label><br />
<input type="hidden" name="id" value="<?php echo $id; ?>" />
<input type="submit" value="SUBMIT" /></p>
</form>

<?php endif; ?>
```

```
</body>
</html>
```

Though there are a couple of complicated things going on under the hood, the user interface shown in Figure 6.6 is a model of simplicity.

Figure 6.6. A middle initial might make him funnier.

Try entering an author name that contains HTML code and special characters, then edit the name using this form. View the source in your browser to see how the special characters were encoded to prevent them interfering with the HTML form tags.

Magic Quotes

While we're on the subject of troublesome special characters, there is another situation in which particular characters in a string can cause problems. Consider the following SQL query:

```
mysql>INSERT INTO author SET
    ->name='Molly O'Reilly',
    ->email='molly@faerie.com';
```

Obviously, the apostrophe in the author's last name will cause problems here, as MySQL can no longer figure out where the author's name ends. The solution in this case would be to use another function provided by PHP: `addslashes`. This function, like `htmlspecialchars`, converts a string's unsafe characters so that they're safe. The difference is that `addslashes` is used to **escape** special characters by putting backslashes before them, as follows:

```
mysql>INSERT INTO author SET
    ->name='Molly O\'Reilly',
    ->email='molly@faerie.com';
```

A backslash tells MySQL to treat the next character (the apostrophe, in this case) as a character in the string, ignoring any special meaning it might normally have. Thus, the above code will correctly insert the name "Molly O'Reilly" into the `author` table.

Why haven't we worried about this problem before now? PHP has a nifty little feature called **magic quotes**, which is enabled by default with the following setting in your `php.ini` file:

```
magic_quotes_gpc = On
```

This setting tells PHP to use the `addslashes` function automatically on any values that are passed with the request for the page. The "`gpc`" in the name stands for "get, post, cookies," which are the three methods by which information may be passed with a request for a Web page. As all the values we've inserted into our database until now have been passed as part of a form submission, the magic quotes feature of PHP has automatically added slashes to them every time. Values retrieved from a MySQL database, however, do not benefit from the magic quotes feature, so we must add slashes before we can use them in any situation where quotes, apostrophes, and other special characters might be a problem.

In some cases, you may not actually *want* to add backslashes to submitted values. For example, if you're going to print out a value that was submitted with a form, and not insert it into a database, then those backslashes could turn out to be quite an eyesore. To undo the work of either the `addslashes` function or the magic quotes feature, you can use yet another function called `stripslashes`.

Complete information about these functions may be found in the PHP Manual[2]. All the scripts in this book are written with the default setting, `magic_quotes_gpc = On` in mind.

 Tip

Do-it-yourself magic quotes

In order to boost server performance, some developers choose to work with magic quotes disabled, and escape special characters themselves only when

---

[2] http://www.php.net/manual

necessary. There are definite security risks to this approach, as failing to escape special characters in a variable that makes its way into a database query can open your site up to some nasty attacks by hackers.

If you're stuck using a Web server with magic quotes disabled, here's a snippet of code that you can add to the top of your PHP scripts that will effectively do the same thing:

```php
<?php
if (!get_magic_quotes_gpc()) {
  $_GET = array_map('addslashes', $_GET);
  $_POST = array_map('addslashes', $_POST);
  $_COOKIE = array_map('addslashes', $_COOKIE);
  $_REQUEST = array_map('addslashes', $_REQUEST);
}
?>
```

This code first uses the built-in function `get_magic_quotes_gpc` to check if magic quotes is enabled. If it isn't, it uses the built-in `array_map` function to apply the `addslashes` function to each element of each of the `$_GET`, `$_POST`, `$_COOKIE`, and `$_REQUEST` arrays, all of which contain data received from the browser.

This does the same job as magic quotes, ensuring that you can write the rest of your script safe in the knowledge that special characters have been escaped in all data received from the browser.

Managing Categories

The roles of the authors and joke categories in the database really are very similar. They both reside in tables of their own, and they both serve to group jokes together in some way. As a result, categories can be handled with the same code we've developed for authors, with one important exception.

When we delete a category, we can't simultaneously delete any jokes that belong to that category, because those jokes may also belong to other categories. We could check each joke to see if it belonged to any other categories, and only delete those that did not, but rather than engage in such a time-consuming process, let's allow for the possibility of including jokes in our database that don't belong to any category at all. These jokes would be invisible to our site visitors, but would remain in the database in case we wanted to assign them to a category later on.

Thus, to delete a category, we also need to delete any entries in the jokecategory table that refer to that category:

File: **deletecat.php (excerpt)**

```
// Delete all joke look-up entries for the
// category along with the entry for the category.
$ok1 = @mysql_query(
    "DELETE FROM jokecategory WHERE categoryid='$id'");
$ok2 = @mysql_query("DELETE FROM category WHERE id='$id'");
```

Other than this one detail, category management is functionally identical to author management. The complete code for the four files involved follows.

File: **cats.php**

```
<!DOCTYPE html PUBLIC "-//W3C//DTD XHTML 1.0 Strict//EN"
    "http://www.w3.org/TR/xhtml1/DTD/xhtml1-strict.dtd">
<html xmlns="http://www.w3.org/1999/xhtml">
<head>
<title>Joke CMS: Manage Categories</title>
<meta http-equiv="content-type"
    content="text/html; charset=iso-8859-1" />
</head>
<body>
<h1>Manage Categories</h1>
<ul>
<?php

$dbcnx = @mysql_connect('localhost', 'root', 'mypasswd');
if (!$dbcnx) {
  exit('<p>Unable to connect to the ' .
      'database server at this time.</p>');
}

if (!@mysql_select_db('ijdb')) {
  exit('<p>Unable to locate the joke ' .
      'database at this time.</p>');
}

$cats = @mysql_query('SELECT id, name FROM category');
if (!$cats) {
  exit('<p>Error retrieving categories from database!<br />'.
      'Error: ' . mysql_error(). '</p>');
}

while ($cat = mysql_fetch_array($cats)) {
```

```
    $id = $cat['id'];
    $name = htmlspecialchars($cat['name']);
    echo "<li>$name ".
        "<a href='editcat.php?id=$id'>Edit</a> | ".
        "<a href='deletecat.php?id=$id'>Delete</a>";
}

?>
</ul>
<p><a href="newcat.php">Add a new category</a></p>
<p><a href="index.html">Return to front page</a></p>
</body>
</html>
```

File: **deletecat.php**

```
<!DOCTYPE html PUBLIC "-//W3C//DTD XHTML 1.0 Strict//EN"
    "http://www.w3.org/TR/xhtml1/DTD/xhtml1-strict.dtd">
<html xmlns="http://www.w3.org/1999/xhtml">
<head>
<title>Joke CMS: Delete Category</title>
<meta http-equiv="content-type"
    content="text/html; charset=iso-8859-1" />
</head>
<body>
<?php

$dbcnx = @mysql_connect('localhost', 'root', 'mypasswd');
if (!$dbcnx) {
  exit('<p>Unable to connect to the ' .
      'database server at this time.</p>');
}

if (!@mysql_select_db('ijdb')) {
  exit('<p>Unable to locate the joke ' .
      'database at this time.</p>');
}

// Delete all joke lookup entries for the
// category along with the entry for the category.
$id = $_GET['id'];
$ok1 = @mysql_query(
    "DELETE FROM jokecategory WHERE categoryid='$id'");
$ok2 = @mysql_query("DELETE FROM category WHERE id='$id'");
if ($ok1 and $ok2) {
  echo '<p>Category deleted successfully!</p>';
} else {
```

```
      echo '<p>Error deleting category from database!<br />'.
          'Error: ' . mysql_error() . '</p>';
    }

    ?>
    <p><a href="cats.php">Return to category list</a></p>
    </body>
    </html>
```

File: **newcat.php**

```
<!DOCTYPE html PUBLIC "-//W3C//DTD XHTML 1.0 Strict//EN"
    "http://www.w3.org/TR/xhtml1/DTD/xhtml1-strict.dtd">
<html xmlns="http://www.w3.org/1999/xhtml">
<head>
<title>Joke CMS: Add New Category</title>
</head>
<body>
<?php if (isset($_POST['name'])):

  // A new category has been entered
  // using the form below.

  $dbcnx = @mysql_connect('localhost', 'root', 'mypasswd');
  if (!$dbcnx) {
    exit('<p>Unable to connect to the ' .
        'database server at this time.</p>');
  }

  if (!@mysql_select_db('ijdb')) {
    exit('<p>Unable to locate the joke ' .
        'database at this time.</p>');
  }

  $name = $_POST['name'];
  $sql = "INSERT INTO category SET name='$name'";
  if (@mysql_query($sql)) {
    echo '<p>New category added</p>';
  } else {
    echo '<p>Error adding new category: ' .
        mysql_error() . '</p>';
  }

?>

<p><a href="<?php echo $_SERVER['PHP_SELF']; ?>">Add another
    category</a></p>
```

```
<p><a href="cats.php">Return to category list</a></p>

<?php else: // Allow the user to enter a new category ?>

<form action="<?php echo $_SERVER['PHP_SELF']; ?>" method="post">
<p>Enter the new category:</p>
<label>Name: <input type="text" name="name" /></label><br />
<input type="submit" value="SUBMIT" />
</form>

<?php endif; ?>

</body>
</html>
```

File: **editcat.php**

```
<!DOCTYPE html PUBLIC "-//W3C//DTD XHTML 1.0 Strict//EN"
    "http://www.w3.org/TR/xhtml1/DTD/xhtml1-strict.dtd">
<html xmlns="http://www.w3.org/1999/xhtml">
<head>
<title>Joke CMS: Edit Category</title>
</head>
<body>
<?php

$dbcnx = @mysql_connect('localhost', 'root', 'mypasswd');
if (!$dbcnx) {
  exit('<p>Unable to connect to the ' .
      'database server at this time.</p>');
}

if (!@mysql_select_db('ijdb')) {
  exit('<p>Unable to locate the joke ' .
      'database at this time.</p>');
}

if (isset($_POST['name'])):
  // The category's details have
  // been updated.

  $name = $_POST['name'];
  $id = $_POST['id'];
  $sql = "UPDATE category SET
          name='$name'
          WHERE id='$id'";
  if (@mysql_query($sql)) {
```

```php
      echo '<p>Category details updated.</p>';
    } else {
      echo '<p>Error updating category details: ' .
          mysql_error() . '</p>';
    }

  ?>

  <p><a href="cats.php">Return to category list</a></p>

  <?php else: // Allow the user to edit the category

    $id = $_GET['id'];
    $cat = @mysql_query("SELECT name FROM category WHERE id='$id'");
    if (!$cat) {
      exit('<p>Error fetching category details: ' .
          mysql_error() . '</p>');
    }

    $cat = mysql_fetch_array($cat);

    $name = $cat["name"];

    // Convert special characters for safe use
    // as an HTML attribute.
    $name = htmlspecialchars($name);

  ?>

  <form action="<?php echo $_SERVER['PHP_SELF']; ?>" method="post">
  <p>Edit the category:</p>
  <label>Name: <input type="text" name="name"
      value="<?php echo $name; ?>" /></label><br />
  <input type="hidden" name="id" value="<?php echo $id; ?>" />
  <input type="submit" value="SUBMIT" /></p>
  </form>

  <?php endif; ?>

  </body>
  </html>
```

Managing Jokes

Along with the addition, deletion, and modification of jokes in our database, we also need to be able to assign categories and authors to our jokes. Furthermore, we're likely to have many more jokes than authors or categories. As a result, to try to display a complete list of jokes, as we did for the authors and categories, could result in an unmanageably long list with no easy way to spot the joke we're after. We need to create a more intelligent method of browsing our library of jokes.

Searching for Jokes

Sometimes, we may know the category, author, or some of the text in a joke with which we want to work, so let's support all of these methods for finding jokes in our database. When we're done, it should work like a simple search engine. The form that prompts the administrator for information about the desired joke must present lists of categories and authors. The code for the form is as follows:

```
<!DOCTYPE html PUBLIC "-//W3C//DTD XHTML 1.0 Strict//EN"
    "http://www.w3.org/TR/xhtml1/DTD/xhtml1-strict.dtd">
<html xmlns="http://www.w3.org/1999/xhtml">
<head>
<title>Joke CMS: Manage Jokes</title>
<meta http-equiv="content-type"
    content="text/html; charset=iso-8859-1" />
</head>
<body>
<h1>Manage Jokes</h1>
<p><a href="newjoke.php">Create New Joke</a></p>
<?php

$dbcnx = @mysql_connect('localhost', 'root', 'mypasswd');
if (!$dbcnx) {
  exit('<p>Unable to connect to the ' .
      'database server at this time.</p>');
}

if (!@mysql_select_db('ijdb')) {
  exit('<p>Unable to locate the joke ' .
      'database at this time.</p>');
}

$authors = @mysql_query('SELECT id, name FROM author');
```

```php
if (!$authors) {
  exit('<p>Unable to obtain author list from the database.</p>');
}

$cats = @mysql_query('SELECT id, name FROM category');
if (!$cats) {
  exit(
      '<p>Unable to obtain category list from the database.</p>');
}
?>

<form action="jokelist.php" method="post">
<p>View jokes satisfying the following criteria:</p>
<label>By author:
<select name="aid" size="1">
  <option selected value="">Any Author</option>
<?php
while ($author = mysql_fetch_array($authors)) {
  $aid = $author['id'];
  $aname = htmlspecialchars($author['name']);
  echo "<option value='$aid'>$aname</option>\n";
}
?>
</select></label><br />
<label>By category:
<select name="cid" size="1">
  <option selected value="">Any Category</option>
<?php
while ($cat = mysql_fetch_array($cats)) {
  $cid = $cat['id'];
  $cname = htmlspecialchars($cat['name']);
  echo "<option value='$cid'>$cname</option>\n";
}
?>
</select></label><br />
<label>Containing text: <input type="text" name="searchtext" />
</label><br />
<input type="submit" value="Search" />
</form>

<p><a href="index.html">Return to front page</a></p>
</body>
</html>
```

Note the \n that appears at the end of the strings output by the echo statements. This is the special code for a new line, and serves to make the HTML code output by this script more readable.[1] Also, note the use of `htmlspecialchars` to ensure that author and category names don't contain any troublesome characters when they're displayed.

The finished form appears in Figure 6.7.

Figure 6.7. Search for a classic.

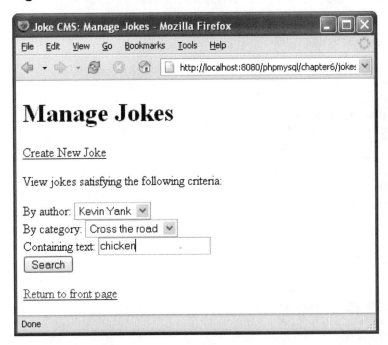

It's up to `jokelist.php` to use the values submitted through the above form to build a list of jokes that satisfies the criteria specified. Obviously, this will be done with a `SELECT` query, but the exact nature of that query will depend on what was entered through the form we defined above. Because the building of this `SELECT` statement is a fairly complicated process, let's work through `jokelist.php` a little at a time.

First, we get the preliminaries out of the way:

---

[1] Other special character codes include `\r` (carriage return) and `\t` (tab). Like variables, these codes only work inside double-quoted strings.

File: **jokelist.php** (excerpt)

```
<!DOCTYPE html PUBLIC "-//W3C//DTD XHTML 1.0 Strict//EN"
    "http://www.w3.org/TR/xhtml1/DTD/xhtml1-strict.dtd">
<html xmlns="http://www.w3.org/1999/xhtml">
<head>
<title>Joke CMS: Manage Jokes</title>
<meta http-equiv="content-type"
    content="text/html; charset=iso-8859-1" />
</head>
<body>
<h1>Manage Jokes</h1>
<?php

$dbcnx = @mysql_connect('localhost', 'root', 'mypasswd');
if (!$dbcnx) {
  exit('<p>Unable to connect to the ' .
      'database server at this time.</p>');
}

if (!@mysql_select_db('ijdb')) {
  exit('<p>Unable to locate the joke ' .
      'database at this time.</p>');
}
```

Now, to start, we define a few strings that, when strung together, form the SELECT query we'd need if no constraints had been selected in the form:

File: **jokelist.php** (excerpt)

```
// The basic SELECT statement
$select = 'SELECT DISTINCT id, joketext';
$from   = ' FROM joke';
$where  = ' WHERE 1=1';
```

You might find the WHERE clause in the above code somewhat confusing. The idea here is for us to be able to build on this basic SELECT statement, depending on the constraints selected in the form. These constraints will require us to add to the FROM and WHERE clauses (portions) of the SELECT statement. But, if no constraints were specified (i.e. the administrator wanted a list of all jokes in the database), there would be no need for a WHERE clause at all! Because it's difficult to add to a WHERE clause that doesn't exist, we needed to come up with a "do nothing" WHERE clause that will always be true. Thus, we have introduced the requirement that 1 equals 1, which fits the bill nicely.[2]

---

[2]In fact, the "do nothing" WHERE clause could just be ' WHERE 1 ', since MySQL considers any positive number true. Feel free to change it if you don't find the idea confusing.

Our next task is to check each of the possible constraints (author, category, and search text) that may have been set in the form, and adjust the SQL accordingly. First, we deal with the possibility that an author was specified. The Any Author option in the form was given a value of "" (the empty string), so, if the value of that form field (stored in $_POST['aid']) is not equal to "", then an author has been specified, and we must adjust our query:

File: **jokelist.php (excerpt)**

```
$aid = $_POST['aid'];
if ($aid != '') { // An author is selected
  $where .= " AND authorid='$aid'";
}
```

.=, the **append operator** is used to tack a new string onto the end of an existing one. In this case, we add to the WHERE clause the condition that the authorid in the joke table must match the author ID selected in the form ($aid).

Next, we handle the specification of a joke category:

File: **jokelist.php (excerpt)**

```
$cid = $_POST['cid'];
if ($cid != '') { // A category is selected
  $from  .= ', jokecategory';
  $where .= " AND id=jokeid AND categoryid='$cid'";
}
```

As the categories associated with a particular joke are stored in the jokecategory table, we need to add this table to the query to create a join. To do this, we simply tack the name of the table onto the end of the $from variable. To complete the join, we need also to specify that the id column (in the joke table) must match the jokeid column (in jokecategory), so we add this condition to the $where variable. Finally, we require the categoryid column (in jokecategory) to match the category ID selected in the form ($cid).

Handling search text is fairly simple, and uses the LIKE SQL operator that we learned way back in Chapter 2:

File: **jokelist.php (excerpt)**

```
$searchtext = $_POST['searchtext'];
if ($searchtext != '') { // Some search text was specified
  $where .= " AND joketext LIKE '%$searchtext%'";
}
```

127

Now that we've built our SQL query, we can use it to retrieve and display our jokes along with links that allow us to edit and delete them, just like we did for authors and joke categories. For readability, we display our jokes in an HTML table:

File: **jokelist.php** (excerpt)

```
?>

<table>
<tr><th>Joke Text</th><th>Options</th></tr>

<?php
$jokes = @mysql_query($select . $from . $where);
if (!$jokes) {
  echo '</table>';
  exit('<p>Error retrieving jokes from database!<br />'.
      'Error: ' . mysql_error() . '</p>');
}

while ($joke = mysql_fetch_array($jokes)) {
  echo "<tr valign='top'>\n";
  $id = $joke['id'];
  $joketext = htmlspecialchars($joke['joketext']);
  echo "<td>$joketext</td>\n";
  echo "<td><a href='editjoke.php?id=$id'>Edit</a> | " .
      "<a href='deletejoke.php?id=$id'>Delete</a></td>\n";
  echo "</tr>\n";
}
?>

</table>

<p><a href="jokes.php">New search</a></p>
</body>
</html>
```

The search results will display as shown in Figure 6.8.

Figure 6.8. A classic is found.

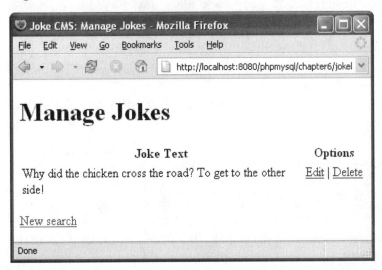

Adding Jokes

With `jokelist.php` out of the way, let's tackle `newjoke.php`, which is linked to from the top of `jokes.php`. This page will be very similar to `newauthor.php` and `newcat.php`. However, in addition to specifying the joke text, the page must allow an administrator to assign an author and categories to a joke. These features make the code of this file worth some examination.

We know from viewing the code of `newauthor.php` that the PHP code that processes the form submission comes before the form code itself. It doesn't have to, but this is the layout we've used so far. Let's begin by looking at the form code, so that the code for handling form submissions makes more sense.

First, we fetch lists of all the authors and categories in the database:

File: **newjoke.php (excerpt)**

```php
<?php
else: // Allow the user to enter a new joke

  $authors = @mysql_query('SELECT id, name FROM author');
  if (!$authors) {
    exit(
        '<p>Unable to obtain author list from the database.</p>');
  }
```

```
$cats = @mysql_query('SELECT id, name FROM category');
if (!$cats) {
  exit('<p>Unable to obtain category list from the ' .
    'database.</p>');
}
?>
```

Next, we create our form. We begin with a standard text area into which we can type the text of the joke:

File: **newjoke.php** (excerpt)

```
<form action="<?php echo $_SERVER['PHP_SELF']; ?>" method="post">
<p>Enter the new joke:<br />
<textarea name="joketext" rows="5" cols="45">
</textarea></p>
```

We'll prompt the administrator to select an author from a drop-down list of the authors in the database:

File: **newjoke.php** (excerpt)

```
<p>Author:
<select name="aid" size="1">
  <option selected value="">Select One</option>
  <option value="">---------</option>
<?php
  while ($author = mysql_fetch_array($authors)) {
    $aid = $author['id'];
    $aname = htmlspecialchars($author['name']);
    echo "<option value='$aid'>$aname</option>\n";
  }
?>
</select></p>
```

A drop-down list won't suffice for the selection of categories, though, because we want the administrator to be able to select multiple categories. Thus, we'll use a series of check boxes—one for each category. Since we have no way to know in advance the number of check boxes we'll need, the matter of naming them becomes an interesting challenge.

What we'll actually do is use a *single* variable for all the check boxes; thus, all the check boxes will have the same name. To be able to receive multiple values from a single variable name, we must make that variable an **array**. Recall from Chapter 3 that an array is a single variable with compartments, each of which can hold a value. To submit a form element as part of an array variable, we simply add a pair of square brackets to the end of the variable name (making it `cats[]` in this case).[3]

With all of our check boxes named the same, we'll need a way to identify which particular check boxes have been selected. To this end, we assign a different value to each check box—the ID of the corresponding category in the database. Thus, the form submits an array that contains the IDs of all the categories to which the new joke should be added.

File: **newjoke.php (excerpt)**

```
<p>Place in categories:<br />
<?php
  while ($cat = mysql_fetch_array($cats)) {
    $cid = $cat['id'];
    $cname = htmlspecialchars($cat['name']);
    echo "<label><input type='checkbox' name='cats[]' " .
        "value='$cid' />$cname</label><br />\n";
  }
?>
</p>
```

And we finish off our form as usual:

File: **newjoke.php (excerpt)**

```
<input type="submit" value="SUBMIT" />
</form>
<?php endif; ?>
```

Figure 6.9 shows what this form will look like.

---

[3]Another way to submit an array is with a `select multiple` tag. Again, you would set the `name` attribute to end with square brackets. What will be submitted is an array of all the `option` values selected from the list by the user. Feel free to experiment with this approach by modifying `new-joke.php` to present the categories in a list.

Figure 6.9. The hits just keep on coming.

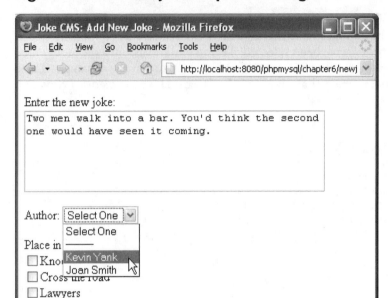

Since we're submitting an array for the first time, the code that processes this form is not totally straightforward. It starts off pretty simply as we add the joke to the `joke` table. As an author is required, we make sure that `$_POST['aid']` contains a value. This prevents the administrator from choosing the Select One option in the author select list (that choice has a value of `""`, the empty string).

File: **newjoke.php (excerpt)**

```php
<?php

$dbcnx = @mysql_connect('localhost', 'root', 'mypasswd');
if (!$dbcnx) {
  exit('<p>Unable to connect to the ' .
       'database server at this time.</p>');
}

if (!@mysql_select_db('ijdb')) {
```

```
    exit('<p>Unable to locate the joke ' .
        'database at this time.</p>');
}

if (isset($_POST['joketext'])):
    // A new joke has been entered
    // using the form.

    $aid = $_POST['aid'];
    $joketext = $_POST['joketext'];

    if ($aid == '') {
        exit('<p>You must choose an author for this joke. Click ' .
            '"Back" and try again.</p>');
    }

    $sql = "INSERT INTO joke SET
        joketext='$joketext',
        jokedate=CURDATE(),
        authorid='$aid'";
    if (@mysql_query($sql)) {
        echo '<p>New joke added</p>';
    } else {
        exit('<p>Error adding new joke: ' . mysql_error() . '</p>');
    }

    $jid = mysql_insert_id();
```

The last line in the above code uses a function that we haven't seen before: `mysql_insert_id`. This function returns the number assigned to the last-inserted entry by the `AUTO_INCREMENT` feature in MySQL. In other words, it retrieves the ID of the newly inserted joke, which we'll need momentarily.

The code that adds the entries to `jokecategory` based on which check boxes were checked is not so simple. First of all, we've never seen how a check box passes its value to a PHP variable before. Also, we need to deal with the fact that these particular check boxes will submit into an array variable.

A typical check box will pass its value to a PHP variable if it is checked, and will do nothing when it is unchecked. Check boxes without assigned values pass `'on'` as the value of their corresponding variables when they are checked. However, we've assigned values to our check boxes (the category IDs), so this is not an issue.

The fact that these check boxes submit into an array actually adds quite a measure of convenience to our code. In essence, what we'll receive from the submitted form is either:

1. an array of category IDs to add the joke to

2. nothing at all (if none of the check boxes were checked)

First, let's handle the latter, special case by creating an empty array when we find that the $_POST['cats'] variable is empty:

```
if (isset($_POST['cats'])) {
  $cats = $_POST['cats'];
} else {
  $cats = array();
}
```

The array function that appears here is used to create a new array in PHP. The parameters that are passed to it become the elements of the array. Because we're not passing parameters to it here, it will simply create an empty array.

Now that we've guaranteed that the $cats variable contains an array, we can use a loop to consider each category ID in the array in turn, and to insert the appropriate entry into the database. Since this array isn't based on a database row, you might wonder how we can access the values in the array. After all, we've usually retrieved an array value using its database column name (e.g. $cat['name']). In this case, our array was created simply by feeding a series of values into the same variable name. When this happens, PHP automatically assigns numerical indices to the values in the array.

For instance, the value of the first check box that was checked will be submitted first into the array and will be accessible as $cat[0]. That is, PHP assigns it an array index of 0. The second check box that is checked will have its value stored with an index of 1, accessible as $cat[1]. So if n check boxes are checked, then the value of the last check box will be in $cat[$n-1]. By counting up through the array indexes as we proceed through a loop in our code, we can process the elements of this array one at a time.

But wait... what is n? We have no way of knowing in advance how many check boxes will be checked, so how should the loop know when to stop counting? Well, there are two ways we can ascertain this value. The first is to use a PHP function called count that takes an array as a parameter and counts the number of elements in it. Here's what our `while` loop would look like if we use this method:

```
$i = 0; // First index
while ($i < count($cats)) { // While we're not at the end
  // process $cats[$i]
  ++$i; // Increment to the next index
}
```

As you can see, this loop uses a counter variable (`$i`), that is, a variable that counts the number of times the loop has executed. The first time through the loop, it will have a value of 0; at the end of the loop we'll add 1 to it. Therefore, the second time through the loop, it will have a value of 1, and so on. Within the loop, we can use this variable as the array index to pull a category ID out of the `$cats` array. The loop stops executing when `$i` reaches `count($cats)`, the number of elements in the `$cats` array. If `$cats` doesn't contain any elements (i.e. no categories were selected), then `$i` will *start out* equal to `count($cats)`, and the contents of the loop won't be executed at all.

This all seems very slick, but there's actually a better method. Instead of using the `count` function, we can keep going until we reach a value of `$i` for which `$cat[$i]` is empty. When we do, we'll know we've reached the end of the list of category IDs:

```
$i = 0; // First index
while (isset($cats[$i])) { // While we're not at the end
  // process $cats[$i]
  ++$i; // Increment to the next index
}
```

This will run a little faster because we don't call a function each time through the loop. Plus, it's a teensy bit more clever, and we programmers have to have our fun when we can!

Going one step further, the especially attentive may recognize this `while` loop as a perfect candidate for replacement with a `for` loop. We introduced `for` loops back in Chapter 3. Here's what the equivalent `for` loop looks like:

```
for ($i = 0; isset($cats[$i]); ++$i) {
  // process $cats[$i]
}
```

Not bad, right? Well, believe it or not, PHP spoils our fun by having a completely separate type of loop that's specialized for looping through arrays, called a **foreach loop**. Here's what the code looks like in this case:

```
foreach ($cats as $catID) {
  // Process $catID
}
```

This `foreach` loop will execute the code inside the loop once *for each* item in the `$cats` array (you see where the `foreach` loop gets its name), and will assign the item for each loop to the variable `$catID`. Since this code is indisputably tidier than the equivalent `while` loop, we'll settle on this as a solution. All that remains is to determine what to do for each selected category ID.

Before we became sidetracked by all these different types of loops, we were about to take our array of category IDs and use it to place our newly-inserted joke into its corresponding categories. A cursory examination of our database layout reveals that we just have to insert an entry into the `jokecategory` table for each category of which that joke should be a member. Recall that each entry in the `jokecat-egory` table consists of a joke ID (`jokeid`) and a category ID (`categoryid`), which together indicate that a particular joke belongs to a particular category. Here's the finished `foreach` loop:

```
  $numCats = 0;
  foreach ($cats as $catID) {
    $sql = "INSERT IGNORE INTO jokecategory
        SET jokeid=$jid, categoryid=$catID";
    $ok = @mysql_query($sql);
    if ($ok) {
      $numCats = $numCats + 1;
    } else {
      echo "<p>Error inserting joke into category $catID: " .
        mysql_error() . '</p>';
    }
  }
?>

<p>Joke was added to <?php echo $numCats; ?> categories.</p>

<p><a href="<?php echo $_SERVER['PHP_SELF']; ?>">Add another
  joke</a></p>
<p><a href="jokes.php">Return to joke search</a></p>
```

The word `IGNORE` in the `INSERT` query used here is a precaution only. Recall that, when we defined the `jokecategory` table, we set the `jokeid` and `category` columns to be the primary key for the table. If somehow the jokeid/categoryid pair that is inserted already exists in the table, an attempt to insert it again would normally cause an error. By adding IGNORE to the command, a reinsert of the same pair is simply ignored by MySQL and no error occurs. This situation should never actually happen, but it's better to be safe than sorry.

Editing and Deleting Jokes

The two files that remain, editjoke.php and deletejoke.php, mirror their author and category counterparts, with minor adjustments. editjoke.php must provide the same author select box and category check boxes as newjoke.php, except that this time they must be initialized to reflect those values stored in the database for the particular joke we've selected. deletejoke.php, meanwhile, must delete the selected joke from the joke table, and must also remove any entries in the jokecategory table for that joke.

As all of this falls within reach of the skills you've developed in the preceding chapters, I'll present the code for these files without comment. Take some time to browse through them and make sure you're comfortable with everything that's going on within.

File: **editjoke.php**

```
<!DOCTYPE html PUBLIC "-//W3C//DTD XHTML 1.0 Strict//EN"
    "http://www.w3.org/TR/xhtml1/DTD/xhtml1-strict.dtd">
<html xmlns="http://www.w3.org/1999/xhtml">
<head>
<title>Joke CMS: Edit Joke</title>
<meta http-equiv="content-type"
    content="text/html; charset=iso-8859-1" />
</head>
<body>
<?php

$dbcnx = @mysql_connect('localhost', 'root', 'mypasswd');
if (!$dbcnx) {
  exit('<p>Unable to connect to the ' .
      'database server at this time.</p>');
}

if (!@mysql_select_db('ijdb')) {
  exit('<p>Unable to locate the joke ' .
      'database at this time.</p>');
}
```

```php
if (isset($_POST['joketext'])):
  // The joke's details have
  // been updated.

  $id = $_POST['id'];
  $aid = $_POST['aid'];
  $joketext = $_POST['joketext'];

  $sql = "UPDATE joke SET
          joketext='$joketext',
          authorid='$aid'
          WHERE id='$id'";
  if (mysql_query($sql)) {
    echo '<p>Joke details updated.</p>';
  } else {
    exit('<p>Error updating joke details: ' .
        mysql_error() . '</p>');
  }

  // Delete all existing entries for this
  // joke from the jokecategory table
  $ok = mysql_query("DELETE FROM jokecategory
                    WHERE jokeid='$id'");
  if (!$ok) {
    exit('<p>Error removing joke from all categories:' .
        mysql_error() . '</p>');
  }

  if (isset($_POST['cats'])) {
    $cats = $_POST['cats'];
  } else {
    $cats = array();
  }

  foreach ($cats as $catID) {
    $sql = "INSERT IGNORE INTO jokecategory
            SET jokeid='$id', categoryid='$catID'";
    $ok = @mysql_query($sql);
    if (!$ok) {
      echo "<p>Error inserting joke into category $catID: " .
          mysql_error() . '</p>';
    }
  }
?>
```

```php
<p><a href="jokes.php">New joke search</a></p>

<?php else: // Allow the user to edit the joke

  $id = $_GET['id'];

  $joke = @mysql_query(
    "SELECT joketext, authorid FROM joke WHERE id='$id'");
  if (!$joke) {
    exit('<p>Error fetching joke details: ' .
        mysql_error() . '</p>');
  }

  $joke = mysql_fetch_array($joke);

  $joketext = $joke['joketext'];
  $authid = $joke['authorid'];

  // Convert HTML special characters
  // in database value for use in
  // an HTML document.
  $joketext = htmlspecialchars($joketext);

  // Get lists of authors and categories for
  // the select box and checkboxes.
  $authors = @mysql_query('SELECT id, name FROM author');
  if (!$authors) {
    exit(
        '<p>Unable to obtain author list from the database.</p>');
  }

  $cats = @mysql_query('SELECT id, name FROM category');
  if (!$cats) {
    exit('<p>Unable to obtain category list from the ' .
        'database.</p>');
  }
?>

<form action="<?php echo $_SERVER['PHP_SELF']; ?>" method="post">
<p>Edit the joke:<br />
<textarea name="joketext" rows="15" cols="45">
<?php echo $joketext; ?></textarea>
<p>Author:
<select name="aid" size="1">
<?php
  while ($author = mysql_fetch_array($authors)) {
```

```php
      $aid = $author['id'];
      $aname = htmlspecialchars($author['name']);
      if ($aid == $authid) {
        echo "<option selected='selected' value='$aid'>" .
            "$aname</option>\n";
      } else {
        echo "<option value='$aid'>$aname</option>\n";
      }
    }
?>
</select></p>
<p>In categories:<br />
<?php
  while ($cat = mysql_fetch_array($cats)) {
    $cid = $cat['id'];
    $cname = htmlspecialchars($cat['name']);

    // Check if the joke is in this category
    $result = @mysql_query(
      "SELECT * FROM jokecategory
        WHERE jokeid='$id' AND categoryid='$cid'");
    if (!$result) {
      exit('<p>Error fetching joke details: ' .
          mysql_error() . '</p>');
    }

    // mysql_num_rows gives the number of entries
    // in a result set. In this case, if the result
    // contains one or more rows, the condition
    // below will evaluate to true to indicate that
    // the joke does belong to the category, and the
    // checkbox should be checked.
    if (mysql_num_rows($result)) {
      echo "<input type='checkbox' checked='checked' " .
          "name='cats[]' value='$cid' />$cname<br />\n";
    } else {
      echo "<input type='checkbox' name='cats[]' value='$cid' " .
          "/>$cname<br />\n";
    }
  }
?>
</p>
<input type="hidden" name="id" value="<?php echo $id; ?>" />
<input type="submit" value="SUBMIT" />
</form>
```

```
<?php endif; ?>

</body>
</html>
```

File: **deletejoke.php**

```
<!DOCTYPE html PUBLIC "-//W3C//DTD XHTML 1.0 Strict//EN"
    "http://www.w3.org/TR/xhtml1/DTD/xhtml1-strict.dtd">
<html xmlns="http://www.w3.org/1999/xhtml">
<head>
<title>Joke CMS: Delete Joke</title>
<meta http-equiv="content-type"
    content="text/html; charset=iso-8859-1" />
</head>
<body>
<?php

$dbcnx = @mysql_connect('localhost', 'root', 'mypasswd');
if (!$dbcnx) {
  exit('<p>Unable to connect to the ' .
      'database server at this time.</p>');
}

if (!@mysql_select_db('ijdb')) {
  exit('<p>Unable to locate the joke ' .
      'database at this time.</p>');
}

// Delete all joke lookup entries for the
// joke along with the entry for the joke.
$id = $_GET['id'];
$ok1 = @mysql_query("DELETE FROM jokecategory WHERE " .
    "jokeid='$id'");
$ok2 = @mysql_query("DELETE FROM joke WHERE id='$id'");
if ($ok1 and $ok2) {
  echo '<p>Joke deleted successfully!</p>';
} else {
  echo '<p>Error deleting joke from database!<br />'.
      'Error: ' . mysql_error() . '</p>';
}

?>
<p><a href="jokes.php">New joke search</a></p>
</body>
</html>
```

Summary

There are a few minor tasks of which our content management system is still incapable. For example, it's unable to provide a listing of all jokes that don't belong to *any* category—something that could come in very handy as the number of jokes in the database grows. You might also like to sort joke listings by various criteria. These particular capabilities require a few more advanced SQL tricks that we'll see in Chapter 9.

If we ignore these little details for the moment, you'll see that you now have a system that allows someone without SQL or database knowledge to administer your database of jokes with ease! Together with a set of PHP-powered pages through which regular site visitors can view the jokes, this content management system allows us to set up a complete database-driven Website that can be maintained by someone with absolutely no database knowledge. And if you think that sounds like a valuable commodity to businesses looking to get on the Web today, you're right!

In fact, only one aspect of our site requires users to have special knowledge (beyond the use of a Web browser): content formatting. For example, it would not be unusual for someone to want to enter a joke that contained more than one paragraph of text. In our current system, this could be accomplished by entering the HTML code for the joke directly into the new joke form. Why is this unacceptable?

As we stated way back in the introduction to this book, one of the most desirable features of a database-driven Website is that the people responsible for adding content to the site need not be familiar with HTML. If we require knowledge of HTML for something as simple as dividing a joke into paragraphs, we have failed to achieve our goal.

In Chapter 7, we'll see how we can make use of some features of PHP to provide a simpler means by which we can format content without requiring site administrators to know the ins and outs of HTML. We'll also bring back the "submit your own joke" link, and discover how we can safely accept content submissions from casual site visitors.

As a bonus in this chapter, you also learned a little more about arrays in PHP. You learned how a set of form elements can submit their values into a single array variable, and you learned how to process that array on the receiving end by looping through it with a `while` loop, a `for` loop, and a `foreach` loop.

7

Content Formatting and Submission

We're almost there! We've designed a database to store jokes, organize them into categories, and track their authors. We've learned how to create a Web page that displays this library of jokes to site visitors. We've even developed a set of Web pages that a site administrator can use to manage the joke library without having to know anything about databases.

In so doing, we've built a site that frees the resident Webmaster from continually having to plug new content into tired HTML page templates, and from maintaining an unmanageable mass of HTML files. The HTML is now kept completely separate from the data it displays. If you want to redesign the site, you simply have to make the changes to the HTML contained in the PHP files that site visitors see. A change to one file (e.g. changing a font) is immediately reflected in the page layouts of all jokes, because all jokes are displayed using that single PHP file. Only one task still requires the use of HTML: **content formatting**.

On any but the simplest of Websites, it will be necessary to allow content (in our case study, jokes) to be formatted. In a simple case, this might merely be the ability to break text into paragraphs. Often, however, content providers will expect facilities such as **boldface** or *italicized* text, hyperlinks, etc.

Our current database and site design already supports all these requirements. A site administrator can include in the text of a joke HTML tags that will have their usual effects on the joke text when it's inserted into a page that a browser requests. However, to eliminate HTML from the system entirely, we must provide some other way to format text.

In this chapter, we'll learn some new PHP functions that provide basic text formatting without the use of HTML. By the time we've finished, we'll have completed a content management system that anyone with a Web browser can use. We'll then take full advantage of this ease of use, and allow site visitors once again to submit their own jokes—this time without the risk that users might fill our site with inappropriate material.

Out with the Old

Before we introduce a new method to format text, we should first disable the old one. A user with no knowledge of HTML might unknowingly include HTML syntax (however invalid) in a plain text document, and if this syntax is still accepted, it could produce unexpected results—or even mess up your finely tuned page layout. Consider the following sentence:

```
A man walked into a bar. <WHACK!>
```

The user who entered this text into the database might be surprised to see the last word (<WHACK!>) missing from the Web page that displayed this content. And while anyone with a basic knowledge of HTML would know that the Web browser discarded that segment of text as an invalid HTML tag, we're trying to cater to users with no knowledge of HTML whatsoever.

In Chapter 6, we saw a PHP function that solved this problem quite neatly: htmlspecialchars. This function, when applied to the text of our joke before it was inserted into a Web page, would convert the string above into the following "HTML-safe" version:

```
A man walked into a bar. &lt;WHACK!&gt;
```

When this string was interpreted by the site visitor's Web browser, it would produce the desired result. As a first step, therefore, we must modify the PHP file on our Website that displays the text of jokes, so that htmlspecialchars is used on all text before it's output to the Web.

Here's the basic code that fetches a joke with a given ID out of the database and formats it for display by converting it to an "HTML-safe" version:

File: **joke.php (excerpt)**

```
// Get the joke text from the database
$id = $_GET['id'];
$joke = @mysql_query(
    "SELECT joketext FROM joke WHERE id='$id'");
if (!$joke) {
  exit('Unable to load the joke from the database.');
}
if (mysql_num_rows($joke) < 1) {
  exit('Could not locate the specified joke ID.');
}
$joke = mysql_fetch_array($joke);
$joketext = $joke['joketext'];

// Filter out HTML code
$joketext = htmlspecialchars($joketext);
```

The only new element in this code is the `mysql_num_rows` function, which takes a MySQL result set number and returns the number of rows in that result set. In this case, we use it to determine if a joke that matched the specified joke ID was found in the database. If one wasn't, we exit with an error message.

We have now neutralized any HTML code that may appear in the site's content. With this clean slate, we are ready to implement a markup language of our own that will let administrators format content.

Regular Expressions

To implement our own markup language, we'll require a script to spot our custom tags in the text of jokes and replace them with their HTML equivalents, before it outputs the joke text to the user's browser. Anyone with experience in regular expressions will know that they're ideal for this sort of work.

A **regular expression** is a string of text containing special codes that allow it to be used with a few PHP functions to search and manipulate other strings of text. This, for example, is a regular expression that searches for the text "PHP" (without the quotes):[1]

```
PHP
```

---

[1]This book covers PHP's support for POSIX Regular Expressions. A more complex, more powerful, but less standardized form of regular expressions called Perl Compatible Regular Expressions (PCRE) is also supported by PHP; however, it's not covered in this book. For more information on PCRE, see http://www.php.net/pcre.

Not much to it, is there? To use a regular expression, you must be familiar with the regular expression functions available in PHP. ereg is the most basic, and can be used to determine whether a regular expression is **satisfied** by a particular text string. Consider this code:

```
$text = 'PHP rules!';

if (ereg('PHP', $text)) {
  echo '$text contains the string "PHP".';
} else {
  echo '$text does not contain the string "PHP".';
}
```

In this example, the regular expression is satisfied because the string stored in variable $text contains "PHP." The above code will thus output the following (note that the single quotes prevent PHP from filling in the value of the variable $text):

```
$text contains the string "PHP".
```

eregi is a function that behaves almost identically to ereg, except that it ignores the case of text when it looks for matches:

```
$text = 'What is Php?';

if (eregi('PHP', $text)) {
  echo '$text contains the string "PHP".';
} else {
  echo '$text does not contain the string "PHP".';
}
```

Again, this outputs the same message, despite the fact that the string actually contains "Php":

```
$text contains the string "PHP".
```

As was mentioned above, there are special codes that may be used in regular expressions. Some of these can be downright confusing and difficult to remember, so if you intend to make extensive use of them, a good reference might come in handy. A tutorial-style reference to standard regular expression syntax may be found at http://www.delorie.com/gnu/docs/regex/regex_toc.html. Let's work our way through a few examples to learn the basic regular expression syntax.

First of all, a caret (^) may be used to indicate the start of the string, while a dollar sign ($) is used to indicate its end:

`PHP`	Matches "PHP rules!" and "What is PHP?"
`^PHP`	Matches "PHP rules!" but not "What is PHP?"
`PHP$`	Matches "I love PHP" but not "What is PHP?"
`^PHP$`	Matches "PHP" but nothing else.

Obviously, you may sometimes want to use `^`, `$`, or other special characters to represent the corresponding character in the search string, rather than the special meaning implied by regular expression syntax. To remove the special meaning of a character, prefix it with a backslash:

`\$\$\$`	Matches "Show me the $$$!" but not "$10".

Square brackets can be used to define a set of characters that may match. For example, the following regular expression will match any string that contains any digit from 1 to 5 inclusive:

`[12345]`	Matches "1a" and "39", but not "a" or "76".

If the character list within the square brackets is preceded with `^`, the set will match anything *but* the characters listed:

`[^12345]`	Matches "1a" and "39", but not "1", or "54".

Ranges of numbers and letters may also be specified:

`[1-5]`	Same as previous.
`^[a-z]$`	Matches any single lowercase letter.
`^[^a-z]$`	Matches any single character *except* a lowercase letter.
`[0-9a-zA-Z]`	Matches any string with a letter or number.

The characters `?`, `+`, and `*` also have special meanings. Specifically, `?` means "the preceding character is optional," `+` means "one or more of the previous character," and `*` means "zero or more of the previous character."

`bana?na`	Matches "banana" and "banna", but not "banaana".
`bana+na`	Matches "banana" and "banaana", but not "banna".
`bana*na`	Matches "banna", "banana", and "banaaana", but not "bnana".
`^[a-zA-Z]+$`	Matches any string of one or more letters and nothing else.

Parentheses may be used to group strings together to apply ?, +, or * to them as a whole:

ba(na)+na Matches "banana" and "banananana",
      but not "bana" or "banaana".

You can provide a number of alternatives within parentheses, separated by pipes (|):

ba(na|ni)+ Matches "bana" and "banina",
     but not "naniba".

And finally, a period (.) matches any character except a new line:

^.+$ Matches any string of one or more characters with no line breaks.

There are more special codes and syntax tricks for regular expressions, all of which should be covered in any reference, such as those mentioned above. For now, we have more than enough for our purposes.

String Replacement with Regular Expressions

We can easily detect the presence of tags in a given text string using `ereg` or `eregi` with the regular expression syntax we've just learned. However, what we need to do is pinpoint those tags, and replace them with appropriate HTML tags. To achieve this, we need to look at a couple more regular expression functions offered by PHP: `ereg_replace` and `eregi_replace`.

`ereg_replace`, like `ereg`, accepts a regular expression and a string of text, and attempts to match the regular expression in the string. In addition, `ereg_replace` takes a second string of text, and replaces every match of the regular expression with that string.

The syntax for `ereg_replace` is as follows:

```
$newstr = ereg_replace(regexp, replacewith, oldstr);
```

Here, *regexp* is the regular expression, and *replacewith* is the string that will replace matches to *regexp* in *oldstr*. The function returns the new string that's the outcome of the replacement operation. In the above, this newly-generated string is stored in $newstr.

eregi_replace, as you might expect, is identical to ereg_replace, except that the case of letters is not considered when searching for matches.

We're now ready to build our custom markup language.

Boldface and Italic Text

Let's start by implementing tags that create **boldface** and *italic* text. Let's say we want [B] to begin bold text and [EB] to end bold text. Obviously, we must replace [B] with <strong> and [EB] with </strong>.[2] Achieving this is a simple application of eregi_replace:[3]

```
$joketext = eregi_replace('\\[b]', '<strong>', $joketext);
$joketext = eregi_replace('\\[eb]', '</strong>', $joketext);
```

Notice that, because [normally indicates the start of a set of acceptable characters in a regular expression, we put a backslash before it in order to remove its special meaning. As backslashes are also used to escape special characters in PHP strings, we must use a double backslash for each single backslash that we wish to have in the regular expression. Without a matching [, the] loses its special meaning, so it doesn't need to be escaped, although you could put a (double) backslash in front of it as well if you wanted to be thorough.

Also notice that, as we're using eregi_replace, which is case insensitive, both [B] and [b] will work as tags in our custom markup language.

Italic text can be achieved in the same way:

```
$joketext = eregi_replace('\\[i]', '<em>', $joketext);
$joketext = eregi_replace('\\[ei]', '</em>', $joketext);
```

Paragraphs

While we could create tags for paragraphs just as we did for boldface and italicized text above, a simpler approach makes even more sense. As users will type the content into a form field that allows them to format text using the enter key, we

---

[2]You may be more accustomed to using <b> and <i> tags; however, I have chosen to respect the most recent HTML standards, which recommend replacing these with <strong> and <em>, respectively, to give the tags semantic meaning.
[3]Experienced developers may object to this use of regular expressions. No, regular expressions are not required for this simple example, and yes, a single regular expression for both tags would be more appropriate than two separate expressions. I'll address both of these issues later in this chapter.

shall take a single new line (\n) to indicate a line break (<br />) and a double new line (\n\n) to indicate a new paragraph (</p><p>). Of course, because Windows computers represent an end-of-line as a new-line-carriage-return pair (\n\r), and Macintosh computers represent it as a carriage-return-new-line pair (\r\n), we must strip out carriage returns first. The code for all this is as follows:

```
// Strip out carriage returns
$joketext = ereg_replace("\r", '', $joketext);
// Handle paragraphs
$joketext = ereg_replace("\n\n", '</p><p>', $joketext);
// Handle line breaks
$joketext = ereg_replace("\n", '<br />', $joketext);
```

That's it! The text will now appear in the paragraphs expected by the user, who hasn't had to learn any custom tags to format the content.

Hyperlinks

While supporting the inclusion of hyperlinks in the text of jokes may seem unnecessary, this feature makes plenty of sense in other applications. Hyperlinks are a little more complicated than the simple conversion of a fixed code fragment into an HTML tag. We need to be able to output a URL, as well as the text that should appear as the link.

Another feature of `ereg_replace` and `eregi_replace` comes into play here. If you surround a portion of the regular expression with parentheses, you can **capture** the corresponding portion of the matched text, and use it in the replace string. To do this, you'll use the code \n, where n is 1 for the first parenthesized portion of the regular expression, 2 for the second, and so on, up to 9 for the 9th. Consider this example:

```
$text = 'banana';
$text = eregi_replace('(.*)(nana)', '\\2\\1', $text);
echo $text; // outputs "nanaba"
```

As before, single backslashes in the string must be written with double backslashes to allow for PHP character escaping.

In the above, \\1 is replaced with **ba** in the replace string, which corresponds to (.*) (zero or more non-new line characters) in the regular expression. \\2 is replaced by **nana**, which corresponds to (nana) in the regular expression.

We can use the same principle to create our hyperlinks. Let's begin with a simple form of link, where the text of the link is the same as the URL. We want to support this syntax:

```
Visit [L]http://www.php.net/[EL].
```

The corresponding HTML code, which we want to output, is as follows:

```
Visit <a href="http://www.php.net/">http://www.php.net/</a>.
```

First, we need a regular expression that will match links of this form. The regular expression is as follows:

```
\[L][-_./a-z0-9!&%#?+,'=:;@~]+\[EL]
```

Again, we've placed backslashes in front of the opening square brackets in [L] and [EL] to indicate that they are to be taken literally. We then use square brackets to list all the characters we wish to accept as part of the URL.[4] I've left out capital letters here, because we'll eventually use the case-insensitive eregi_replace function, so they would be redundant. We place a + after the square brackets to indicate that the URL will be composed of one or more characters taken from this list.

To output our link, we'll need to capture the URL and output it both as the href attribute of the a tag, and as the text of the link. To capture the URL, we surround the corresponding portion of our regular expression with parentheses:

```
\[L]([-_./a-z0-9!&%#?+,'=:;@~]+)\[EL]
```

We convert the link with the following code:

File: **joke.php (excerpt)**

```
$joketext = eregi_replace(
    '\\[L]([-_./a-z0-9!&%#?+,\'=:;@~]+)\\[EL]',
    '<a href="\\1">\\1</a>', $joketext);
```

Note that in addition to doubling the existing backslashes in our regular expression, we had to escape the quote (') in the regular expression with a backslash (\') to prevent PHP from thinking it indicated the end of the regular expression

---

[4]I have not included a space in the list of characters I want to allow in a link URL. Although Microsoft Internet Explorer supports such URLs, spaces in the path or file name portions of a URL should be replaced with the code %20, and spaces in the query string should be replaced by +. If you want to allow spaces in your URLs, feel free to add a space to the list of characters in square brackets.

string. Meanwhile, \\1 in the replacement string is replaced by the URL for the link, and the output is as expected!

We'd also like to support hyperlinks whose link text differs from the URL. Let's say the form of our link is as follows:

```
Check out [L=http://www.php.net/]PHP[EL].
```

Here's our regular expression:

```
\[L=([-_./a-z0-9!&%#?+,'=:;@~]+)]([^\[]+)\[EL]
```

Quite a mess, isn't it? Squint at it for a little while, and you'll see it achieves exactly what we need it to, capturing both the URL (\\1) and the text (\\2) for the link. This code describes the link text as one or more characters, none of which is an opening square bracket ([^\[]+). The PHP code that performs the substitution is as follows:

File: joke.php (excerpt)

```
$joketext = eregi_replace(
    '\\[L=([-_./a-z0-9!&%#?+,\'=:;@~]+)]([^\\[]+)\\[EL]',
    '<a href="\\1">\\2</a>', $joketext);
```

Matching Tags

A nice side-effect of the regular expressions we developed to read hyperlinks is that they will only find matched pairs of [L] and [EL] tags. A [L] tag missing its [EL] or vice versa will not be detected, and will appear unchanged in the finished document, allowing the person updating the site to spot the error and fix it.

In contrast, the PHP code we developed for boldface and italic text in the section called "Boldface and Italic Text" will convert unmatched [B] and [I] tags into unmatched HTML tags! This can lead to ugly situations in which, for example, the entire text of a joke starting from an unmatched tag will be displayed in bold—possibly even spilling into subsequent content on the page.

We can rewrite our code for bold and italic text in the same style we used for hyperlinks. This solves the problem by only processing matched pairs of tags:

```
$joketext = eregi_replace(
    '\[B]([^\[]+)\[EB]', '<strong>\\1</strong>',
    $joketext);
$joketext = eregi_replace(
```

```
'\[I]([^\[]+)\[EI]', '<em>\\1</em>',
  $joketext);
```

Nested tags

One weakness of these regular expressions is that they represent the content between the tags as a series of characters that doesn't contain an opening square bracket ([^\[]+). As a result, nested tags (tags within tags) will not work correctly in this system.

Ideally, we would like to be able to tell the regular expression to capture characters following the opening tag until it reaches a matching closing tag. Unfortunately, the + and * special characters in POSIX regular expressions are what we call **greedy**, which means they'll match as many characters as they can. Consider this example:

```
This text contains [B]two[EB] bold [B]words[EB]!
```

Now, if didn't restrict the characters that can appear between tags, we might come up with a regular expression like this one:

```
\[B](.+)\[EB]
```

Nice and simple, right? Unfortunately, because the + is greedy, the regular expression will match only one pair of tags in the above example—and it's not the pair you might expect! Here's the results:

```
This text contains <strong>two[EB]
bold[B]words</strong>!
```

As you can see, the greedy + plowed right through the first closing tag and the second opening tag to find the second closing tag in its attempt to match as many characters as possible. What we need in order to support nested tags are non-greedy versions of + and ., and for that you need the more complex Perl-Compatible Regular Expressions (PCRE)[3].

If unmatched tags aren't much of a concern for you, however, you can actually simplify your code by not using regular expressions at all! PHP's str_replace function works a lot like ereg_replace, except that it only searches for strings—not patterns.

```
$newstr = str_replace(searchfor, replacewith, oldstr);
```

We can therefore rewrite our bold/italic code as follows:

---

[3] http://www.php.net/pcre

```
$joketext = str_replace('[B]', '<strong>', $joketext);
$joketext = str_replace('[EB]', '</strong>', $joketext);

$joketext = str_replace('[I]', '<em>', $joketext);
$joketext = str_replace('[EI]', '</em>', $joketext);
```

One difference remains between this and our regular expression code. We used `eregi_replace` in our previous code to match both lowercase [b] and uppercase [B] tags, as that function was case-insensitive. `str_replace` is case-sensitive, so we need to make a further modification to allow uppercase tags.

If you're lucky enough to be using PHP 5, you can simply use the new `str_ireplace` function:

```
$joketext = str_ireplace('[B]', '<strong>', $joketext);
$joketext = str_ireplace('[EB]', '</strong>', $joketext);

$joketext = str_ireplace('[I]', '<em>', $joketext);
$joketext = str_ireplace('[EI]', '</em>', $joketext);
```

For backwards compatibility with PHP 4, however, you can use the following code:

File: **joke.php (excerpt)**

```
$joketext = str_replace(
    array('[b]', '[B]'), '<strong>', $joketext);
$joketext = str_replace(
    array('[eb]', '[EB]'), '</strong>', $joketext);

$joketext = str_replace(
    array('[i]', '[I]'), '<em>', $joketext);
$joketext = str_replace(
    array('[ei]', '[EI]'), '</em>', $joketext);
```

`str_replace` lets you specify an array of search strings, so the above code will replace [b] or [B] with , [eb] or [EB] with , and so on. For more information about the intricacies of `str_replace`, refer to the PHP manual[4].

While this code looks more complicated than the original version with `eregi_replace`, `str_replace` is much more efficient because it doesn't need to interpret your search string for regular expression codes. Whenever `str_replace`

---

[4] http://www.php.net/str_replace

(or `str_ireplace` in PHP 5) can do the job, you should use it instead of `ereg_replace` or `eregi_replace`.

The `joke.php` file included in the code archive makes use of `str_replace`; feel free to replace it with the regular expression code above if you're worried about unmatched tags.

Splitting Text into Pages

While no joke is likely to be so long that it will require more than one page, many content-driven sites (like sitepoint.com) provide lengthy content that is best presented broken into pages. Yet another regular expression function in PHP makes this exceedingly easy to do.

`split` is a function that takes a regular expression and a string of text, and uses matches for the regular expression to break the text into an array. Consider the following example:

```
$regexp = "[ \n\t\r]+"; // One or more whitespace chars
$text = "This is a\ntest.";
$textarray = split($regexp, $text);
echo $textarray[0] . '<br />'; // Outputs "This<br />"
echo $textarray[1] . '<br />'; // Outputs "is<br />"
echo $textarray[2] . '<br />'; // Outputs "a<br />"
echo $textarray[3] . '<br />'; // Outputs "test.<br />"
```

As you might expect, there is also a `spliti` function that is case-insensitive.

If we search for a `[PAGEBREAK]` tag instead of a whitespace character, and we display only the page in which we're interested (indicated by a `$_GET['page']` variable passed with the page request, for example), instead of all of the resulting portions of the text, we'll have succeeded in our goal.[5]

---

[5]The real reason for using regular expressions here is to allow `[PAGEBREAK]` to be case insensitive; that is, we want `[pagebreak]` or even `[Pagebreak]` to work just as well. If you are happy with requiring that the tag be typed in uppercase, you can actually use PHP's `explode` function instead. It works just like `split`, but it searches for a specific string rather than a pattern defined by a regular expression. See the PHP manual [http://www.php.net/explode] for details. Unlike `str_replace`, `explode` cannot accept an array as its search argument, nor is there an `explodei` function available in PHP 5 (see the section called "Matching Tags").

File: **joke.php** (excerpt)

```
// If no page specified, default to the first page ($page = 0)
if (!isset($_GET['page'])) {
  $page = 0;
} else {
  $page = $_GET['page'];
}

// Split the text into an array of pages
$textarray = spliti('\[PAGEBREAK]', $joketext);

// Select the page we want
$joketext = $textarray[$page];
```

Obviously, we'll want to provide a way for users to move between pages. Let's put a link to the previous page at the top of the current page, and a link to the next page at the bottom.

However, if this is the first page, clearly we won't need a link to the previous page. We know we're on the first page if $page equals zero.

Likewise, we don't need a link to the next page on the last page of content. To detect the last page, we need to use the count function that I introduced briefly in Chapter 6. count takes an array and returns the number of elements it contains. When count is passed our array of pages, it will tell us how many pages there are. If there are ten pages, then $textarray[9] will contain the last page. Thus, we know we're on the last page if $page equals count($textarray) minus one.

The code for the links that will turn our pages looks like this:

File: **joke.php** (excerpt)

```
$PHP_SELF = $_SERVER['PHP_SELF'];

if ($page != 0) {
  $prevpage = $page - 1;
  echo "<p><a href=\"$PHP_SELF?id=$id&amp;page=$prevpage\">".
     'Previous Page</a></p>';
}

echo "<p>$joketext</p>";

if ($page < count($textarray) - 1) {
  $nextpage = $page + 1;
  echo "<p><a href=\"$PHP_SELF?id=$id&amp;page=$nextpage\">".
```

```
       'Next Page</a></p>';
}
```

Putting it all Together

The completed code that will output our joke text (with all special character, multi-page, and custom tag conversion in place) is as follows:

File: **joke.php**

```
<!DOCTYPE html PUBLIC "-//W3C//DTD XHTML 1.0 Strict//EN"
    "http://www.w3.org/TR/xhtml1/DTD/xhtml1-strict.dtd">
<html xmlns="http://www.w3.org/1999/xhtml">
<head>
<title>The Internet Joke Database</title>
<meta http-equiv="content-type"
    content="text/html; charset=iso-8859-1" />
</head>
<body>
<?php

$dbcnx = @mysql_connect('localhost', 'root', 'mypasswd');
if (!$dbcnx) {
  exit('<p>Unable to connect to the ' .
      'database server at this time.</p>');
}

if (!@mysql_select_db('ijdb')) {
  exit('<p>Unable to locate the joke ' .
      'database at this time.</p>');
}

// Get the joke text from the database
$id = $_GET['id'];
$joke = @mysql_query(
    "SELECT joketext FROM joke WHERE id='$id'");
if (!$joke) {
  exit('Unable to load the joke from the database.');
}
if (mysql_num_rows($joke) < 1) {
  exit('Could not locate the specified joke ID.');
}
$joke = mysql_fetch_array($joke);
$joketext = $joke['joketext'];

// Filter out HTML code
```

```
$joketext = htmlspecialchars($joketext);

// If no page specified, default to the first page ($page = 0)
if (!isset($_GET['page'])) {
  $page = 0;
} else {
  $page = $_GET['page'];
}

// Split the text into an array of pages
$textarray = spliti('\[PAGEBREAK]', $joketext);

// Select the page we want
$joketext = $textarray[$page];

// Bold and italics
$joketext = str_replace(array('[b]', '[B]'), '<strong>',
    $joketext);
$joketext = str_replace(array('[eb]', '[EB]'), '</strong>',
    $joketext);
$joketext = str_replace(array('[i]', '[I]'), '<em>', $joketext);
$joketext = str_replace(array('[ei]', '[EI]'), '</em>',
    $joketext);

// Paragraphs and line breaks
$joketext = ereg_replace("\r", '', $joketext);
$joketext = ereg_replace("\n\n", '</p><p>', $joketext);
$joketext = ereg_replace("\n", '<br />', $joketext);

// Hyperlinks
$joketext = eregi_replace(
  '\\[L]([-_./a-z0-9!&%#?+,\'=:;@~]+)\\[EL]',
  '<a href="\\1">\\1</a>', $joketext);
$joketext = eregi_replace(
  '\\[L=([-_./a-z0-9!&%#?+,\'=:;@~]+)]([^\\[]+)\\[EL]',
  '<a href="\\1">\\2</a>', $joketext);

$PHP_SELF = $_SERVER['PHP_SELF'];

if ($page != 0) {
  $prevpage = $page - 1;
  echo "<p><a href=\"$PHP_SELF?id=$id&amp;page=$prevpage\">".
      'Previous Page</a></p>';
}

echo "<p>$joketext</p>";
```

```
if ($page < count($textarray) - 1) {
  $nextpage = $page + 1;
  echo "<p><a href=\"$PHP_SELF?id=$id&amp;page=$nextpage\">".
      'Next Page</a></p>';
}

?>
<p><a href="index.php">Back to the front page</a></p>
</body>
</html>
```

While we're at it, let's create a front page for the site that allows visitors to select a joke category to view:

File: **index.php**

```
<!DOCTYPE html PUBLIC "-//W3C//DTD XHTML 1.0 Strict//EN"
    "http://www.w3.org/TR/xhtml1/DTD/xhtml1-strict.dtd">
<html xmlns="http://www.w3.org/1999/xhtml">
<head>
<title>The Internet Joke Database</title>
<meta http-equiv="content-type"
    content="text/html; charset=iso-8859-1" />
</head>
<body>
<h1>Welcome to the Internet Joke Database!</h1>
<p>Please select a category:</p>
<ul>
<?php

$dbcnx = @mysql_connect('localhost', 'root', 'mypasswd');
if (!$dbcnx) {
  exit('<p>Unable to connect to the ' .
      'database server at this time.</p>');
}

if (!@mysql_select_db('ijdb')) {
  exit('<p>Unable to locate the joke ' .
      'database at this time.</p>');
}

$cats = @mysql_query('SELECT id, name FROM category');
if (!$cats) {
  exit('<p>Error retrieving categories from database!<br />' .
      'Error: ' . mysql_error() . '</p>');
}
```

```
while ($cat = mysql_fetch_array($cats)) {
  $id = $cat['id'];
  $name = htmlspecialchars($cat['name']);

  echo "<li><a href='jokelist.php?cat=$id'>$name</a></li>";
}

?>
</ul>
<p>Or <a href="jokelist.php">view all jokes</a> in the
  database.</p>
</body>
</html>
```

And here's the page that it uses to display the list of jokes:

File: **jokelist.php**

```
<!DOCTYPE html PUBLIC "-//W3C//DTD XHTML 1.0 Strict//EN"
    "http://www.w3.org/TR/xhtml1/DTD/xhtml1-strict.dtd">
<html xmlns="http://www.w3.org/1999/xhtml">
<head>
<title>The Internet Joke Database</title>
<meta http-equiv="content-type"
    content="text/html; charset=iso-8859-1" />
</head>
<body>
<?php

$dbcnx = @mysql_connect('localhost', 'root', 'mypasswd');
if (!$dbcnx) {
  exit('<p>Unable to connect to the ' .
      'database server at this time.</p>');
}

if (!@mysql_select_db('ijdb')) {
  exit('<p>Unable to locate the joke ' .
      'database at this time.</p>');
}

$jokessql =
    'SELECT joke.id, LEFT(joketext, 20), jokedate, name, email
    FROM joke, author, jokecategory
    WHERE authorid=author.id AND jokeid=joke.id';

if (isset($_GET['cat'])) { // Category filter specified
```

```php
  $cat = $_GET['cat'];
  $jokessql .= " AND categoryid='$cat'";

  // Get category name
  $catresult = @mysql_query(
      "SELECT name from category WHERE id='$cat'");
  if (!$catresult) {
    exit('<p>Error retrieving category name from database!' .
        '<br />Error: ' . mysql_error() . '</p>');
  }
  if (mysql_num_rows($catresult) < 1)
  {
    exit('<p>Couldn\'t find specified category in the ' .
        'database!</p>');
  }
  $catdetail = mysql_fetch_array($catresult);
  $catname = htmlspecialchars($catdetail['name']);
} else {
  $catname = 'All';
}

?>
<h1><?php echo $catname; ?> Jokes</h1>

<table>
<tr><th>Joke Text</th><th>Author</th><th>Date</th></tr>

<?php
$jokes = @mysql_query($jokessql);
if (!$jokes) {
  echo('</table>');
  exit('<p>Error retrieving jokes from database!<br />' .
      'Error: ' . mysql_error() . '</p>');
}

while ($joke = mysql_fetch_array($jokes)) {

  $id = $joke['id'];
  $joketext = $joke['LEFT(joketext, 20)'];

  // If the joke text is 20 characters long, add "..." to the end
  // of it to indicate that it is actually longer. strlen()
  // returns string length!
  if (strlen($joketext) == 20) {
    $joketext .= "...";
  }
```

```
// Remove any custom tags (even partial ones!) in the joke text.
// They are not needed in this preview.
$joketext = ereg_replace(
  '\\[(B|EB|I|EI|L|L=|L=[-_./a-z0-9!&%#?+,\'=:;@~]+|EL|E)?(]|$)',
    '', $joketext);

// Finally, make it safe to display in an HTML document
$joketext = htmlspecialchars($joketext);

$author = htmlspecialchars($joke['name']);
$email = htmlspecialchars($joke['email']);
$jdate = $joke['jokedate'];

echo "<tr valign=\"top\">\n";
echo "<td><a href=\"joke.php?id=$id\">$joketext</a></td>\n";
echo "<td><a href=\"mailto:$email\">$author</a></td>\n";
echo "<td>$jdate</td>\n";
echo "</tr>\n";
}
?>

</table>
<p><a href="index.php">Back to front page</a></p>
</body>
</html>
```

Automatic Content Submission

It seems a shame to have spent so much time and effort on a content management system that's so easy that anyone can use it, if the only people who are actually *allowed* to use it are the site administrators. Furthermore, while it's extremely convenient for an administrator not to have to edit HTML to make updates to the site's content, he or she must still transcribe submitted documents into the "add new joke" form, and convert any formatted text into the custom formatting language we developed above—a tedious and mind-numbing task to say the least.

What if we put the "add new joke" form in the hands of casual site visitors? If you recall, we actually did this in Chapter 4 when we provided a form through which users could submit their own jokes. At the time, this was simply a device that demonstrated how INSERT statements could be made from within PHP scripts. We did not include it in the code we developed from scratch in this chapter because of the inherent security risks involved. After all, who wants to open the content of his or her site for just anyone to tamper with?

But new joke submissions don't have to appear on the site immediately. What if we added a new column to the `joke` table called `visible` that could take one of two values: `Y` and `N`? Newly submitted jokes could automatically be set to `N`, and could be prevented from appearing on the site if we simply add `WHERE visible='Y'` to any query of the `joke` table for which the results are intended for public access. Jokes with `visible` set to `N` would wait in the database for review by a content manager, who could edit each joke before making it visible, or deleting it out of hand.

To create a column that can contain either of two values, of which one is the default, we'll need a new MySQL column type called `ENUM`:

```
mysql>ALTER TABLE joke ADD COLUMN
    ->visible ENUM('N', 'Y') NOT NULL;
```

Since we declared this column as required (`NOT NULL`), the first value listed within the parentheses (`'N'` in this case) is the default value, which is assigned to new entries if no value is specified in the `INSERT` statement. All that's left for you to do is modify the administration system to allow hidden jokes to be shown. A simple check box in the "add joke" and "edit joke" forms should do the trick. You also may want to modify the joke search form to allow administrators to search only for visible or hidden jokes.

With new jokes hidden from the public eye, the only security detail that remains is author identification. We want to be able to identify which author in the database submitted a particular joke, but it's inappropriate to rely on the old drop-down list of authors in the "add new joke" form, since any author could pose as any other. Obviously, some sort of user name/password authentication scheme is required. We'll see how such a system can be built in Chapter 12.

You can then require authors to correctly enter their email addresses and passwords when they submit a joke to the database. You might even like to give them a password-protected "control center," where they can view the status of the jokes they've submitted to the site, and even update details like their names and email addresses. All of this is within reach with the power of PHP.

Summary

While it would be interesting to delve into the details of the content-submission system described above, you should already have all the skills necessary to build it yourself. Want to let users rate the jokes on the site? How about letting joke authors make changes to their jokes, but requiring an administrator to approve the changes before they go live on the site? The power and complexity of the system is limited only by your imagination.

At this point, you should be equipped with all the basic skills and concepts you need to build your very own database-driven Website. In the rest of this book, I'll cover more advanced topics that will help optimize your site's performance. Oh, and of course we'll explore more exciting features of PHP and MySQL.

In Chapter 8, we'll take a step away from our joke database and have a close-up look at MySQL server maintenance and administration. We'll learn how to make backups of our database (a critical task for any Web-based company), to administer MySQL users and their passwords, and to log into a MySQL server if you've forgotten your password.

8

MySQL Administration

At the core of any well-designed, content-driven site is a relational database. In this book, we've used the MySQL Relational Database Management System (RDBMS) to create our database. MySQL is a popular choice among Web developers not only because it's free for noncommercial use on all platforms, but also because MySQL servers are fairly simple to set up. As I demonstrated in Chapter 1, armed with proper instructions, a new user can get a MySQL server up and running in less than 30 minutes—under ten if you practice a little!

If all you want is to have a MySQL server around so you can play with a few examples and experiment a little, then the initial installation process we went through in Chapter 1 is likely all you'll need. If, on the other hand, you want to set up a database backend to a real, live Website—perhaps a site upon which your company depends—then there are a few more things you'll need to learn how to do before you can rely on a MySQL server day-in and day-out.

Backups of data that's important to you or your business should be an essential item on the administrator's list of priorities. Unfortunately, because setting up backups isn't the most interesting part of an administrator's duties, such procedures are usually arranged once out of necessity and deemed "good enough" for all applications. If, until now, your answer to the question, "Should we back up our databases?" has been, "It's okay; they'll be backed up along with everything else," you really should stick around. I'll show you why a generic file backup solution is inadequate for many MySQL installations, and I'll demonstrate the "right" way to back up and restore a MySQL database.

In Chapter 1, we set up the MySQL server so that you could connect as `root` with a password you chose. This `root` MySQL user (which, incidentally, has nothing to do with the root user on Linux and similar systems) had read/write access to all databases and tables. In many organizations, it's necessary to create users whose access is limited to particular databases and tables, and to restrict that access in some way (e.g. read-only access to a particular table). In this chapter, we'll learn how to facilitate such restrictions using two new MySQL commands: `GRANT` and `REVOKE`.

In some situations, such as power outages, MySQL databases can become damaged. Such damage need not always send you scrambling for your backups, however. We'll finish off our review of MySQL database administration by learning how to use the MySQL database check and repair utility to fix simple database corruptions.

Backing up MySQL Databases

Like Web servers, most MySQL servers are expected to remain online 24 hours a day, seven days a week. This makes backups of MySQL database files problematic. Because the MySQL server uses memory caches and buffers to improve the efficiency of updates to the database files stored on disk, these files may be in an inconsistent state at any given time. Since standard backup procedures involve merely copying system and data files, backups of MySQL data files cannot be relied upon, as they can't guarantee that the files that are copied are in a fit state to be used as replacements in the event of a crash.

Furthermore, as many databases receive new information at all hours of the day, standard backups can provide only "snapshots" of database data. Any information stored in the database that's changed after the last backup will be lost in the event that the MySQL data files are destroyed or become unusable. In many situations, such as when a MySQL server is used to track customer orders on an ecommerce site, this is an unacceptable loss.

Facilities exist in MySQL to keep up-to-date backups that are not adversely affected by server activity at the time at which the backups are generated. Unfortunately, they require you to set up a backup scheme specifically for your MySQL data, completely apart from whatever backup measures you have established for the rest of your data. As with any good backup system, however, you'll appreciate it when the time comes to use it.

Database Backups using `mysqldump`

In addition to `mysqld`, the MySQL server, and `mysql`, the MySQL client, a MySQL installation comes with many useful utility programs. We've seen `mysqladmin`, which is responsible for the control and retrieval of information about an operational MySQL server, for example.

`mysqldump` is another such program. When run, it connects to a MySQL server (in much the same way as the `mysql` program or the PHP language does) and downloads the complete contents of the database you specify. It then outputs these as a series of SQL `CREATE TABLE` and `INSERT` commands that, if run in an empty MySQL database, would create a MySQL database with exactly the same contents as the original.

If you redirect the output of `mysqldump` to a file, you can store a "snapshot" of the database as a backup. The following command (typed all on one line) connects to the MySQL server running on `myhost` as user `root` with password `mypass`, and saves a backup of the database called `ijdb` into the file `ijdb_backup.sql`:[1]

```
mysqldump -h myhost -u root -pmypass ijdb > ijdb_backup.sql
```

To restore this database after a server crash, you would use these commands:

```
mysqladmin -h myhost -u root -pmypass create ijdb
mysql -h myhost -u root -pmypass ijdb < ijdb_backup.sql
```

The first command uses the `mysqladmin` program to create the database; alternatively, you can do this at the MySQL command line. The second connects to the MySQL server using the usual `mysql` program, and feeds in our backup file as the commands to be executed.

In this way, we can use `mysqldump` to create backups of our databases. `mysqldump` connects through the MySQL server to perform backups, rather than by accessing directly the database files in the MySQL data directory. The backup it produces is guaranteed to be a valid copy of the database, not merely a snapshot of the

---

[1]To run `mysqldump` and the other MySQL utility programs, you need to be in the `bin` directory of your MySQL installation, or that directory must be added to the system path. On Linux and similar systems, you can also place symbolic links to the required programs into your `/usr/local/bin` directory.

database files, which may be in a state of flux as long as the MySQL server is online.

But how do we bridge the gap between these snapshots to maintain a database backup that's always up to date? The solution is simple: instruct the server to keep an update log.

Incremental Backups using Update Logs

As I mentioned above, many situations in which MySQL databases are used would make the loss of data—any data—unacceptable. In cases like these, we need a way to bridge the gaps between the backups we made using `mysqldump` as described above. The solution is to instruct the MySQL server to keep an **update log**. An update log is a record of all SQL queries that were received by the database, and which modified the contents of the database in some way. This includes `INSERT`, `UPDATE`, and `CREATE TABLE` statements (among others), but doesn't include `SELECT` statements.

The basic idea is that you can restore the contents of the database at the very moment at which a disaster occurred. This restoration involves the application of a backup (made using `mysqldump`), followed by the application of the contents of the update logs that were generated after that backup was made.

You can also edit update logs to undo mistakes that may have been made. For example, if a co-worker comes to you after accidentally issuing a `DROP TABLE` command, you can edit your update log to remove that command before you restore the database using your last backup and the log application. In this way, you can even keep changes to other tables that were made *after* the accident. And, as a precaution, you should probably also revoke your co-worker's `DROP` privileges (see the next section to find out how).

When you launch MySQL from the command prompt, you can tell it to keep update logs with the `--log-update` switch. For example, on Linux systems:

```
safe_mysqld --log-update=update
```

The above command starts the MySQL server and tells it to create files named `update.001`, `update.002`, and so on, in the server's data directory (`/usr/loc-al/mysql/data` if you set up the server on Linux according to the instructions in Chapter 1). A new file will then be created each time the server flushes its log files; in practice, this occurs whenever the server is restarted. If you want to store your update logs somewhere else (usually a good idea—if the disk that contains your data directory dies, you don't want it to take your backups with it!), you can specify the full path to the update files.

If you run your MySQL server full-time, you probably have your system set up to launch the MySQL server at startup. The addition of command-line options to the server can be difficult in this case. A simpler way to have update logs created is to add the option to the MySQL configuration file, my.cnf, which you should have created in your system's /etc directory on Linux. For Windows users, the my.cnf file should be located in the root of the C: drive; alternatively, it may be named my.ini and placed in the Windows directory. To set MySQL to create update logs by default, simply add a log-update line below [mysqld] in your my.cnf file.

```
[mysqld]
log-update=/backups/mysql/update
```

Feel free to specify a location to which you'd like the server to write the update logs. Save the file and restart your MySQL server. From now on, the server will behave by default as if you'd specified the --log-update option on the command line.

Obviously, update logs can take up a lot of space on an active server. For this reason, and because MySQL will not delete old log files automatically as it creates new ones, it's up to you to manage your update log files. The following UNIX shell script, for example, tells MySQL to flush its log files, then deletes all update files that were last modified more than a week ago.

```
#!/bin/sh

/usr/local/mysql/bin/mysqladmin -u root —pmypasswd flush-logs
find /backups/mysql/ -name "update.[0-9]*" -type f -mtime +6 \
  | xargs rm -f
```

This first step (flushing the log files) creates a new update log in case the current one is about to be deleted. This deletion will occur if the server has been online, and has not received any queries that changed the database contents, for over a week. If you're an experienced user, it should be fairly easy to set up a script that uses cron[2] or the Windows Task Scheduler to perform a database backup periodically (say, once a week), and to delete old update logs. If you need a little help

---

[2]cron is a well-known task scheduling utility available on most Linux and UNIX-based systems. To learn how to set up cron tasks, begin by typing man crontab at your server's command prompt.

with this, speak to your Web host, system administrator, or local guru, or post a message to the SitePoint Forums[1] (we'll be glad to help!).

If you've made a backup and a copy of the update logs since the backup was made, then the restoration of your database should be fairly simple. After you create the empty database and apply the backup as described in the previous section, apply the update logs, using the `--one-database` command-line option for `mysql`. This command instructs the server to run only those queries in the update log that pertain to the database you want to restore (`ijdb` in this example):

```
mysql -u root -pmypasswd --one-database ijdb < update.100
mysql -u root -pmypasswd --one-database ijdb < update.102
...
```

MySQL Access Control

In Chapter 2, I mentioned that the database called `mysql`, which appears on every MySQL server, is used to keep track of users, their passwords, and what they're allowed to do. Until now, however, we've always logged into the server as the `root` user, which gives us access to all databases and tables.

If your MySQL server will only be accessed through PHP, and you're careful about who's given the password to the `root` MySQL account, then the `root` account may be sufficient for your needs. However, in cases where a MySQL server is shared among many users (for example, if a Web host wishes to use a single MySQL server to provide a database to each of its users), it's usually a good idea to set up user accounts with more restricted access.

The MySQL access control system is fully documented in Chapter 6 of the MySQL Reference Manual[2]. In essence, user access is governed by the contents of five tables in the `mysql` database: `user`, `db`, `host`, `tables_priv`, and `columns_priv`. If you plan to edit these tables directly using `INSERT`, `UPDATE`, and `DELETE` statements, I'd suggest you read the relevant section of the MySQL manual first. But, for us mere mortals, MySQL provides a simpler method to manage user access. Using `GRANT` and `REVOKE`—nonstandard commands provided by MySQL—you can create users and set their privileges without worrying about the details of how they'll be represented in the tables mentioned above.

---

[1] http://www.sitepointforums.com/
[2] http://dev.mysql.com/doc/mysql/en/Privilege_system.html

Using GRANT

The GRANT command, which is used to create new users, assign user passwords, and add user privileges, looks like this:

```
mysql>GRANT privilege [(columns)] ON what
    ->TO user [IDENTIFIED BY 'password']
    ->[WITH GRANT OPTION];
```

As you can see, there are a lot of blanks to be filled in with this command. Let's describe each of them in turn, then review some examples to gain an idea of how they work together.

privilege is the privilege you wish to grant with this command. The privileges you can specify can be sorted into three groups:

❑ **Database/Table/Column privileges**

ALTER	Modify existing tables (e.g. add/remove columns) and indexes.
CREATE	Create new databases and tables.
DELETE	Delete table entries.
DROP	Delete tables and/or databases.
INDEX	Create and/or delete indexes.
INSERT	Add new table entries.
LOCK TABLES	Lock tables for which the user has SELECT privileges (see Chapter 9).
SELECT	View/search table entries.
SHOW DATABASES	View a list of available databases.
UPDATE	Modify existing table entries.

❑ **Global administrative privileges**

FILE	Read and write files on the MySQL server machine.

PROCESS   View and/or kill server threads that belong to other users.

RELOAD   Reload the access control tables, flush the logs, etc.

SHUTDOWN   Shut down the MySQL server.

❏ **Special privileges**

ALL   The user is allowed to do anything (like root), except grant privileges.

USAGE   The user is only allowed to log in—nothing else.

Some of these privileges apply to features of MySQL that we have not yet seen, but most should be familiar to you.

what defines the areas of the database sever to which the privileges apply. `*.*` means the privileges apply to all databases and tables. `dbName.*` means the privileges apply to all tables in the database called `dbName`. `dbName.tblName` means the privileges apply only to the table called `tblName` in the database called `dbName`. You can even specify privileges for individual table columns—simply place a list of the columns between the parentheses that follow the privileges to be granted (we'll see an example of this in a moment).

user specifies the user to which these privileges should apply. In MySQL, a user is specified both by the user name given at login, and the host name/IP address of the machine from which the user connects. The two values are separated by the @ sign (i.e. *user@host*). Both values may contain the `%` wild card character, but you need to put quotes around any value that does (e.g. `kevin@"%"` will allow the user name `kevin` to log in from any host and use the privileges you specify).

password specifies the password that's required to connect the user to the MySQL server. As indicated by the square brackets above, the `IDENTIFIED BY 'password'` portion of the `GRANT` command is optional. Any password specified here will replace the existing password for that user. If no password is specified for a new user, a password will not be required to connect.

The optional `WITH GRANT OPTION` portion of the command specifies that the user be allowed to use the `GRANT/REVOKE` commands to give to another user any privileges granted to him or her. Be careful with this option—the repercussions are not always obvious! A WITH GRANT OPTION user can give the option to other users in order to trade privileges with them.

Let's consider a few examples. To create a user named dbmgr that can connect from server.host.net with password managedb and have full access to the database named ijdb only (including the ability to grant access to that database to other users), use this GRANT command:

```
mysql>GRANT ALL ON ijdb.*
    ->TO dbmgr@server.host.net
    ->IDENTIFIED BY 'managedb'
    ->WITH GRANT OPTION;
```

Subsequently, to change that user's password to funkychicken, use:

```
mysql>GRANT USAGE ON *.*
    ->TO dbmgr@server.host.net
    ->IDENTIFIED BY 'funkychicken';
```

Notice that we haven't granted any additional privileges (the USAGE privilege doesn't let a user do anything besides log in), but the user's existing privileges remain unchanged.

Now, let's create a new user named jess, who will connect from various machines in the host.net domain. Say she's responsible for updating the names and email addresses of authors in the database, but may need to refer to other database information at times. As a result, she will have read-only (i.e. SELECT) access to the ijdb database, but will be able to UPDATE the name and email columns of the author table. Here are the commands:

```
mysql>GRANT SELECT ON ijdb.*
    ->TO jess@"%.host.net"
    ->IDENTIFIED BY "jessrules";
mysql>GRANT UPDATE (name, email) ON ijdb.author
    ->TO jess@"%.host.net";
```

Notice that, in the first command, we used the % (wild card) character in the host name to indicate the host from which Jess could connect. Notice also that we haven't given her the ability to pass her privileges to other users, as we didn't put WITH GRANT OPTION on the end of the command. The second command demonstrates how privileges are granted for specific table columns—it lists the column(s), separated by commas, in parentheses after the privilege(s) being granted.

Using REVOKE

The REVOKE command, as you'd expect, is used to strip previously granted privileges from a user. The syntax for the command is as follows:

```
mysql>REVOKE privilege [(columns)]
    ->ON what FROM user;
```

All the fields in this command work just as they do in GRANT above.

To revoke the DROP privileges of a co-worker of Jess's (for instance, if he or she has demonstrated a habit of occasionally deleting tables and databases by mistake), you would use this command:

```
mysql>REVOKE DROP ON *.* FROM idiot@"%.host.net";
```

Revoking a user's login privileges is about the only thing that can't be done using GRANT and REVOKE. The following commands will definitely prevent a user from doing anything of consequence besides logging in:

```
mysql>REVOKE ALL PRIVILEGES ON *.* FROM idiot@"%.host.net";
mysql>REVOKE GRANT OPTION ON *.* FROM idiot@"%.host.net";
```

But, to remove a user completely, you'll need to delete the corresponding entry in the user table:

```
mysql>DELETE FROM mysql.user
    ->WHERE User="idiot" AND Host="%.host.net";
```

Access Control Tips

As a result of the way the access control system in MySQL works, there are a couple of idiosyncrasies of which you should be aware before you launch into user creation.

When you create users that can log into the MySQL server only from the computer on which that server is running (i.e. you require them to use Telnet or SSH to log into the server and run the MySQL client from there, or to communicate using server-side scripts like PHP), you may ask yourself what the *user* part of the GRANT command should be. Imagine the server is running on www.host.net. Should you set up the user as *username*@www.host.net, or *username*@localhost?

The answer is that you can't rely on either one to handle all connections. In theory, if, when connecting, the user specifies the host name either with the `mysql` client, or with PHP's `mysql_connect` function, that host name will have to match the entry in the access control system. However, as you probably don't want to force your users to specify the host name a particular way (in fact, users of the `mysql` client likely won't want to specify the host name at all), it's best to use a workaround.

For users who need the ability to connect from the machine on which the MySQL server is running, it's best to create two user entries in the MySQL access system: one with the actual host name of the machine (e.g. *username*@`www.host.net`), the other with `localhost` (e.g. *username*@`localhost`). Of course, you will have to grant/revoke all privileges to both of these user entries individually, but this is the only workaround that you can really rely upon.

Another problem commonly faced by MySQL administrators is that user entries whose host names contain wild cards (e.g. `jess@%.host.net` above) may fail to work. When a failure occurs, it's usually due to the way MySQL prioritizes the entries in the access control system. Specifically, it orders entries so that more specific host names appear first (e.g. `www.host.net` is completely specific, `%.host.net` is less specific, and `%` is totally unspecific).

In a fresh installation, the MySQL access control system contains two anonymous user entries (these allow connections to be made from the local host using any user name—the two entries support connections from `localhost` and the server's actual host name[3], as described above), and two `root` user entries. The problem described above occurs when the anonymous user entries take precedence over our new entry because their host name is more specific.

Let's look at the abridged contents of the user table on `www.host.net`, our fictitious MySQL server, after we add Jess's entry. The rows are sorted in the order in which the MySQL server considers them when it validates a connection:

```
+---------------+------+------------------+
| Host          | User | Password         |
+---------------+------+------------------+
| localhost     | root | (encrypted value) |
| www.host.net  | root | (encrypted value) |
| localhost     |      |                  |
```

---

[3]On Windows installations of MySQL, the second entry's hostname is set to either `%` or `build` (depending on the MySQL version), not the server's host name. It therefore does not contribute to the problem described here. It does, however, permit connections with any user name from any computer, so it's a good idea to delete it anyway.

```
| www.host.net |      |                   |
| %.host.net   | jess | (encrypted value) |
+--------------+------+-------------------+
```

As you can see, since Jess's entry has the least specific host name, it comes last in the list. When Jess attempts to connect from `www.host.net`, the MySQL server matches her connection attempt to one of the anonymous user entries (a blank `User` value matches anyone). Since these anonymous entries don't require a password, and presumably Jess enters her password, MySQL rejects the connection attempt. Even if Jess managed to connect without a password, she would be given the very limited privileges that are assigned to anonymous users, as opposed to the privileges assigned to her entry in the access control system.

The solution to this problem is either to make your first order of business as a MySQL administrator the deletion of those anonymous user entries (`DELETE FROM mysql.user WHERE User=""`), or to give two more entries to all users who need to connect from `localhost` (i.e. entries for `localhost` and the actual host name of the server):

```
+--------------+------+-------------------+
| Host         | User | Password          |
+--------------+------+-------------------+
| localhost    | root | (encrypted value) |
| www.host.net | root | (encrypted value) |
| localhost    | jess | (encrypted value) |
| www.host.net | jess | (encrypted value) |
| localhost    |      |                   |
| www.host.net |      |                   |
| %.host.net   | jess | (encrypted value) |
+--------------+------+-------------------+
```

As it's excessive to maintain three user entries (and three sets of privileges) for each user, I recommend that you remove the anonymous users unless you have a particular need for them:

```
+--------------+------+-------------------+
| Host         | User | Password          |
+--------------+------+-------------------+
| localhost    | root | (encrypted value) |
| www.host.net | root | (encrypted value) |
| %.host.net   | jess | (encrypted value) |
+--------------+------+-------------------+
```

Locked Out?

Like locking your keys in the car, forgetting your password after you've spent an hour installing and tweaking a new MySQL server can be an embarrassment—to say the least! Fortunately, if you have root access to the computer on which the MySQL server is running, or if you can log in as the user you set up to run the MySQL server (mysql if you followed the Linux installation instructions in Chapter 1), all is not lost. The following procedure will let you regain control of the server.

First, you must shut down the MySQL server. As you'd normally do this using mysqladmin, which requires your forgotten password, you'll instead need to kill the server process to shut it down. Under Windows, use the task manager to find and end the MySQL process, or simply stop the MySQL service if you have installed it as such. Under Linux, use the ps command, or look in the server's PID file in the MySQL data directory, to determine the process ID of the MySQL server, then terminate it with this command:

```
shell%kill pid
```

pid is the process ID of the MySQL server. This should be enough to stop the server. Do *not* use kill -9 unless absolutely necessary, as this may damage your table files. If you're forced to do so, however, the next section provides instructions on how to check and repair those files.

Now that the server's down, you can restart it by running safe-mysqld (mysqld-opt or mysqld-nt under Windows, or mysqld_safe under Mac OS X) with the --skip-grant-tables command line option. This instructs the MySQL server to allow unrestricted access to anyone. Obviously, you'll want to run the server in this mode as infrequently as possible, to avoid the inherent security risks.

Once you're connected, change your root password to something you'll remember:

```
mysql>UPDATE mysql.user SET Password=PASSWORD("newpassword")
    ->WHERE User="root";
```

Finally, disconnect, and instruct the MySQL server to reload the grant tables to begin requiring passwords:

```
mysqladmin flush-privileges
```

That does it—and nobody ever has to know what you did. As for locking your keys in your car, you're on your own there.

Checking and Repairing MySQL Data Files

In power outages, situations where you need to `kill -9` the MySQL server process, or when Jess's friend `idiot@%.host.net` kicks the plug out of the wall, there is a risk that your MySQL data files may be damaged. This situation can arise if the server is in the middle of making changes to the files at the time of the disturbance, as the files may be left in a corrupt or inconsistent state. Since this type of damage can be subtle, it can go undetected for days, weeks, or even months. As a result, by the time you do finally discover the problem, all your backups may contain the same corruption.

Chapter 4 of the MySQL Reference Manual[3] describes the `myisamchk` utility that comes with MySQL, and how you can use it to check and repair your MySQL data files. While that chapter is recommended reading for anyone who wants to set up a heavy-duty preventative maintenance schedule for their MySQL server, we'll cover all the essentials here.

Before we go any further, though, it's important to realize that the `myisamchk` program expects to have sole access to the MySQL data files that it checks and modifies. If the MySQL server works with the files at the same time, and makes a modification to a file that `myisamchk` is in the middle of checking, `myisamchk` might incorrectly detect an error and try to fix it—which in turn could trip up the MySQL server! Thus, to avoid making things worse instead of better, it's usually a good idea to shut down the MySQL server while you're working on the data files. Alternatively, shut down the server just long enough to make a copy of the files, then do the work on the copies. When you're done, shut down the server again briefly to replace the files with the new ones, and perhaps apply any update logs that were made in the interim.

The MySQL data directory isn't too difficult to understand. It contains a subdirectory for each database, and each of these subdirectories contains the data files for the tables in the corresponding database. Each table is represented by three files that have the same name as the table, but three different extensions. The *tblName*.`frm` file is the table definition, which keeps track of the columns contained in the table, and their types. The *tblName*.`MYD` file contains all the table data. The *tblName*.`MYI` file contains any indexes for the table. For example, it might contain the lookup table that helps the table's primary key column speed up queries based on this table.

---

[3] http://dev.mysql.com/doc/mysql/en/Table_maintenance.html

To check a table for errors, just run `myisamchk` (in the MySQL `bin` directory) and provide either the location of these files and the name of the table, or the name of the table index file:

```
myisamchk /usr/local/mysql/var/dbName/tblName
myisamchk /usr/local/mysql/var/dbName/tblName.MYI
```

Or, on Windows:

```
myisamchk C:\mysql\data\dbName\tblName
myisamchk C:\mysql\data\dbName\tblName.MYI
```

Either of the above will perform a check of the specified table. To check all tables in the database, use a wild card:

```
myisamchk /usr/local/mysql/var/dbName/*.MYI
```

To check all databases in all tables, use two:

```
myisamchk /usr/local/mysql/var/*/*.MYI
```

Without any options, `myisamchk` performs a normal check of the table files. If you suspect problems with a table, and a normal check fails to bring anything to light, you can perform a much more thorough (but much slower!) check using the `--extend-check` option:

```
myisamchk --extend-check /path/to/tblName
```

Checking for errors is nondestructive, so you don't have to worry that you might make an existing problem worse if you perform a check on your data files. Repair operations, on the other hand, while usually safe, will make changes to your data files that cannot be undone. For this reason, I strongly recommend that you make a copy of any damaged table files before you attempt to repair them. As usual, make sure your MySQL server is shut down before you make copies of live data files.

There are three types of repair that you can use to fix a problem with a damaged table. These should be tried in order with fresh copies of the data files each time (i.e. don't try the second recovery method on a set of files that result from a failed attempt of the first recovery method). If at any point you get an error message that indicates that a temporary file can't be created, delete the file to which the message refers and try again—the offending file is a remnant of a previous repair attempt.

The three repair methods can be executed as follows:

```
myisamchk --recover --quick /path/to/tblName
myisamchk --recover /path/to/tblName
myisamchk --safe-recover /path/to/tblName
```

The first is the quickest, and fixes the most common problems; the last is the slowest, and fixes a few problems that the other methods do not.

If these methods fail to resurrect a damaged table, there are a couple more tricks you can try before you give up:

❏ If you suspect that the table index file (`*.MYI`) is damaged beyond repair, or even missing entirely, it can be regenerated from scratch and used with your existing data (`*.MYD`) and table form (`*.frm`) files. To begin, make a copy of your table data (`tblName.MYD`) file. Restart your MySQL server and connect to it, then delete the contents of the table with the following command:

```
mysql>DELETE FROM tblName;
```

This command doesn't just delete the contents of your table; it also creates a brand new index file for that table. Log out and shut down the server again, then copy your saved data file (`tblName.MYD`) over the new (empty) data file. Finally, perform a standard repair (the second method above), and use `myisamchk` to regenerate the index data based on the contents of the data and table form files.

❏ If your table form file (`tblName.frm`) is missing or damaged beyond repair, but you know the table well enough to reproduce the `CREATE TABLE` statement that defines it, you can generate a new `.frm` file and use it with your existing data and index files. If the index file is no good, use the above method to generate a new one afterwards. First, make a copy of your data and index files, then delete the originals and remove any record of the table from the data directory.

Start up the MySQL server and create a new table using exactly the same `CREATE TABLE` statement. Log out and shut down the server, then copy your two saved files over the top of the new, empty files. The new `.frm` file should work with them, but perform a standard table repair—the second method above—for good measure.

Summary

Admittedly, this chapter hasn't been the usual nonstop, action-packed code-fest to which you may have become accustomed by now. But our concentration on these topics—the back up and restoration of MySQL data, the administration of the MySQL access control system, and table checking and repair—has armed you with the tools you'll need in order to set up a MySQL database server that will stand the test of time, not to mention the constant traffic that your site will endure during that period.

In Chapter 9, we'll get back to the fun stuff and learn some advanced SQL techniques that can make a relational database server do things you may never have thought possible.

9

Advanced SQL Queries

As we worked through our example of the Internet Joke Database Website, we had opportunities to explore most aspects of Structured Query Language (SQL). From the basic form of a `CREATE TABLE` query, to the two syntaxes of `INSERT` queries, you probably know many of these commands by heart now.

In an effort to tie up some loose ends in this chapter, we'll look at a few more SQL tricks that we haven't seen before, either because they were too advanced, or simply because "it didn't come up." As is typical, most of these will expand on our knowledge of what is already the most complex and potentially confusing SQL command available to us: the `SELECT` query.

Sorting SELECT Query Results

Long lists of information are always easier to use when they're provided in some kind of order. To find a single author in a list from our `author` table, for example, could become an exercise in frustration if we had more than a few dozen registered authors in our database. While at first it might appear that they are sorted in order of database insertion, with the oldest records first and the newest records last, you'll quickly notice that deleting records from the database leaves invisible gaps in this order; these gaps are filled by the insertion of newer entries.

SELECT queries offer no reliable built-in result-sorting capabilities. Fortunately, there is another, optional part of the SELECT query that lets us specify a column by which our table of results can be sorted. Let's say we wanted to print out a listing of the entries in our author table for future reference. As you'll recall, this table has three columns: id, name, and email. Since id isn't really interesting in and of itself (it just provides a means to associate entries in this table with entries in the joke table), we will usually list only the remaining two columns when we work with this table. Here's a short list of a table of authors:

```
mysql>SELECT name, email FROM author;
+----------------+----------------------+
| name           | email                |
+----------------+----------------------+
| Joan Smith     | joan@example.com     |
| Michael Yates  | yatesy@example.com   |
| Kevin Yank     | kevin@sitepoint.com  |
| Amy Mathieson  | amym@example.com     |
+----------------+----------------------+
```

As you can see, the entries are not sorted in any particular order. This result is fine for a short list like this, but it would be easier to find a particular author's email address (that of Amy Mathieson, for example) in a very long list of authors—say a few hundred or so—if the authors' names appeared in alphabetical order. Here's how we'd create that ordering:

```
mysql>SELECT name, email FROM author ORDER BY name;
+----------------+----------------------+
| name           | email                |
+----------------+----------------------+
| Amy Mathieson  | amym@example.com     |
| Joan Smith     | joan@example.com     |
| Kevin Yank     | kevin@sitepoint.com  |
| Michael Yates  | yatesy@example.com   |
+----------------+----------------------+
```

The entries now appear sorted alphabetically by their names. Just as we can add a WHERE clause to a SELECT statement to narrow down the list of results, we can also add an ORDER BY clause to specify a column by which a set of results should be sorted. The addition of the keyword DESC after the name of the sort column allows us to sort the entries in descending order:

```
mysql>SELECT name, email FROM author ORDER BY name DESC;
+----------------+----------------------+
| name           | email                |
+----------------+----------------------+
```

```
| Michael Yates  | yatesy@example.com  |
| Kevin Yank     | kevin@sitepoint.com |
| Joan Smith     | joan@example.com    |
| Amy Mathieson  | amym@example.com    |
+----------------+---------------------+
```

You can actually use a comma-separated list of several column names in the ORDER BY clause, to have MySQL sort the entries by the first column, then sort any sets of tied entries by the second, and so on. Any of the columns listed in the ORDER BY clause may use the DESC keyword to reverse the sort order.

Obviously, in a large table, MySQL must do a lot of work to sort the result set. You can ease this burden by setting up **indexes** for columns (or sets of columns) that you expect to use to sort result sets. When you index a column, the database invisibly creates and maintains a sorted list of the entries in that column, along with their locations in the table. Whenever you INSERT a new entry or UPDATE an existing entry, the database will update the index accordingly. When the database is asked to sort results based on that column, all it needs to do is to refer to the index for the pre-sorted list of entries.

To create an index, you can use a CREATE INDEX query or an ALTER TABLE ADD INDEX query. The following two queries are equivalent, and both create an index for the name column of the author table:

```
mysql>CREATE INDEX name ON author (name);
Query OK, 4 rows affected (0.28 sec)
Records: 4  Duplicates: 0  Warnings: 0
```

```
mysql>ALTER TABLE author ADD INDEX name (name);
Query OK, 4 rows affected (0.28 sec)
Records: 4  Duplicates: 0  Warnings: 0
```

In both query formats, you place in parentheses the list of columns you want to use for the index. In this example, we're creating an index for a single column.

Removing an index is equally easy, and can again be done with either of two query types:

```
mysql>DROP INDEX name ON author;
Query OK, 4 rows affected (0.16 sec)
Records: 4  Duplicates: 0  Warnings: 0
```

```
mysql>ALTER TABLE author DROP INDEX name;
Query OK, 4 rows affected (0.28 sec)
Records: 4  Duplicates: 0  Warnings: 0
```

All of these queries are described in Appendix A. A more detailed look at indexes and how they can be used to speed up queries can be found in the article *Optimizing your MySQL Application*[1] on sitepoint.com.

Setting LIMITs

Often, you might work with a large database table, but only be interested in a few entries within it. Let's say you wanted to track the popularity of different jokes on your site. You could add a column named `timesviewed` to your `joke` table. Start it with a value of zero for new jokes, and add one to the value of the requested joke every time the joke page is viewed, to keep count of the number of times each joke in your database has been read.

The query that adds one to the `timesviewed` column of a joke with a given ID is as follows:

```
$sql = "UPDATE joke SET timesviewed=timesviewed+1
    WHERE id='$id'";
if (!mysql_query($sql)) {
  echo "<p>Error adding to times viewed for this joke!</p>\n";
}
```

You might use this joke view counter to present a "Top 10 Jokes" list on the front page of your site, for example. Using `ORDER BY timesviewed DESC` to list the jokes from highest `timesviewed` to lowest, we would just have to pick the first ten values from the top of the list. But if we have thousands of jokes in our database, the retrieval of that entire list in order to obtain just ten results would be quite wasteful in terms of the processing time and server system resources, such as memory and CPU load, required.

However, if we use a `LIMIT` clause, we can specify a certain number of results to be returned. In this example, we need only the first ten:

```
$sql = "SELECT * FROM joke ORDER BY timesviewed DESC LIMIT 10";
```

Although it's much less interesting, we could get rid of the word `DESC` and retrieve the ten least popular jokes in the database.

---

[1] http://www.sitepoint.com/article/optimizing-mysql-application

Often, you want to let users view a long list of entries—for example, the results of a search—but wish to display only a few at a time.[1] Think of the last time you went looking through pages of search engine results to find a particular Website. You can use a LIMIT clause to do this sort of thing—simply specify the result with which the list will begin, and the maximum number of results to display. The query below, for example, will list the twenty-first to twenty-fifth most popular jokes in the database:

```
$sql = "SELECT * FROM joke ORDER BY timesviewed DESC
    LIMIT 20, 5";
```

Remember, the first entry in the list of results is entry number zero. Thus, the twenty-first entry in the list is entry number 20.

LOCKing TABLES

Notice how, in the UPDATE query given above, and repeated here for convenience, we take the existing value of timesviewed and add one to it to set the new value.

```
$sql = "UPDATE joke SET timesviewed=timesviewed+1
    WHERE id='$id'";
```

If you hadn't known that you were allowed to use this short cut, you might have performed a separate SELECT to get the current value, added one to it, then performed an UPDATE using that newly calculated value. Besides the fact that this would have required two queries instead of one, and thus would take about twice as long, there is a danger to using this method. What if, while that new value was being calculated, someone else viewed the same joke? The PHP script would be run a second time for that new request. When it performed the SELECT to get the current value of timesviewed, it would retrieve the same value the first script did, because the value would not yet have been updated. Both scripts would then add one to the same value, and write the new value into the table. See what happens? Two users view the joke, but the timesviewed counter increments by just one!

In some situations, this kind of fetch-calculate-update procedure cannot be avoided, and the possibility of interference between simultaneous requests of this nature must be dealt with. Other situations in which this procedure may be necessary include cases in which you need to update several tables in response to

---

[1] I have written an article that explores this technique in greater detail at sitepoint.com, entitled *Object Oriented PHP: Paging Result Sets* [http://www.sitepoint.com/article/php-paging-result-sets].

a single action (e.g. updating inventory and shipping tables in response to a sale on an ecommerce Website).

By **locking** the table or tables with which you're working in a multiple-query operation, you can obtain exclusive access for the duration of that operation, and prevent potentially damaging interference from concurrent operations. The syntax that locks a table is fairly simple:

```
LOCK TABLES tblName {READ | WRITE}
```

As shown, when you lock a table, you must specify whether you want a **read lock** or a **write lock**. The former prevents other processes from making changes to the table, but allows others to read the table. The latter stops all other access to the table.

When you're finished with a table you've locked, you must release the lock to give other processes access to the table again:

```
UNLOCK TABLES
```

A LOCK TABLES query implicitly releases whatever locks you may already have. Therefore, to safely perform a multi-table operation, you must lock all the tables you'll use with a single query. Here's what the PHP code might look like for the ecommerce application we mentioned above:

```
mysql_query('LOCK TABLES inventory WRITE, shipping WRITE');

// Perform the operation...

mysql_query('UNLOCK TABLES');
```

For simple databases that require the occasional multi-table operation, table locking, as described here, will do the trick. More demanding applications, however, can benefit from the increased performance and crash-proof nature of **transactions**.

Transactions in MySQL

Many high-end database servers (e.g. Oracle, MS SQL Server, etc.) support a feature called **transactions**, which lets you perform complex, multi-query operations in a single, uninterrupted step. Consider what would happen if your server were struck by a power failure halfway through a database update in response to a client order. For example, the server might have crashed after it updated your `shipping` table, but before it updated your `inventory` table, in response to a customer's order.

Transactions allow a group of table updates such as this to be defined so that they all occur, or none of them will. You can also manually cancel a transaction halfway through if the logic of your application requires it.

MySQL 4.x includes built-in support for **InnoDB tables**, which support transactions, in addition to the foreign key constraints I mentioned in Chapter 6. A full discussion of transactions is outside the scope of this book; please refer to the MySQL Reference Manual for a full description of InnoDB tables[3] and transaction support[4].

Column and Table Name Aliases

In some situations, it may be more convenient to refer to MySQL columns and tables using different names. Let's take the example of a database used by an airline's online booking system; this example actually came up in the SitePoint Forums. The database structure can be found in `airline.sql` in the code archive if you want to follow along.

To represent the flights offered by the airline, the database contains two tables: `flight` and `city`. Each entry in the `flight` table represents an actual flight between two cities—the origin and destination of the flight. Obviously, `origincityid` and `destinationcityid` are columns in the `flight` table; other columns record things like the date and time of the flight, the type of aircraft, the flight numbers, and the various fares.

The `city` table contains a list of all the cities to which the airline flies. Thus, both the `origincityid` and `destinationcityid` columns in the `flight` table will just contain IDs referring to entries in the `city` table.

Now, consider these queries. To retrieve a list of flights with their origins, here's what you do:

---

[3] http://dev.mysql.com/doc/mysql/en/InnoDB.html
[4] http://dev.mysql.com/doc/mysql/en/Transactional_Commands.html

```
mysql>SELECT flight.number, city.name
    ->FROM flight, city
    ->WHERE flight.origincityid=city.id;
+---------+-----------+
| number  | name      |
+---------+-----------+
| CP110   | Montreal  |
| QF2026  | Melbourne |
| CP226   | Sydney    |
| QF2027  | Sydney    |
+---------+-----------+
```

To obtain a list of flights with their destinations, the query is very similar:

```
mysql>SELECT flight.number, city.name
    ->FROM flight, city
    ->WHERE flight.destinationcityid=city.id;
+---------+-----------+
| number  | name      |
+---------+-----------+
| CP226   | Montreal  |
| QF2027  | Melbourne |
| CP110   | Sydney    |
| QF2026  | Sydney    |
+---------+-----------+
```

Now, what if we wanted to list both the origin and destination of each flight with a single query? That's pretty reasonable, right? Here's a query you might try:

```
mysql>SELECT flight.number, city.name, city.name
    ->FROM flight, city
    ->WHERE flight.origincityid=city.id
    ->AND flight.destinationcityid=city.id;
Empty set (0.02 sec)
```

Why doesn't this work? Have another look at the query, and this time focus on what it actually says, rather than what you expect it to do. It tells MySQL to join the flight and city tables and list the flight number, city name, and city name (yes, twice!) of all entries obtained, by matching up the origincityid with the city id and the destinationcityid with the city id. In other words, the origincityid, destinationcityid, and city id must all be equal! This results in a list of all flights where the origin and the destination are the same! Unless your airline offers scenic flights, there aren't likely to be any entries that match this description (thus, the "Empty set" result above).

What we need is a way to be able to return two different entries from the `city` table—one for the origin and one for the destination—for each result. If we had two copies of the table, one called `origin` and one called `destination`, this would be much easier to do, but why maintain two tables that contain the same list of cities? The solution is to give the `city` table two different temporary names (**aliases**) for the purposes of this query.

If we follow the name of a table with `AS alias` in the `FROM` portion of the `SELECT` query, we can give it a temporary name by which we can refer to it elsewhere in the query. Here's that first query again (to display flight numbers and origins only), but this time we've given the `city` table an alias: `origin`.

```
mysql>SELECT flight.number, origin.name
   ->FROM flight, city AS origin
   ->WHERE flight.origincityid=origin.id;
```

This doesn't actually change the way the query works—in fact, it doesn't change the results at all—but, for long table names, it can save some typing. Consider, for example, if we had given aliases of `f` and `o` to `flight` and `city`, respectively. The query would be much shorter as a result.

Let's now return to our problem query. If we refer to the `city` table twice, using different aliases, we can use a three-table join (in which two of the tables are actually one and the same) to get the effect we want:

```
mysql>SELECT flight.number, origin.name, destination.name
   ->FROM flight, city AS origin, city AS destination
   ->WHERE flight.origincityid=origin.id
   ->AND flight.destinationcityid=destination.id;
+---------+-----------+-----------+
| number  | name      | name      |
+---------+-----------+-----------+
| CP110   | Montreal  | Sydney    |
| QF2026  | Melbourne | Sydney    |
| CP226   | Sydney    | Montreal  |
| QF2027  | Sydney    | Melbourne |
+---------+-----------+-----------+
```

You can also define aliases for column names. We could use this, for example, to differentiate the two `name` columns in our result table above:

```
mysql>SELECT f.number, o.name AS origin, d.name AS destination
   ->FROM flight AS f, city AS o, city AS d
   ->WHERE f.origincityid=o.id AND f.destinationcityid=d.id;
+---------+-----------+---------------+
```

```
| number  | origin    | destination |
+---------+-----------+-------------+
| CP110   | Montreal  | Sydney      |
| QF2026  | Melbourne | Sydney      |
| CP226   | Sydney    | Montreal    |
| QF2027  | Sydney    | Melbourne   |
+---------+-----------+-------------+
```

GROUPing SELECT Results

In Chapter 2, we saw the following query, which tells us how many jokes are stored in our joke table:

```
mysql>SELECT COUNT(*) FROM joke;
+----------+
| COUNT(*) |
+----------+
|        4 |
+----------+
```

The MySQL function COUNT used in this query belongs to a special class of functions called **summary functions** or **group-by functions**, depending on where you look. A complete list of these functions is provided in Chapter 13 of the MySQL Manual[5] and in Appendix B. Unlike other functions, which affect individually each entry in the result of the SELECT query, summary functions group together all the results and return a single result. In the above example, for instance, COUNT returns the total number of result rows.

Let's say you wanted to display a list of authors along with the number of jokes they have to their names. Your first instinct might be to retrieve a list of all the authors' names and IDs, then use COUNT to count the number of results when you SELECT the jokes with each author's ID. The PHP code (presented without error handling, for simplicity) would look something like this:

```php
// Get a list of all the authors
$authors = @mysql_query('SELECT name, id FROM author');
if (!$authors) {
  exit('<p>Error retriving author list.</p>');
}

// Process each author
while ($author = mysql_fetch_array($authors)) {
```

---

[5] http://dev.mysql.com/doc/mysql/en/GROUP-BY-Functions.html

```
$name = $author['name'];
$id = $author['id'];

// Get count of jokes attributed to this author
$result = @mysql_query(
  "SELECT COUNT(*) AS numjokes FROM joke WHERE authorid='$id'");
if (!$result) {
  exit('<p>Error retriving jokes for author.</p>');
}
$row = mysql_fetch_array($result);
$numjokes = $row['numjokes'];

// Display the author & number of jokes
echo "<p>$name ($numjokes jokes)</p>";
}
```

Note the use of AS in the second query above to give a friendlier name (numjokes) to the result of COUNT(*).

This technique will work, but will require $n+1$ separate queries (where n is the number of authors in the database). Having the number of queries rely on a number of entries in the database is always something we want to avoid, as a large number of authors would make this script unreasonably slow and resource-intensive. Fortunately, another advanced feature of SELECT comes to the rescue!

If you add a GROUP BY clause to a SELECT query, you can tell MySQL to group the query results into sets, the results in each set sharing a common value(s) in the specified column(s). Summary functions like COUNT then operate on those groups—not on the entire result set as a whole. The next query, for example, lists the number of jokes attributed to each author in the database:

```
mysql>SELECT author.name, COUNT(*) AS numjokes
    ->FROM joke, author
    ->WHERE authorid=author.id
    ->GROUP BY authorid;
+------------+----------+
| name       | numjokes |
+------------+----------+
| Kevin Yank |        3 |
| Joan Smith |        1 |
+------------+----------+
```

If we group the results by author ID (authorid), we receive a breakdown of results for each author. Note that we could have specified GROUP BY author.id and achieved the same result (since, as stipulated in the WHERE clause, these columns must be equal). `GROUP BY author.name` would also work in most cases, but, as you can't guarantee that two different authors won't have the same name, in which case their results would be lumped together, it's best to stick to the ID columns, which are guaranteed to be unique for each author.

LEFT JOINs

We can see from the results above that Kevin Yank has three jokes to his name, and Joan Smith has one. What these results do not show is that there is a third author, Amy Mathieson, who doesn't have *any* jokes to her name. Since there are no entries in the `joke` table with `authorid` values that match her author ID, there will be no results that satisfy the `WHERE` clause in the query above, and she will therefore be excluded from the table of results.

About the only practical way to overcome this challenge with the tools we've seen so far would be to add another column to the `author` table and simply store the number of jokes attributed to each author in that column. Keeping that column up to date, however, would be a real pain, because we'd have to remember to update it every time a joke was added to, removed from, or changed (if, for example, the value of `authorid` was changed) in the `joke` table. To keep things synchronized, we'd have to use `LOCK TABLES` whenever we made such changes, as well. Quite a mess, to say the least!

MySQL provides another method for joining tables, which fetches information from multiple tables at once. Called a **left join**, it's designed for just this type of situation. To understand how left joins differ from standard joins, we must first recall how standard joins work.

Figure 9.1. Standard joins take all possible combinations of rows.

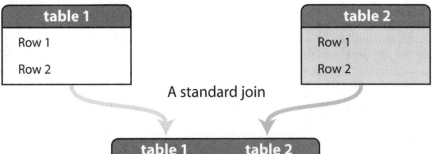

As shown in Figure 9.1, MySQL performs a standard join of two tables by listing all possible combinations of the rows of those tables. In a simple case, a standard join of two tables with two rows apiece will contain four rows: row 1 of table 1 with row 1 of table 2, row 1 of table 1 with row 2 of table 2, row 2 of table 1 with row 1 of table 2, and row 2 of table 1 with row 2 of table 2. With all of these result rows calculated, MySQL then looks to the WHERE clause for guidance on which rows should actually be kept (e.g. those where the authorid column from table 1 matches the id column from table 2).

The reason why the above solution does not suit our purposes is that we'd like to also include rows in table 1 (i.e. author) that don't match any rows in table 2 (i.e. joke). A left join does exactly what we need—it forces a row to appear in the results for each row in the first (left-hand) table, even if no matching entries are found in the second (right-hand) table. Such **forced rows** are given NULL values for all of the columns in the right-hand table.

To perform a left join between two tables in MySQL, separate the two table names in the FROM clause with LEFT JOIN instead of a comma. Then follow the second table's name with ON *condition*, where *condition* specifies the criteria for matching rows in the two tables (i.e. what you would normally put in the

WHERE clause). Here's our revised query for listing authors and the number of jokes to their credit:

```
mysql>SELECT author.name, COUNT(*) AS numjokes
    ->FROM author LEFT JOIN joke ON authorid=author.id
    ->GROUP BY authorid;
+-----------------+----------+
| name            | numjokes |
+-----------------+----------+
| Amy Mathieson   |        1 |
| Kevin Yank      |        3 |
| Joan Smith      |        1 |
+-----------------+----------+
```

Wait just a minute! Suddenly Amy Mathieson has one joke? That can't be right! In fact, it is—but only because the query is wrong. COUNT(*) counts the number of rows returned for each author. If we look at the ungrouped results of the LEFT JOIN, we can see what's happened:

```
mysql>SELECT author.name, joke.id AS jokeid
    ->FROM author LEFT JOIN joke ON authorid=author.id;
+-----------------+--------+
| name            | jokeid |
+-----------------+--------+
| Kevin Yank      |      1 |
| Kevin Yank      |      2 |
| Kevin Yank      |      4 |
| Joan Smith      |      3 |
| Amy Mathieson   |   NULL |
+-----------------+--------+
```

See? Amy Mathieson *does* have a row—the row is forced because it doesn't have any matching rows in the right-hand table of the LEFT JOIN (joke). The fact that the joke ID value is NULL doesn't affect COUNT(*)—it still counts it as a row. If, instead of *, you specify an actual column name (say, joke.id) for the COUNT function to look at, it will ignore NULL values in that column, and give us the count we want:

```
mysql>SELECT author.name, COUNT(joke.id) AS numjokes
    ->FROM author LEFT JOIN joke ON authorid=author.id
    ->GROUP BY authorid;
+-----------------+----------+
| name            | numjokes |
+-----------------+----------+
| Amy Mathieson   |        0 |
```

```
| Kevin Yank     |        3 |
| Joan Smith     |        1 |
+----------------+----------+
```

Limiting Results with HAVING

What if we wanted a list of *only* those authors that had no jokes to their name? Once again, let's look at the query that most users would try first:

```
mysql>SELECT author.name, COUNT(joke.id) AS numjokes
   ->FROM author LEFT JOIN joke ON authorid=author.id
   ->WHERE numjokes=0
   ->GROUP BY authorid;
ERROR 1054: Unknown column 'numjokes' in 'where clause'
```

By now, you're probably not surprised that it didn't work as expected. The reason why WHERE numjokes=0 didn't do the job has to do with the way MySQL processes result sets. First, MySQL produces the raw, combined list of authors and jokes from the author and joke tables. Next, it processes the WHERE clause and the ON portion of the FROM clause so that only the relevant rows in the list are returned (in this case, rows that match authors with their jokes). Finally, MySQL processes the GROUP BY clause by grouping the results according to their authorid, COUNTing the number of entries in each group that have non-NULL joke.id values, and producing the numjokes column as a result.

Notice that the numjokes column isn't actually created until the GROUP BY clause is processed, and *that* doesn't happen until after the WHERE clause does its thing! If you wanted to exclude jokes that contained the word "chicken" from the count, you could use the WHERE clause without a problem, because that exclusion doesn't rely on a value that the GROUP BY clause is responsible for producing. Conditions that affect the results after grouping takes place, however, must appear in a special HAVING clause. Here's the corrected query:

```
mysql>SELECT author.name, COUNT(joke.id) AS numjokes
   ->FROM author LEFT JOIN joke ON authorid=author.id
   ->GROUP BY authorid
   ->HAVING numjokes=0;
+----------------+----------+
| name           | numjokes |
+----------------+----------+
| Amy Mathieson  |        0 |
+----------------+----------+
```

Some conditions work both in the HAVING and the WHERE clauses. For example, if we wanted to exclude a particular author by name, we could do so by using `author.name!='Author Name'` in either the WHERE or the HAVING clause, because, regardless of whether you filter out the author before or after you group the results, the same results are returned. In such cases, it is always best to use the WHERE clause, because MySQL is better at optimizing such queries internally so they happen faster.

Summary

In this chapter, we rounded out your knowledge of Structured Query Language (SQL), as supported by MySQL. We focused predominantly on features of SELECT that allow you to view information stored in a database with an unprecedented level of flexibility and power. With judicious use of the advanced features of SE-LECT, you can have MySQL do what it does best—and lighten the load on PHP in the process.

There are still a few isolated query types that we haven't seen, and MySQL offers a whole library of built-in functions to do things like calculate dates and format text strings (see Appendix B). To become truly proficient with MySQL, you should also have a firm grasp on the various column types offered by MySQL. The TIMESTAMP type, for example, can be a real time-saver (no pun intended). All of these are fully documented in the MySQL Manual, and briefly covered in Appendix C.

10 Binary Data

All the examples of database-driven Websites we've seen so far have dealt with sites based around textual data. Jokes, authors, categories… all of these things can be fully represented with strings of text. But, what if you ran, say, an online digital photo gallery to which people could upload pictures taken with digital cameras? For this idea to work, we need to be able to let visitors to our site upload their photos, and we need to be able to keep track of them.

In this chapter, we'll develop a system whereby users can upload binary files (images, documents… whatever!) and have them stored on your Web server for display on your site. There are several things you need to learn on the way, though, and I'll also cover all these in this chapter: working with files in PHP, handling uploaded files in PHP, and storing and retrieving binary data in MySQL.

As we learn to juggle files with PHP, we'll also take the opportunity to relieve some of the load on your Web server with the help of semi-dynamic pages.

Semi-Dynamic Pages

As the owner of a successful—or soon-to-be so—Website, site traffic is probably something you'd like to encourage. Unfortunately, high site traffic is just the kind of thing that a Web server administrator dreads—especially when that site is primarily composed of dynamically generated, database-driven pages. Such pages take a great deal more horsepower from the computer that runs the Web server software than do plain, old HTML files, because every page request is like a miniature program that runs on that computer.

While some pages of a database-driven site must always display current-to-the-second data culled from the database, others do not. Consider the front page of a Website like sitepoint.com. Typically, it presents a sort of "digest" of what's new and fresh on the site. But how often does that information actually change? Once an hour? Once a day? Once a *week*? And how important is it that visitors to your site see those changes the instant they occur? Would your site really suffer if changes took effect after a slight delay?

By converting high-traffic dynamic pages into **semi-dynamic** equivalents—static pages that are regenerated dynamically at regular intervals to freshen their content—you can significantly reduce the toll that the database-driven components of your site take on your Web server's performance.

Say you have `index.php`, your front page, which provides a summary of new content on your site. Through examination of server logs, you'll probably find that this is one of the most requested pages on your site. If you ask yourself some of the questions above, you'll realize that this page doesn't have to be dynamically generated for every request. As long as it's updated every time new content is added to your site, it'll be as dynamic as it needs to be. With a PHP script, you can generate a static snapshot of the dynamic page's output and put this snapshot online, in place of the dynamic version, as `index.html`.

This little trick will require some reading, writing, and juggling of files. PHP is perfectly capable of accomplishing this task, but we have not yet seen the functions we'll need:

fopen	This function opens a file for reading and/or writing. This file can be stored on the server's hard disk, or PHP can load it from a URL just like a Web browser would.
fclose	This function tells PHP you're finished reading/writing a particular file and releases it for other programs or scripts to use.
fread	The `fread` function reads data from a file into a PHP variable. It allows you to specify how much information (i.e. how many characters or bytes) to read.

fwrite   fwrite writes data from a PHP variable into a file.

copy   This function performs a run-of-the-mill file copy operation.

unlink   unlink deletes a file from the hard disk.

Do you see where we're headed? If not, don't worry—you will in a moment.

Create a file called generateindex.php. It will be the responsibility of this file to load index.php, the dynamic version of your front page, as a Web browser would, then to write the static version of the file as an updated version of index.html. If anything goes wrong in this process, you want to avoid the potential destruction of the good copy of index.html, so we'll make this script write the new static version into a temporary file (tempindex.html), then copy it over index.html if all is well.

We start out by setting some PHP variables to configure the URL of the PHP script we wish to load, the temporary file name to use in the process, and the name of the static page we wish to create:

File: **generateindex.php (excerpt)**

```
<?php
  $srcurl = 'http://localhost/index.php';
  $tempfilename = 'tempindex.html';
  $targetfilename = 'index.html';
?>
```

Next up, we have the standard HTML boilerplate. After all, this script, too, must send something to the browser so you know what's going on.

File: **generateindex.php (excerpt)**

```
<!DOCTYPE html PUBLIC "-//W3C//DTD XHTML 1.0 Strict//EN"
    "http://www.w3.org/TR/xhtml1/DTD/xhtml1-strict.dtd">
<html xmlns="http://www.w3.org/1999/xhtml">
<head>
<title>Generating <?php echo $targetfilename; ?></title>
<meta http-equiv="content-type"
    content="text/html; charset=iso-8859-1" />
</head>
<body>
<p>Generating <?php echo $targetfilename; ?>...</p>
```

Now, to do the real work. We start out by using `unlink` to delete the temporary file, in case it was previously left lying around by a failed execution of this script. We use the PHP error suppression operator (@) to avoid displaying an error message if the file doesn't exist, as in most cases, it won't.

File: **generateindex.php (excerpt)**

```php
<?php
  @unlink($tempfilename);
```

Now we can load the dynamic page (`index.php`) by requesting its URL with `fopen`. Since we're requesting the file as a URL, rather than directly using its file name, the PHP script will be processed by the Web server before we receive it, so what we'll get is essentially a static HTML page. The `'r'` parameter indicates that we intend only to read from this file, not to write to it.

File: **generateindex.php (excerpt)**

```php
$dynpage = fopen($srcurl, 'r');
if (!$dynpage) {
  exit("<p>Unable to load $srcurl. Static page update " .
      "aborted!</p>");
}
```

We must then use the `fread` function to read the contents of the URL into a PHP variable. The second argument indicates how much data we are willing to read; we set it to 1MB, so that things don't get out of hand if `index.php` goes haywire and sends out a massive page. Having done that, we close the connection, using `fclose`, to free up resources.

File: **generateindex.php (excerpt)**

```php
$htmldata = fread($dynpage, 1024 * 1024);
fclose($dynpage);
```

With the page contents tucked away in the `$htmldata` variable, we now want to write them into a static HTML file. The first step is to open that file with `fopen`, this time passing `'w'` as the second parameter to indicate that we will write to the file:

File: **generateindex.php (excerpt)**

```php
$tempfile = fopen($tempfilename, 'w');
if (!$tempfile) {
  exit("<p>Unable to open temporary file ($tempfilename) for " .
      "writing. Static page update aborted!</p>");
}
```

We use `fwrite` to write the data, and then `fclose` to close the file:

File: **generateindex.php (excerpt)**

```
fwrite($tempfile, $htmldata);
fclose($tempfile);
```

With the static page written into a temporary file, we now want to copy the temporary file over the previous version of the static file using `fcopy`. We can then delete the temporary file with `unlink`:

File: **generateindex.php (excerpt)**

```
$ok = copy($tempfilename, $targetfilename);
unlink($tempfilename);
?>
<p>Static page successfully updated!</p>
</body>
</html>
```

Now, whenever `generateindex.php` is executed (say, when a browser requests it), a fresh copy of `index.html` will be generated from `index.php`. Moving `index.php` and `generateindex.php` into a restricted-access directory will ensure that only site administrators have the ability to update the front page of your site. Expand this script to generate all semi-dynamic pages on your site, and add an "update semi-dynamic pages" link to your content management system!

If you'd rather have your front page update automatically, you'll need to set up your server to run `generateindex.php` at regular intervals—for instance, every hour. Under recent versions of Windows, you can use the Task Scheduler to run `php.exe` (a standalone version of PHP included with the Windows PHP distribution) automatically every hour. Just create a batch file called `generateindex.bat` that contains this line of text:

File: **generateindex.bat**

```
@C:\PHP\php.exe C:\WWW\generateindex.php
```

Adjust the paths and file names as necessary, then set up Task Scheduler to run `generateindex.bat` every hour. In some older versions of Windows, you'll need to set up 24 tasks to be run daily at the appropriate times. Done!

Under Linux, or other UNIX-based platforms, you can do a similar thing with `cron`—a program installed on just about every UNIX system out there that lets you define tasks to be run at regular intervals. Type `man crontab` at your system command prompt to read about how you can set up tasks for `cron`.

The task you'll set cron to run will be very similar to the Windows task discussed above. However, the standalone version of PHP that you'll need doesn't come with the PHP Apache module we compiled way back in Chapter 1. You'll need to compile it separately, from the same package we used to compile the Apache module. Instructions are provided with the package and on the PHP Website[1], but feel free to post in the SitePoint Forums if you need help!

For experienced cron users in a hurry, here's what the line in your crontab file should look like:

```
0 0-23 * * * php /path/to/generateindex.php > /dev/null
```

Handling File Uploads

Okay, we can now juggle files we've created ourselves, but the next piece of the puzzle is to accept files uploaded by visitors to your site, and handle them just as deftly.

We'll start with the basics: let's write an HTML form that allows users to upload files. HTML makes this quite easy with its input type="file" tag. By default, however, only the name of the file selected by the user is sent. To have the file itself submitted with the form data, we need to add enctype="multipart/form-data" to the form tag:

```
<form action="fileupload.php" method="post"
    enctype="multipart/form-data">
  <p><label>Select file to upload:
    <input type="file" name="upload" /></label></p>
  <p><input type="submit" value="Submit" /></p>
</form>
```

As we can see, a PHP script (fileupload.php, in this case) will handle the data submitted with the form above. Information about uploaded files appears in an array called $_FILES that's automatically created by PHP. As you'd expect, an entry in this array called $_FILES['upload'] (from the name attribute of the input tag) will contain information about the file uploaded in this example. However, instead of storing the contents of the uploaded file, $_FILES['upload'] contains yet another array. We therefore use a second set of square brackets to select the information we want:

---

[1] http://www.php.net/

$_FILES['*upload*']['tmp_name']

This takes the name of the file stored on the Web server's hard disk in the directory set by the TEMP environment variable (e.g. C:\Windows\TEMP\ on most Windows 9x systems), unless it has been specified explicitly using the upload_tmp_dir setting in your php.ini file. This file is only kept as long as the PHP script responsible for handling the form submission is in operation. So, if you want to use it for any tasks later on (e.g. storing it for display on the site), you need to make a copy of it somewhere else. To do this, use the copy function described in the previous section.

$_FILES['*upload*']['name']

This takes the name of the file on the client machine, before it was submitted. If you make a permanent copy of the temporary file, you might want to give it its original name instead of the automatically-generated temporary file name described above.

$_FILES['*upload*']['size']

This takes the size (in bytes) of the file.

$_FILES['*upload*']['type']

This takes the MIME type (e.g. text/plain, image/gif, etc.) of the file.

Remember, 'upload' is just the name attribute of the input tag that submitted the file, so the actual names of these variables will depend on that attribute.

You can use these variables to decide whether to accept or reject an uploaded file. For example, in a photo gallery we would only really be interested in JPEG and possibly GIF files. These files have MIME types of image/pjpeg and image/gif respectively, but to cater to differences between browsers,[1] you should use regular expressions to validate the uploaded file's type:

```
if (eregi('^image/p?jpeg(;.*)?$', $_FILES['upload']['type'])
    or eregi('^image/gif(;.*)?$', $_FILES['upload']['type'])) {
  // Handle the file…
} else {
  echo "<p>Please submit a JPEG or GIF image file.</p>\n";
}
```

See Chapter 7 for help with regular expression syntax.

---

[1]The exact MIME type depends on the browser in use. Internet Explorer uses the standards-compliant image/pjpeg for JPEG images, while Mozilla uses image/jpeg. Stranger yet, Opera 6 uses image/jpeg; name="*filename*.jpg"!

While you can use a similar technique to disallow files that are too large (by checking the $_FILES['upload']['size'] variable), this is not usually a good idea. Before this value can be checked, the file is already uploaded and saved in the temporary directory. If you try to reject files because you have limited disk space and/or bandwidth, the fact that large files can still be uploaded, even though they're deleted almost immediately, may be a problem for you.

Instead, you can tell PHP in advance the maximum file size you wish to accept. There are two ways to do this. The first is to adjust the upload_max_filesize setting in your php.ini file. The default value is 2MB, so if you want to accept uploads larger than that, you'll immediately need to change that value.[2]

The second method is to include a hidden input field in your form with the name MAX_FILE_SIZE, and the maximum file size you want to accept with this form as its value. For security reasons, this value cannot exceed the upload_max_filesize setting in your php.ini, but it does provide a way for you to accept different maximum sizes on different pages. The following form, for example, will allow uploads of up to 1 kilobyte (1024 bytes):

```
<form action="fileupload.php" method="post"
    enctype="multipart/form-data">
  <input type="hidden" name="MAX_FILE_SIZE" value="1024" />
  <p><label>Select file to upload:
    <input type="file" name="uploadedfile" /></label></p>
  <p><input type="submit" name="submit" value="Submit" /></p>
</form>
```

Note that the hidden MAX_FILE_SIZE field must come before any input type="file" tags in the form, so that PHP is apprised of this restriction before it receives any submitted files. Note also that this restriction can easily be circumvented by a malicious user who simply writes his or her own form without the MAX_FILE_SIZE field. For fail-safe security against large file uploads, use the upload_max_filesize setting in php.ini.

Assigning Unique File Names

As we said above, to keep an uploaded file, we need to copy it to another directory. And while we have access to the name of each uploaded file with its $_FILE['upload']['name'] variable, we have no guarantee that two files with

---

[2] A second restriction, affecting the total size of form submissions, is enforced by the post_max_size setting in php.ini. Its default value is 8MB, so if you want to accept *really* big uploads, you'll need to modify that setting, too.

the same name will not be uploaded. In such a case, storage of the file with its original name may result in newer uploads overwriting older ones.

For this reason, you'll usually want to adopt a scheme that allows you to assign a unique file name to every uploaded file. Using the system time (which we can access using the PHP `time` function), we can easily produce a name based on the number of seconds since January 1, 1970. But what if two files happen to be uploaded within one second of each other? To help guard against this possibility, we'll also use the client's IP address (automatically stored in `$_SERVER['REMOTE_ADDR']` by PHP) in the file name. Since we're unlikely to receive two files from the same IP address within one second of each other, this is an acceptable solution for our purposes.

```php
// Pick a file extension
if (eregi('^image/p?jpeg(;.*)?$',
    $_FILES['upload']['type'])) {
  $extension = '.jpg';
} else {
  $extension = '.gif';
}

// The complete path/filename
$filename = 'C:/Uploads/' . time() .
    $_SERVER['REMOTE_ADDR'] . $extension;

// Copy the file (if it is deemed safe)
if (is_uploaded_file($_FILES['upload']['tmp_name']) and
    copy($_FILES['upload']['tmp_name'], $filename)) {
  echo "<p>File stored successfully as $filename.</p>";
} else {
  echo "<p>Could not save file as $filename!</p>";
}
```

Important to note is my use of the `is_uploaded_file` function to check if the file is "safe." All this function does is return true if the file name it is passed as a parameter (`$_FILES['upload']['tmp_name']` in this case) was in fact uploaded as part of a form submission. If a malicious user loaded this script and manually specified a file name such as `/etc/passwd`, and we had not used `is_uploaded_file` to check that `$_FILES['upload']` really referred to an uploaded file, our script might be used to copy sensitive files on our server into a directory from which they would become publicly accessible over the Web! Thus, before you ever trust a PHP variable that you expect to contain the file name of an uploaded file, be sure to use `is_uploaded_file` to check it.

A second trick I've used here is to combine `is_uploaded_file` and `copy` together as the condition of an `if` statement. If the result of `is_uploaded_file` is false, PHP knows immediately that the entire condition will be false when it identifies the `and` operator separating the two function calls. To save time, it won't even bother running `copy`, so the file won't get copied when `is_uploaded_file` returns false. On the other hand, if `is_uploaded_file` returns true, PHP goes ahead and copies the file. The result of `copy` then determines whether the success or error message is displayed. Similarly, if we had used the `or` operator instead of `and`, a successful result from the first part of the condition would cause PHP to skip the second part. This characteristic of `if` statements is known as **short-circuit evaluation**, and works in other conditional structures such as `while` and `for` loops, too.

Finally, note in the above script that I have used UNIX-style forward slashes (/) in the path, despite it being a Windows path. If I'd used backslashes I'd have had to replace them with double-backslashes (\\) so that PHP didn't think we were escaping special characters. However, PHP is smart enough to convert forward slashes in a file path to backslashes when it's running on a Windows system. As, under UNIX, we can also use single slashes (/) as usual, the adoption of forward slashes in general for file paths in PHP will make your scripts more portable.

Recording Uploaded Files in the Database

So, we've created a system whereby visitors can upload JPEG and GIF images and have them saved on our server... but wasn't this book supposed to be about database-driven Websites? If we used the system as it stands now, someone would have to collect the submitted images out of the folder in which they're saved, then add them to the Website by hand! If you think back to Chapter 7, when we developed a system that site visitors could use to submit jokes and have them stored in the database ready for quick approval by an administrator, you'll know there must be a better way!

MySQL has several column types that allow you to store binary data. In database parlance, these column types let us store BLOBs (Binary Large OBjects). However, the storage of potentially large files in a relational database is not usually a good idea. While there is convenience in having all the data located in one place, large files lead to large databases, and large databases lead to reduced performance and much larger backup files.

The best alternative is usually to store the *file names* in the database. As long as you remember to delete files when you delete their corresponding entries in the database, everything should work just the way you need it to. Since we've seen all the SQL code involved in this time and again, I'll leave the details to you. As usual, the SitePoint Forum community is there to offer a helping hand if you need it.

In cases where you're dealing with relatively small files—for example, head shots for use in a staff directory—the storage of data in MySQL is, however, quite practical. In the rest of this chapter, I'll demonstrate how to use PHP to store binary files uploaded over the Web in a MySQL database, and how to retrieve those files for download or display.

Binary Column Types

As with most database-driven Web applications, the first thing to consider is the layout of the database. For each of the files that's stored in our database, we will store the file name, the MIME type (e.g. image/pjpeg for JPEG image files), a short description of the file, and the binary data itself. Here's the CREATE TABLE statement that must be entered in MySQL to create the table:

```
mysql>CREATE TABLE filestore (
    ->    id INT NOT NULL PRIMARY KEY AUTO_INCREMENT,
    ->    filename VARCHAR(255) NOT NULL,
    ->    mimetype VARCHAR(50) NOT NULL,
    ->    description VARCHAR(255) NOT NULL,
    ->    filedata MEDIUMBLOB
    ->);
```

Most of this syntax should be familiar to you; however, the MEDIUMBLOB column type is new. If you consult the MySQL Column Type Reference in Appendix C, you'll find that MEDIUMBLOB is the same as MEDIUMTEXT, except that it performs case-sensitive searches and sorts. In fact, from MySQL's point of view, there is no difference between binary data and blocks of text—both are just long strings of bytes to be stored in the database. The reason we'll use MEDIUMBLOB instead of MEDIUMTEXT is simply to anticipate the situation in which we might need to compare the contents of one binary file with another. In such cases, we'd want the comparison to be case sensitive, as binary files may use byte patterns that are equivalent to alphabetical letters, and we'd want to distinguish the byte pattern that represents 'A' from that which represents 'a'.

MEDIUMBLOB is one of several BLOB column types designed to store variable-length binary data (BLOB stands for Binary Large OBject). These column types differ from one another only in two aspects: the maximum size of the data a particular value in the column can contain, and the number of bytes used to store the length of each data value. The different binary column types are listed with these details in Table 10.1.

Table 10.1. Binary Column Types in MySQL

Column Type	Maximum Size	Space Required Per Entry
TINYBLOB	255B	Data size + 1 byte
BLOB	65KB	Data size + 2 bytes
MEDIUMBLOB	16.7MB	Data size + 3 bytes
LONGBLOB	4.3GB	Data size + 4 bytes

As you can see, the table we created above will be able to store files up to 16.7MB in size. If you think you'll need larger files, you can bump the `filedata` column up to a `LONGBLOB`. Each file will occupy one more byte in the database, because MySQL will require that extra byte in order to record larger file sizes, but you'll be able to store files up to 4.3GB in size—assuming that your operating system allows files of this size!

Storing Files

The next step is to create a PHP script that lets users upload files and store them in the database. You can hold off copying the code in the next two sections—I'll present it all as a complete script at the end of the chapter. Here's the code for the form—there should be no surprises here:

File: **filestore.php (excerpt)**

```
<form action="<?php echo $_SERVER['PHP_SELF']; ?>"
    method="post" enctype="multipart/form-data">
  <p><label>Upload File:<br />
    <input type="file" name="upload" /></label></p>
  <p><label>File Description:<br />
    <input type="text" name="desc" maxlength="255" /></label></p>
  <p><input type="submit" value="Upload" /></p>
</form>
```

As you should already know from our work in this chapter, this form will create a temporary file on the server and store the name of that file in `$_FILES['upload']['tmp_name']`. It also creates `$_FILES['upload']['name']` (the original name of the file), $_FILES['upload']['size'] (the file size in bytes), and $_FILES['upload']['type'] (the MIME type of the file).

Inserting the file into the database is a relatively straightforward process: open the temporary file, read the data it contains into a PHP variable, then use that variable in a standard MySQL INSERT query. Again, we make use of is_uploaded_file to make sure the file name we use does, in fact, correspond to an uploaded file before we do any of this. Here's the code:

File: **filestore.php (excerpt)**

```php
// Bail out if the file isn't really an upload.
if (!is_uploaded_file($_FILES['upload']['tmp_name'])) {
  exit('There was no file uploaded!');
}
$uploadfile = $_FILES['upload']['tmp_name'];
$uploadname = $_FILES['upload']['name'];
$uploadtype = $_FILES['upload']['type'];
$uploaddesc = $_POST['desc'];

// Open file for binary reading ('rb')
$tempfile = fopen($uploadfile, 'rb');

// Read the entire file into memory using PHP's
// filesize function to get the file size.
$filedata = fread($tempfile, filesize($uploadfile));

// Prepare for database insert by adding backslashes
// before special characters.
$filedata = addslashes($filedata);

// Create the SQL query.
$sql = "INSERT INTO filestore SET
    filename = '$uploadname',
    mimetype = '$uploadtype',
    description = '$uploaddesc',
    filedata = '$filedata'";

// Perform the insert.
$ok = @mysql_query($sql);
if (!$ok) {
  exit('Database error storing file: ' . mysql_error());
}
```

Viewing Stored Files

Armed with the code that accepts file uploads and stores them in a database, you're halfway home. But you still need to be able to pull that data out of the database to use it. For our purposes, this will mean sending the file to a requesting browser.

Once again, this turns out to be a relatively straightforward process. We simply retrieve the data for the requested file from the database and send it on to the Web browser. The only tricky part is to send the browser information *about* the file:

the file size   so that the browser can display accurate download progress information to the user

the file type   so that the browser knows what to do with the data it receives, e.g. display it as a Web page, a text file, an image, or offer to save the file

the file name   if we don't specify this, the browser will assume all files downloaded from our script have the same file name as the script

All this information is sent to the browser using **HTTP headers**—special lines of information that precede the transmission of the file data itself. Sending HTTP headers via PHP is quite easy using the `header` function, but as headers must be sent before plain content, any calls to this function must come before anything is output by your script.

The **file size** is specified with a `content-length` header:

File: **filestore.php (excerpt)**

```
header('content-length: ' . strlen($filedata));
```

`strlen` is a built-in PHP function that returns the length of the given string. Since binary data is just a string of bytes as far as PHP is concerned, you can use this function to count the length, in bytes, of the file data.

The **file type** is specified with a `content-type` header:

File: **filestore.php (excerpt)**

```
header("content-type: $mimetype");
```

Finally, the **file name** is specified with a `content-disposition` header:

```
header("content-disposition: inline; filename=$filename");
```

You could use the script below to fetch a file with a given ID from the database, and send it to the browser:

```
$id = $_GET['id'];

// User is retrieving a file
$sql = "SELECT filename, mimetype, filedata
    FROM filestore WHERE id = '$id'";
$result = @mysql_query($sql);
if (!$result) {
  exit('Database error: ' . mysql_error());
}

$file = mysql_fetch_array($result);
if (!$file) {
  exit('File with given ID not found in database!');
}

$filename = $file['filename'];
$mimetype = $file['mimetype'];
$filedata = $file['filedata'];

header("content-disposition: inline; filename=$filename");
header("content-type: $mimetype");
header('content-length: ' . strlen($filedata));

echo $filedata;
exit();
```

One final trick we can add to this code is to allow a file to be downloaded, instead of viewed, if the user so desires. Web standards suggest that the way to do this is to send a `content-disposition` of `attachment` instead of `inline`. Here's the modified code. It checks if the variable `$action` equals `'dnld'`, which would indicate that this special file type should be sent:

```
$sql = "SELECT FileName, MimeType, FileData
        FROM filestore WHERE ID = '$id'";
$result = @mysql_query($sql);
if (!$result) die("Database error: " . mysql_error());

$file = mysql_fetch_array($result);
if (!$file) {
```

```
  exit('File with given ID not found in database!');
}

$filename = $file['FileName'];
$mimetype = $file['MimeType'];
$filedata = $file['FileData'];
$disposition = 'inline';

if ($action == 'dnld')
  $disposition = 'attachment';

header("content-disposition: $disposition; filename=$filename");
header("content-type: $mimetype");
header('content-length: ' . strlen($filedata));

echo $filedata;
exit();
```

Unfortunately, many browsers do not respect the content-disposition header. Netscape 4, Internet Explorer 5, and all Opera browsers, for example, will decide what to do with a file based on the content-type header.

To ensure the correct behavior in as many browsers as possible, we can use the built-in $_SERVER['HTTP_USER_AGENT'] variable to identify the browser in use. We can coerce Opera 7 and Internet Explorer 5 browsers to display the download dialog by sending a made-up content-type of application/x-download:

File: **filestore.php (excerpt)**

```
$disposition = 'inline';

if ($action == 'dnld') {
  $disposition = 'attachment';
  if (strpos($_SERVER['HTTP_USER_AGENT'], 'MSIE 5') or
      strpos($_SERVER['HTTP_USER_AGENT'], 'Opera 7')) {
    $mimetype = 'application/x-download';
  }
}

header("content-disposition: $disposition; filename=$filename");
```

The strpos function used here is a built-in PHP function that takes two strings and searches for the second string within the first. If it doesn't find it, it returns false, but if it does, it returns the position of the second string in the first as an integer.

Older versions of Opera and Netscape 4 are best left to their own devices; when you mess with the `content-type` header, these browsers display binary files as plain text in the browser window, and display an error message, respectively.

The Complete Script

Below, you'll find the complete example script. It combines all the elements given above with some simple code that will list the files in the database and allow them to be deleted. As always, this file is available in the code archive.

As you look at the code, you may notice two spots in which I've used this command:

File: **filestore.php (excerpt)**

```php
header('location: '. $_SERVER['PHP_SELF']);
```

As described above, the `header` function sends an HTTP header to the browser. We've seen the `content-type`, `content-length`, and `content-disposition` headers already. The above line sends a `location` header, which redirects the browser to the specified URL. As it specifies `$_SERVER['PHP_SELF']` as the URL, this line redirects the browser to the same page.

"What's the point of that?" you might wonder. Well, I use this line after the script adds or deletes a file in the database. In such cases, the action—add or delete—is specified either by a form submission or by a query string in the page's URL. If the script simply took the requested action and immediately displayed the updated list of files, the user could repeat that action inadvertently by refreshing the page! To avoid this kind of error, we instead redirect the browser to a page that is identical in every way, except that the request doesn't involve a form submission, and the URL doesn't contain a query string (`$_SERVER['PHP_SELF']`). Thus, the user can refresh the file list that's produced with no ill effects.

File: **filestore.php**

```php
<?php

$dbcnx = @mysql_connect('localhost', 'root', 'mypasswd');
if (!$dbcnx) {
  exit('<p>Unable to connect to the ' .
      'database server at this time.</p>');
}

if (!@mysql_select_db('ijdb')) {
```

```
   exit('<p>Unable to locate the joke ' .
       'database at this time.</p>');
}

if (isset($_GET['action'])) {
  $action = $_GET['action'];
} else {
  $action = '';
}

if (($action == 'view' or $action == 'dnld') and
    isset($_GET['id'])) {
  $id = $_GET['id'];

  // User is retrieving a file
  $sql = "SELECT filename, mimetype, filedata
      FROM filestore WHERE id = '$id'";
  $result = @mysql_query($sql);
  if (!$result) {
    exit('Database error: ' . mysql_error());
  }

  $file = mysql_fetch_array($result);
  if (!$file) {
    exit('File with given ID not found in database!');
  }

  $filename = $file['filename'];
  $mimetype = $file['mimetype'];
  $filedata = $file['filedata'];
  $disposition = 'inline';

  if ($action == 'dnld') {
    $disposition = 'attachment';
    if (strpos($_SERVER['HTTP_USER_AGENT'], 'MSIE 5') or
        strpos($_SERVER['HTTP_USER_AGENT'], 'Opera 7')) {
      $mimetype = 'application/x-download';
    }
  }

  header("content-disposition: $disposition; filename=$filename");
  header("content-type: $mimetype");
  header('content-length: ' . strlen($filedata));

  echo $filedata;
  exit();
```

```php
} elseif ($action == 'del' and isset($_GET['id'])) {
  $id = $_GET['id'];

  // User is deleting a file
  $sql = "DELETE FROM filestore WHERE id = '$id'";
  $ok = @mysql_query($sql);
  if (!$ok) {
    exit('Database error: ' . mysql_error());
  }

  header('location: ' . $_SERVER['PHP_SELF']);
  exit();

} elseif (isset($_FILES['upload'])) {

  // Bail out if the file isn't really an upload.
  if (!is_uploaded_file($_FILES['upload']['tmp_name'])) {
    exit('There was no file uploaded!');
  }
  $uploadfile = $_FILES['upload']['tmp_name'];
  $uploadname = $_FILES['upload']['name'];
  $uploadtype = $_FILES['upload']['type'];
  $uploaddesc = $_POST['desc'];

  // Open file for binary reading ('rb')
  $tempfile = fopen($uploadfile, 'rb');

  // Read the entire file into memory using PHP's
  // filesize function to get the file size.
  $filedata = fread($tempfile, filesize($uploadfile));

  // Prepare for database insert by adding backslashes
  // before special characters.
  $filedata = addslashes($filedata);

  // Create the SQL query.
  $sql = "INSERT INTO filestore SET
      filename = '$uploadname',
      mimetype = '$uploadtype',
      description = '$uploaddesc',
      filedata = '$filedata'";

  // Perform the insert.
  $ok = @mysql_query($sql);
  if (!$ok) {
```

```php
    exit('Database error storing file: ' . mysql_error());
  }

  header('location: ' . $_SERVER['PHP_SELF']);
  exit();

}

// Default page view: lists stored files

$sql = 'SELECT id, filename, mimetype, description
    FROM filestore';
$filelist = @mysql_query($sql);
if (!$filelist) {
  exit('Database error: ' . mysql_error());
}
?>
<!DOCTYPE html PUBLIC "-//W3C//DTD XHTML 1.0 Strict//EN"
    "http://www.w3.org/TR/xhtml1/DTD/xhtml1-strict.dtd">
<html xmlns="http://www.w3.org/1999/xhtml">
<head>
<title>PHP/MySQL File Repository</title>
<meta http-equiv="content-type"
    content="text/html; charset=iso-8859-1" />
</head>
<body>

<h1>PHP/MySQL File Repository</h1>

<form action="<?php echo $_SERVER['PHP_SELF']; ?>"
    method="post" enctype="multipart/form-data">
  <p><label>Upload File:<br />
    <input type="file" name="upload" /></label></p>
  <p><label>File Description:<br />
    <input type="text" name="desc" maxlength="255" /></label></p>
  <p><input type="submit" value="Upload" /></p>
</form>

<p>The following files are stored in the database:</p>
<table>
<tr>
  <th>Filename</th>
  <th>Type</th>
  <th>Description</th>
</tr>
<?php
```

```php
if (mysql_num_rows($filelist) > 0) {
  while ($f = mysql_fetch_array($filelist)) {
    ?>

<tr valign="top">
  <td>
    <a href="<?php echo $_SERVER['PHP_SELF'];
        ?>?action=view&id=<?php echo $f['id']; ?>">
      <?php echo $f['filename']; ?></a>
  </td>
  <td><?php echo $f['mimetype']; ?></td>
  <td><?php echo $f['description']; ?></td>
  <td>
    [<a href="<?php echo $_SERVER['PHP_SELF'];
        ?>?action=dnld&id=<?php echo $f['id']; ?>"
      >Download</a> |
    <a href="<?php echo $_SERVER['PHP_SELF'];
        ?>?action=del&id=<?php echo $f['id']; ?>"
      onclick="return confirm('Delete this file?');"
      >Delete</a>]
  </td>
</tr>

    <?php
  }
} else {
  ?>
  <tr><td colspan="3">No Files!</td></tr>
  <?php
}
?>
</table>
</body>
</html>
```

This example demonstrates all the techniques you need in order to juggle binary files with PHP and MySQL, and I invite you to think of some creative uses of this code. Consider, for example, a file archive to which users must provide a user name and password before they are allowed to view or download the files. If a user enters an incorrect user name/password combination, your script can display an error page instead of sending the file data. Another possibility would be a script that sends different files depending on the details provided by the form.

Large File Considerations

In systems like that developed above, large files present some unique challenges to the developer. I'll explain these here briefly, but fully developed solutions to these problems are beyond the scope of this book.

MySQL Packet Size

By default, MySQL does not accept commands (packets) that are longer than 1MB. This default puts a reasonably severe limit on the maximum file size you can store, unless you're prepared to write your file data in 1MB chunks, using an INSERT followed by several UPDATEs. You can increase the maximum packet size by setting the max_allowed_packet option in your my.cnf (or my.ini) file. Refer to the MySQL manual[2] for more information on this issue.

PHP Script Timeout

PHP is configured by default to kill PHP scripts that run for more than 30 seconds. For large downloads over slow connections, this limit will be reached fairly quickly! Use PHP's set_time_limit function to set an appropriate time limit for the download, or simply set the time limit to zero, which allows the script to run to completion, however long it takes. Don't do this unless you're positive your script will always terminate, and not run into an infinite loop!

Summary

In this chapter, we explored the methodologies for storing binary data (e.g. image files, encryption keys, programs for download) in MySQL databases, and retrieving it again for dynamic display on the Web. We also developed a complete, but admittedly simple, online file storage system to test out these techniques.

---

[2] http://www.mysql.com/doc/en/Packet_too_large.html

11

Cookies and Sessions in PHP

Cookies and sessions are two of those mysterious technologies that are almost always made out to be more intimidating and complex than they really are. In this chapter, I'll debunk those myths by explaining in simple language what they are, how they work, and what they can do for you. I'll also provide practical examples to demonstrate each, with hints as to how these can be expanded to add exciting new features to your own Website!

Cookies

Most computer programs these days preserve some form of **state** when you close them. Whether it be the position of the application window, or the names of the last five files that you worked with, the settings are usually stored in a small file somewhere on your system, so they can be read back the next time the program is run. When Web developers took Web design to the next level, and moved from static pages to complete, interactive, online applications, there was a need for similar functionality in Web browsers—so cookies were born.

A **cookie** is a name/value pair associated with a given Website, and stored on the computer that runs the client (browser). Once it's set by a Website, all future page requests to that same site will also include the cookie, until it **expires**. Other Websites cannot access the cookies set by your site, and vice versa, so, contrary to popular belief, they're a relatively safe place to store personal information. Cookies in and of themselves cannot violate a user's privacy.

Illustrated in Figure 11.1 is the life cycle of a PHP-generated cookie.

❶ First, a Web browser requests a URL that corresponds to a PHP script. Within that script is a call to the `setcookie` function that's built into PHP.

❷ The page produced by the PHP script is sent back to the browser, along with an HTTP `set-cookie` header that contains the name (e.g. `mycookie`) and value pair of the cookie to be set.

❸ When it receives this HTTP header, the browser creates and stores the specified value as a cookie named `mycookie`.

❹ Subsequent page requests to that Website contain an HTTP `cookie` header that sends the name/value pair (`mycookie=value`) to the script requested.

❺ Upon receipt of a page request with a cookie header, PHP automatically creates an entry in the `$_COOKIE` array with the name of the cookie (`$_COOKIE['mycookie']`) and its value.

Figure 11.1. The life cycle of a cookie.

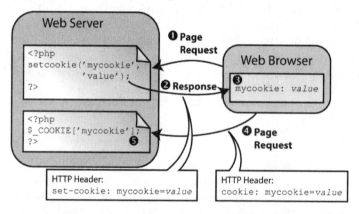

In other words, the PHP `setcookie` function lets you set a variable that will automatically be set by subsequent page requests from the same browser! Before we examine an actual example, let's take a close look at the `setcookie` function.

```
setcookie(name[, value[, expirytime[, path[, domain[, secure]]]]])
```

Like the `header` function we saw in Chapter 10, the `setcookie` function adds HTTP headers to the page, and thus *must be called before any of the actual page content is sent*. Any attempt to call `setcookie` after page content—HTML, for example—has been sent to the browser, will produce a PHP error message.

The only required parameter for this function is *name*, which specifies the name of the cookie. Calling `setcookie` with only the *name* parameter will actually delete the cookie that's stored on the browser, if it exists. The *value* parameter allows you to create a new cookie, or modify the value stored in an existing one.

By default, cookies will remain stored on the browser, and thus will continue to be sent with page requests until the browser is closed by the user. If you want the cookie to persist beyond the current browser session, you must set the *expirytime* parameter to show the number of seconds from January 1, 1970 to the time at which you want the cookie to be deleted automatically. The current time in this format can be obtained using the PHP `time` function. Thus, a cookie could be set to expire in one hour, for example, by setting *expirytime* to `time() + 3600`. To delete a cookie that has a preset expiry time, change this expiry time to represent a point in the past (e.g. one year ago: `time() − 3600 * 24 * 365`). Here's an example:

```
// Set a cookie to expire in 1 year
setcookie('mycookie', 'somevalue', time() + 3600 * 24 * 365);

// Delete it
setcookie('mycookie', '', time() − 3600 * 24 * 365);
```

The *path* parameter lets you restrict access to the cookie to a given path on your server. For instance, if you set a path of `'/~kyank/'` for a cookie, only requests for pages in the ~kyank directory (and its subdirectories) will include the cookie as part of the request. Note the trailing "/", which prevents other scripts in other directories beginning with /~kyank (such as /~kyankfake/) from accessing the cookie. This is helpful if you're sharing a server with other users, and each user has a home directory. It allows you to set cookies without exposing your visitors' data to the scripts of other users on your server.

The *domain* parameter serves a similar purpose; it restricts the cookie's access to a given domain. By default, a cookie will be returned only to the host from which it was originally sent. Large companies, however, commonly have several host names for their Web presence (e.g. `www.example.com` and `support.example.com`). To create a cookie that is accessible by pages on both servers, you would set the *domain* parameter to `'.example.com'`. Note the leading ".", which prevents another site at `example.com` from accessing your cookies on the basis that their domain ends with `example.com`.

The *secure* parameter, when set to 1, indicates that the cookie should be sent only with page requests that happen over a secure (SSL) connection (i.e. with a URL that starts with `https://`).

While all parameters except *name* are optional, you must specify values for earlier parameters if you want to specify values for later ones. For instance, you can't call setcookie with a *domain* value if you don't also specify some value for the *expirytime* parameter. To omit parameters that require a value, you can set string parameters (*value, path, domain*) to ' ' (the empty string) and numerical parameters (*expirytime* and *secure*) to 0.

Let's now look at an example of cookies in use. Imagine you want to display a special welcome message to people on their first visit to your site. You could use a cookie to indicate that someone had been to your site before, and only display the message when the cookie was not set. Here's the code:

```
if (!isset($_COOKIE['visited'])) {
  echo 'Welcome to my Website! Click here for a tour!';
}
setcookie('visited', '1', time() + 3600 * 24 * 365);
```

At first glance, this code would seem to do exactly what we want it to. Unfortunately, it runs into a common pitfall—the welcome message is printed out before setcookie is called. Instead of setting the cookie, PHP displays an error message to inform you that HTTP headers cannot be added after page content has already been sent.

To fix the problem, we call setcookie before we print out the message:

```
setcookie('visited', '1', time() + 3600 * 24 * 365);
if (!isset($_COOKIE['visited'])) {
  echo 'Welcome to my Website! Click here for a tour!';
}
```

This may seem wrong at first glance. If you've never worked with cookies before, you might think that the welcome message will never be printed out, because the cookie is always set before the if statement. However, if you think back to the cookie life cycle, you'll realize that the cookie isn't actually set until the browser receives the Web page that's generated by this script. So the cookie that is created by the setcookie line above won't actually exist until the next time a page is requested.

Instead of simply tracking whether or not the user has visited before, you could track the number of times he or she has visited. Here's the complete example containing all the HTML tags. Notice how I've structured the document to ensure that setcookie happens before any page content is output.

```php
<?php
if (!isset($_COOKIE['visits'])) {
  $_COOKIE['visits'] = 0;
}
$visits = $_COOKIE['visits'] + 1;
setcookie('visits', $visits, time() + 3600 * 24 * 365);
?>
<!DOCTYPE html PUBLIC "-//W3C//DTD XHTML 1.0 Strict//EN"
    "http://www.w3.org/TR/xhtml1/DTD/xhtml1-strict.dtd">
<html xmlns="http://www.w3.org/1999/xhtml">
<head>
<title>Cookie counter</title>
<meta http-equiv="content-type"
    content="text/html; charset=iso-8859-1" />
</head>
<body>
<?php
if ($visits > 1) {
  echo "This is visit number $visits.";
} else { // First visit
  echo 'Welcome to my Web site! Click here for a tour!';
}
?>
</body>
</html>
```

Before you go overboard using cookies, be aware that browsers place a limit on the number and size of cookies allowed per Website. Most browsers will start deleting old cookies to make room for new ones after you've set 20 cookies from your site. Browsers also enforce a maximum combined size for all cookies from all Websites, so an especially cookie-heavy site might cause your own site's cookies to be deleted. For these reasons, you should never store information in a cookie if your application relies on that information being available later on. Instead, cookies are best used for convenient features like automatically logging in a user. If the cookie that contains a visitor's automatic login details is deleted before that person's next visit, he or she can simply reenter the user name and password by hand.

PHP Sessions

Because of the limitations I've just described, cookies are not appropriate for storing large amounts of information. Also, because of the negative impressions that many people have of cookies, it's not uncommon for users to disable cookies in their browsers. If you run an ecommerce Website that uses cookies to store the items in a user's shopping cart as the user makes his or her way through your site, this can be a big problem.

Sessions were developed in PHP as the solution to all these issues. Instead of storing all your (possibly large) data as cookies in the Web browser, sessions let you store the data on your Web server. The only thing that's stored in the browser is a single cookie that contains the user's **session ID**—a variable for which PHP watches on subsequent page requests, and uses to load the stored data that's associated with that session.

Unless configured otherwise, a PHP session automatically sets in the user's browser a cookie that contains the session ID—a long string of letters and numbers that serves to identify that user uniquely for the duration of his or her visit to your site. The browser then sends that cookie along with every request for a page from your site, so that PHP can determine to which of potentially numerous sessions-in-progress the request belongs. Using a set of temporary files that are stored on the Web server, PHP keeps track of the variables that have been registered in each session, and their values.

One of the big selling points of PHP sessions is that they also work when cookies are disabled! If PHP detects that cookies are disabled in the user's browser, it will automatically add the session ID as a query string variable on all the relative links on your page, thus passing the session ID onto the next page. Be aware that all of the pages on your site need to be PHP files for this to work, because PHP won't be able to add the session ID to links on non-PHP pages. Also, for this feature to work, `session.use_trans_sid` must be enabled in your `php.ini` file (see below).

Before you can go ahead and use the spiffy session-management features in PHP, you need to ensure that the relevant section of your `php.ini` file has been set up properly. If you're using a server that belongs to your Web host, it's probably safe to assume this has been done for you. Otherwise, open your `php.ini` file in a text editor and look for the section marked `[Session]` (say *that* ten times fast!). Beneath it, you'll find twenty-some options that begin with the word `session`. Most of them are just fine as they are, but here are a few crucial ones you'll want to check:

```
session.save_handler      = files
session.save_path         = C:\WINDOWS\TEMP
session.use_cookies       = 1
session.use_trans_sid     = 1
```

`session.save_path` tells PHP where to create the temporary files used to track sessions. It must be set to a directory that exists on the system, or you'll get ugly error messages when you try to create a session on one of your pages. Under Linux, `/tmp` is a popular choice. In Windows, you could use `C:\WINDOWS\TEMP`, or some other directory if you prefer (I use `D:\PHP\SESSIONS`). With these adjustments made, restart your Web server software to allow the changes to take effect.

You're now ready to start working with PHP sessions. But before we jump into an example, let's quickly look at the most common session management functions in PHP. To tell PHP to look for a session ID, or to start a new session if none is found, you simply call `session_start`. If an existing session ID is found when this function is called, PHP restores the variables that belong to that session. Since this function attempts to create a cookie, it must come before any page content is sent to the browser, just as we saw for `setcookie` above.

```
session_start();
```

To create a session variable, which will be available on all pages in the site when accessed by the current user, simply set a value in the special `$_SESSION` array. For example, the following will store the variable called pwd in the current session:

```
$_SESSION['pwd'] = 'mypassword';
```

To remove a variable from the current session, use PHP's unset function:

```
unset($_SESSION['pwd']);
```

Finally, should you want to end the current session and delete all registered variables in the process, you can clear all the stored values and use `session_destroy`:

```
$_SESSION = array();
session_destroy();
```

For more detailed information on these and the other session-management functions in PHP, see the relevant section of the PHP Manual[1]. Now that we have these basic functions under our belt, let's put them to work in a simple example.

---

[1] http://www.php.net/session

A Simple Shopping Cart

This example will consist of two PHP scripts:

☐ a product catalogue, through which you can add items to your shopping cart

☐ a checkout page, which displays the contents of the user's shopping cart for confirmation

From the checkout page, the order could then be submitted to a processing system that would handle the details of payment acceptance and shipping arrangements. That system is beyond the scope of this book, and will not be discussed here, but if you'd like to try one, I'd recommend playing with PayPal[2], which is quite easy to set up.

As in Chapter 10, we'll look at various important fragments of code first, after which I'll present the full script, so don't bother typing any of the following snippets into your editor.

Let's start with the list of items we'll have for sale in our online store:

```
<table border="1">
  <thead>
    <tr>
      <th>Item Description</th>
      <th>Price</th>
    </tr>
  </thead>
  <tbody>
    <tr>
      <td>Canadian-Australian Dictionary</td>
      <td>$24.95</td>
    </tr>
    <tr>
      <td>As-new parachute (never opened)</td>
      <td>$1,000.00</td>
    </tr>
    <tr>
      <td>Songs of the Goldfish (2CD Set)</td>
      <td>$19.99</td>
    </tr>
    <tr>
```

---

[2] https://developer.paypal.com/

```
      <td>Ending PHP4 (O'Wroxey Press)</td>
      <td>$34.95</td>
    </tr>
  </tbody>
</table>
<p>All prices are in imaginary dollars.</p>
```

Now, instead of hard-coding the items, we'll place them in a PHP array and generate the page dynamically. Arrays are created with the built-in PHP function array, by listing the elements to be included in the array as the parameters of the function. Items and their prices would normally be stored in a database, but I'm using this method so we can focus on sessions. You should already know all you need to put together a database-driven product catalogue, so I'll leave that to you.

Here's the code for our dynamically generated product catalogue:

File: **catalog.php** (excerpt)

```php
<?php
$items = array(
    'Canadian-Australian Dictionary',
    'Used Parachute (never opened)',
    'Songs of the Goldfish (2CD Set)',
    'Ending PHP4 (O\'Wroxey Press)');
$prices = array(24.95, 1000, 19.99, 34.95);
?>
<table border="1">
  <thead>
    <tr>
      <th>Item Description</th>
      <th>Price</th>
    </tr>
  </thead>
  <tbody>
<?php
  for ($i = 0; $i < count($items); $i++) {
    echo '<tr>';
    echo '<td>' . $items[$i] . '</td>';
    echo '<td>$' . number_format($prices[$i], 2) . '</td>';
    echo '</tr>';
  }
?>
  </tbody>
</table>
<p>All prices are in imaginary dollars.</p>
```

This code produces the HTML we saw above. The table row for each item is created using a `for` loop that counts through the `$items` array (the function `count` returns the number of items in the array). `for` loops were introduced in Chapter 3, and we saw how to use them with the `count` function in Chapter 6. We also use PHP's built-in `number_format` function to display the prices with two digits after the decimal point (see the PHP Manual[3] for more information about this function).

Now, we're going to store the list of items the user placed in the shopping cart in yet another array. Because we'll need this variable to persist throughout a user's visit to your site, we'll store it using PHP sessions. Here's the code that's responsible:

File: **catalog.php (excerpt)**

```
session_start();
if (!isset($_SESSION['cart'])) {
  $_SESSION['cart'] = array();
}
```

`session_start` either starts a new session (and sets the session ID cookie), or restores the variables registered in the existing session, if one exists. The code then checks if `$_SESSION['cart']` exits, and, if it doesn't, initializes it to an empty array to represent the empty cart.

We can now print out the number of items in the user's shopping cart:

File: **catalog.php (excerpt)**

```
<p>Your shopping cart contains <?php
    echo count($_SESSION['cart']); ?> items.</p>
```

Now, the user's shopping cart is going to stay very empty if we don't provide a way to add items to it, so let's modify the `for` loop that displays our table of items to provide a Buy link on the end of each row:

File: **catalog.php (excerpt)**

```
<?php
  for ($i = 0; $i < count($items); $i++) {
    echo '<tr>';
    echo '<td>' . $items[$i] . '</td>';
    echo '<td>$' . number_format($prices[$i], 2) . '</td>';
    echo '<td><a href="' . $_SERVER['PHP_SELF'] .
        '?buy=' . $i . '">Buy</a></td>';
```

[3] http://www.php.net/number_format

```
    echo '</tr>';
  }
?>
```

Now each product in our catalogue has a link back to the catalogue with buy=*n* in the query string, where *n* is the index of the item that's to be added to the shopping cart in the $items array. We can then watch for the $_GET['buy'] variable in our script. When it occurs, we'll add the item to the $_SESSION['cart'] array before redirecting the browser back to the same page, but without a query string, thereby ensuring that refreshing the page doesn't repeatedly add the item to the cart.

File: **catalog.php** (excerpt)

```
if (isset($_GET['buy'])) {
  // Add item to the end of the $_SESSION['cart'] array
  $_SESSION['cart'][] = $_GET['buy'];
  header('location: ' . $_SERVER['PHP_SELF']);
  exit();
}
```

Now, this works just fine if the user has cookies enabled, but when cookies are disabled, PHP's automatic link adjustment doesn't affect the header function, so the session ID gets lost at this point. Fortunately, if PHP identifies that cookies are disabled, it creates a constant named SID, a string of the form PHPSESSID=*somevalue*, which will pass on the session ID. We can make our code compatible with disabled cookie support as follows:

File: **catalog.php** (excerpt)

```
if (isset($_GET['buy'])) {
  // Add item to the end of the $_SESSION['cart'] array
  $_SESSION['cart'][] = $_GET['buy'];
  header('location: '. $_SERVER['PHP_SELF'] . '?' . SID);
  exit();
}
```

All that's left is to add a View your cart link to the appropriate page, and we'll have completed the catalogue script. Here is the complete code for this page:

```
<?php
session_start();
if (!isset($_SESSION['cart'])) {
  $_SESSION['cart'] = array();
}
if (isset($_GET['buy'])) {
  // Add item to the end of the $_SESSION['cart'] array
```

```php
  $_SESSION['cart'][] = $_GET['buy'];
  header('location: ' . $_SERVER['PHP_SELF'] . '?' . SID);
  exit();
}
?>
<!DOCTYPE html PUBLIC "-//W3C//DTD XHTML 1.0 Strict//EN"
    "http://www.w3.org/TR/xhtml1/DTD/xhtml1-strict.dtd">
<html xmlns="http://www.w3.org/1999/xhtml">
<head>
<title>Product catalog</title>
<meta http-equiv="content-type"
    content="text/html; charset=iso-8859-1" />
</head>
<body>
<p>Your shopping cart contains <?php
    echo count($_SESSION['cart']); ?> items.</p>
<p><a href="cart.php">View your cart</a></p>
<?php
$items = array(
    'Canadian-Australian Dictionary',
    'As-new parachute (never opened)',
    'Songs of the Goldfish (2CD Set)',
    'Ending PHP4 (O\'Wroxey Press)');
$prices = array(24.95, 1000, 19.99, 34.95);
?>
<table border="1">
  <thead>
    <tr>
      <th>Item Description</th>
      <th>Price</th>
    </tr>
  </thead>
  <tbody>
<?php
  for ($i = 0; $i < count($items); $i++) {
    echo '<tr>';
    echo '<td>' . $items[$i] . '</td>';
    echo '<td>$' . number_format($prices[$i], 2) . '</td>';
    echo '<td><a href="' . $_SERVER['PHP_SELF'] .
        '?buy=' . $i . '">Buy</a></td>';
    echo '</tr>';
  }
?>
  </tbody>
</table>
<p>All prices are in imaginary dollars.</p>
```

```
</body>
</html>
```

The code for cart.php is very similar to the product catalogue. All it does is take the $_SESSION['cart'] variable (after loading the session, of course), and use the numbers stored there to print out the corresponding items from the $items array. We also provide a link that loads the page with query string empty=1, and causes the script to unset the $_SESSION['cart'] variable, which results in a new, empty shopping cart. Here's the code:

```php
<?php
session_start();
if (!isset($_SESSION['cart'])) {
  $_SESSION['cart'] = array();
}
if (isset($_GET['empty'])) {
  // Empty the $_SESSION['cart'] array
  unset($_SESSION['cart']);
  header('location: ' . $_SERVER['PHP_SELF'] . '?' . SID);
  exit();
}
?>
<!DOCTYPE html PUBLIC "-//W3C//DTD XHTML 1.0 Strict//EN"
    "http://www.w3.org/TR/xhtml1/DTD/xhtml1-strict.dtd">
<html xmlns="http://www.w3.org/1999/xhtml">
<head>
<title>Shopping cart</title>
<meta http-equiv="content-type"
    content="text/html; charset=iso-8859-1" />
</head>
<body>
<h1>Your Shopping Cart</h1>
<?php
$items = array(
  'Canadian-Australian Dictionary',
  'As-new parachute (never opened)',
  'Songs of the Goldfish (2CD Set)',
  'Ending PHP4 (O\'Wroxey Press)');
$prices = array( 24.95, 1000, 19.99, 34.95 );
?>
<table border="1">
  <thead>
    <tr>
      <th>Item Description</th>
      <th>Price</th>
    </tr>
```

```
  </thead>
  <tbody>
<?php
  $total = 0;
  for ($i = 0; $i < count($_SESSION['cart']); $i++) {
    echo '<tr>';
    echo '<td>' . $items[$_SESSION['cart'][$i]] . '</td>';
    echo '<td align="right">$';
    echo number_format($prices[$_SESSION['cart'][$i]], 2);
    echo '</td>';
    echo '</tr>';
    $total = $total + $prices[$_SESSION['cart'][$i]];
  }
?>
  </tbody>
  <tfoot>
    <tr>
      <th align="right">Total:</th><br>
      <th align="right">$<?php echo number_format($total, 2); ?>
      </th>
    </tr>
  </tfoot>
</table>
<p><a href="catalog.php">Continue Shopping</a> or
<a href="<?php echo $_SERVER['PHP_SELF']; ?>?empty=1">Empty your
  cart</a></p>
</body>
</html>
```

Summary

In this chapter, you learned about the two main methods of creating persistent variables—those variables that continue to exist from page to page in PHP. The first stores the variable in the visitor's browser in the form of a **cookie**. By default, cookies terminate at the end of the browser session, but by specifying an expiry time, they can be preserved indefinitely. Unfortunately, cookies are fairly unreliable because you have no way of knowing when the browser might delete your cookies, and because some users configure their browsers to disable cookies. Obviously, cookies are not something that should be relied upon.

Sessions, on the other hand, free you from all the limitations of cookies. Their functioning doesn't rely on cookies, and they let you store an unlimited number of potentially large variables. Sessions are an essential building block in modern ecommerce applications, as we demonstrated in our simple shopping cart example.

12

Structured PHP Programming

Techniques to better **structure your code** are useful in all but the simplest of PHP projects. The PHP language offers many facilities to help you do this, the most powerful being its object oriented programming (OOP) features, which are explored in depth in *The PHP Anthology: Object Oriented PHP Solutions*[1] by Harry Fuecks. OOP is a big topic, and requires you to change drastically the way you think about solving problems in PHP. Thankfully, the more basic features of PHP already offer many opportunities for structuring your code.

In this chapter, I'll explore some *simple* ways to keep your code **manageable** and **maintainable** without requiring you to become a programming wizard.

What is Structured Code?

Structured code is an umbrella term that I'll use throughout this chapter to describe code that has been written with organization in mind.

Up until this point, most of our attention has been trained on what PHP can do for us, and what commands we need to use to get things done. In every case, I've tried to present the most straightforward way to tackle any problem, and if an example did what we wanted it to do, it was considered successful.

---

[1] http://www.sitepoint.com/books/phpant1/

In the real world, though, your experience with a piece of code won't end with you getting it to work. Over time, you'll need to revisit working code to make changes dictated by new requirements and evolving technology. Often, you'll also spot opportunities to reuse some old code in another project. These activities can be incredibly tedious and even aggravating if your code was written to "just work." Structured code won't run any better than unstructured code, but, as we'll see, it's a whole lot easier to work with!

Entire books have been dedicated to structured code—most famously, *Design Patterns* (Addison-Wesley, ISBN: 0-321-12742-0) by "the Gang of Four"—but it doesn't have to take months of research to understand the fundamentals. With a few handy features of the PHP language, you can begin to write structured code today.

The Need for Structured Code

Before I hit you with a pile of advice on how to organize your code, allow me to explain and illustrate the perils of relying on unstructured code for nontrivial PHP projects. If you have been involved in a practical PHP project of any kind, chances are that you will be painfully familiar with at least one of these issues:

Too Much Code

From one perspective, the whole point of server-side languages like PHP is to reduce the sheer quantity of code that goes into your average Website. Consider that before the advent of server-side programming, a site with 1,000 jokes would typically consist of at least 1,000 files, each containing the HTML code to display one article in a Web browser. As a PHP developer, you could be forgiven for finding it hard to believe Websites were ever built that way.

Thanks to PHP, you can dump all that raw content into a nice, efficient database and build the site with a mere handful of PHP files. Instead of a file for every joke, you can have *one* file for *all* jokes!

Why, then, do so many PHP developers fall into the trap of writing the same code over and over again when dealing with pieces of PHP code that are useful in several places on a site? For example, to display a "Top 10 Jokes" listing on every page of a site, many PHP developers would copy the code to fetch that list from the database into each of the PHP files that make up the site!

Structured code techniques let you write the code once and share it between the different PHP files that need it. Not only does this cut down on the volume of code that you have to write, but when it comes time to make changes to your site, this approach saves you having to search endlessly through your files looking for every occurrence of the fragment you need to change.

Finding What You Need

As interpreted scripting languages go, PHP is fast. An average Web server can blaze through thousands of lines of PHP code in the blink of an eye. Your average Web *developer*, on the other hand, reads code a wee bit slower. I've had to maintain more than one massive PHP script in my time, and when faced with a swirling miasma of unstructured code that does twenty different things, I curse the name of the original developer (yes, even when it was me!).

Just as it's easier to find a plumber in the Yellow Pages thanks to the alphabetized categories, it's easier to work on a PHP site when the code is broken up into chunks, each of which has a specific job to do. Instead of spending half your development time squinting at your monitor as you scroll up and down through monolithic scripts composed of PHP intertwined with HTML, structured code will ensure that you can always find the specific bit you want to work on.

Understanding How It Works

Have you ever come back to a project after several months (or years!) of working on something else? If that project was written with poorly structured code, you probably felt like a squirrel in winter that forgot where it buried all its acorns! The same thing can happen in team situations when you need to work on code that was originally written by someone else.

The issues inherent in unstructured code are magnified many times over when you are not intimately familiar with the code in question. Judicious placement of comments in the code can help, but in the maintenance of large projects, it can be a challenge even to find the *comments* you're interested in, let alone the specific lines of code.

Structured code has the admirable quality of being largely self-documenting. The code that controls all database access for your site will likely be called `db.inc.php`. The database query that fetches the top ten jokes for display on your home page will control the number of records it fetches with a constant called `TOP_JOKES_COUNT`. You'll know a "Log out" link will only display when a user is logged in because it's surrounded by an `if` statement with the `loggedIn` function as its condition.

Most developers hate breaking stride to write comments. Since structured code is most often self-explanatory, fewer pesky comments are needed!

My mission in this chapter is to supply some simple tools you can use to avoid the problems described above in any small to medium-sized PHP project.

Realize that, as the complexity of a project increases, so does the complexity of the measures you need to take to protect yourself from these snafus. As a result, getting the full benefit of this book will require some discipline on your part. I can only show you the hammer; I can't keep you from pounding in nails with your forehead!

Include Files

Often, even very simple PHP-based Websites need the same piece of code in several places. **Include files** (also known as just **includes**) save you from having to write the same code over and over again in such cases.

On database driven Websites, for example, almost every PHP script must establish a database connection as its first order of business. At its simplest, the code for establishing that connection will look something like this:

```
$dbcnx = @mysql_connect('localhost', 'root', 'mypasswd');
if (!$dbcnx) {
  exit('Error connecting to the site database.');
}
if (!@mysql_select_db('ijdb', $dbcnx)) {
  exit('Error opening the site database.');
}
```

At seven lines long, it's not the most cumbersome chunk of code ever, but having to type it at the top of every page can get annoying in a hurry. Many new PHP developers will often omit essential error checking (e.g. by leaving out the two exit() lines in the above) to save typing, which can result in a lot of lost time looking for the cause when an error *does* occur. Others will make heavy use of the clipboard to copy pieces of code like this from existing scripts for use in new ones. Some even use features of their text editor software to store useful pieces of code like this as "snippets" for frequent use.

But what happens when the database password, or some other detail of the code changes? Suddenly you're on a treasure hunt to find every occurrence of the code in your site and make the necessary change—a task that can be especially frustrating if you've used several variations of the code that you need to track down and update.

Figure 12.1. Include files allow several scripts to share common code.

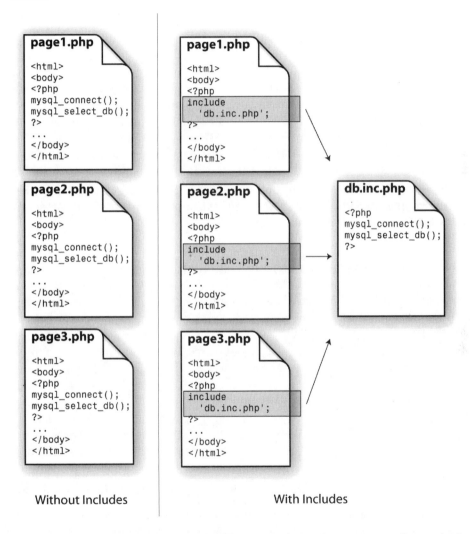

Without Includes | With Includes

Figure 12.1 illustrates how include files can help in this situation. Instead of repeating the code fragment in every file that needs it, write it just once in a separate file, known as an **include file**. That file can then be **included** in any other PHP files that need to use it!

Let's go back to our database connection example to see how this works in detail. First, create a file called db.inc.php[1] and place the database connection code inside it.

File: **db.inc.php**

```php
<?php
$dbcnx = @mysql_pconnect('localhost', 'root', 'mypasswd');
if (!$dbcnx) {
  exit('Error connecting to the site database.');
}
if (!@mysql_select_db('database', $dbcnx)) {
  exit('Error opening the site database.');
}
?>
```

As you can see, include files are just like normal PHP files, but typically they contain snippets of code that are only useful within the context of a larger script. Here's how you can put db.inc.php to use:

File: **top10.php**

```php
<!DOCTYPE html PUBLIC "-//W3C//DTD XHTML 1.0 Strict//EN"
  "http://www.w3.org/TR/xhtml1/DTD/xhtml1-strict.dtd">
<html xmlns="http://www.w3.org/1999/xhtml">
<head>
<title>Top 10 Jokes</title>
<meta http-equiv="Content-Type"
  content="text/html; charset=iso-8859-1" />
</head>
<body>
<p>The top 10 jokes on our site are:</p>
<?php
include 'db.inc.php';

$result = @mysql_query(
```

---

[1] The current convention is to name include files with a .inc.php extension. This allows you easily to identify them among ordinary PHP scripts, while at the same time ensuring that they are identified and processed as PHP scripts by the Web server and by whatever development tools you use. In practice, you can name include files however you like. Previously, it was common to simply give include files a .inc extension, but unless the Web server was specifically configured to process such files as PHP scripts or to protect them from being downloaded, users who guessed the names of your include files could download them as plain text and gain access to sensitive information, such as database passwords, that appeared in the source code.

```
    "SELECT * FROM joke ORDER BY timesviewed DESC LIMIT 10");
if (!$result) {
  exit('Error fetching jokes from the site database.');
}
while ($joke = mysql_fetch_array($result)) {
  echo '<p>' . $joke['joketext'] . '</p>';
}
?>
</body>
</html>
```

As you can see, the code to include a file is a simple one-liner:

File: **top10.php** (excerpt)

```
include 'db.inc.php';
```

You simply type `include`, followed by the name of the file to include as a text string.[2] You can of course use a variable or a more complex PHP expression instead of a string, but that flexibility is rarely needed.

When PHP encounters the `include` statement, it puts the current script on hold and runs the specified PHP script. When it's finished, it returns to the original script and picks up where it left off.

Included scripts have access to any variables that exist within the including script when the include occurs, and vice-versa. This is illustrated in the following example, in which the include file `calculate-area.inc.php` uses the $x and $y variables from `show-area.php` to calculate the value of $total, then `show-area.php` outputs that value:

File: **show-area.php**

```
<!DOCTYPE html PUBLIC "-//W3C//DTD XHTML 1.0 Strict//EN"
  "http://www.w3.org/TR/xhtml1/DTD/xhtml1-strict.dtd">
<html xmlns="http://www.w3.org/1999/xhtml">
<head>
<title>Area Example</title>
<meta http-equiv="Content-Type"
  content="text/html; charset=iso-8859-1" />
</head>
<body>
<?php
```

---

[2]You will often see includes coded with parentheses surrounding the file name, as if `include` were a function. These parentheses, when used, only serve to complicate the file name expression, and are therefore not used in this book. The same goes for `echo`, another popular one-liner.

```
$x = 3;
$y = 5;
include 'calculate-area.inc.php';
echo "<p>Area: $area</p>"; // Outputs 15
?>
</body>
</html>
```

File: **calculate-area.inc.php**

```
<?php
$area = $x * $y;
?>
```

While potentially useful, you usually should avoid deliberately sharing variables across include files in this way, because it can make your code difficult to understand. In the example above, a developer looking at show-area.php can't immediately tell what $x and $y are for, nor is it obvious where $area is getting its value.

It's also all too easy inadvertently to overwrite an important variable in the main file by setting it in the include file. If you must use variables within an include file, try to choose variable names that aren't likely to clash with including scripts. A good technique is to start variable names with an underscore when they're not meant for use outside the include file (e.g. $_variable).

Include files are the simplest way to structure PHP code. Because of their simplicity, they are also the most widely used method. Even very simple Web applications can benefit greatly from the use of include files.

Types of Includes

The include statement shown above is actually only one of four statements that you can use to include another PHP file in a currently-running script:

☐ include

☐ require

☐ include_once

☐ require_once

include and require are almost identical. The only difference between them is what happens when the specified file cannot be included (i.e. if it does not exist, or if the Web server doesn't have permission to read it). With include, a warning is displayed[3] and the script continues to run. With require, an error is displayed and the script stops.

In general, therefore, you should use require whenever the main script will not work without the script to be included. I do recommend using include whenever possible, however. Even if the db.inc.php file for your site cannot be loaded, for example, you might still want to let the script for your front page continue to load. None of the content from the database will display, but the user might be able to use the Contact Us link at the bottom of the page to let you know about the problem!

include_once and require_once work just like include and require, respectively, but if the specified file has already been included (using *any* of the four statements described here) at least once for the page request, the statement will be ignored. This is handy for include files that do something that only needs to be done once, like connecting to the database.

Figure 12.2 shows include_once in action. In the figure, index.php includes two files: head.inc.php and list.inc.php. Both of these files use include_once to include db.inc.php, as they both need a database connection in order to do their job. As shown, PHP will ignore the attempt to include db.inc.php in list.inc.php because the file was already included in head.inc.php. As a result, only one database connection is created.

---

[3]In production environments, warnings and errors are usually disabled in php.ini. In such environments, a failed include has no visible effect (aside from the lack of whatever content would normally have been generated by the include file), while a failed require causes the page to stop at the point of failure. When a failed require occurs before any content is sent to the browser, the unlucky user will see nothing but a blank page!

Figure 12.2. Use `include_once` to avoid opening a second database connection.

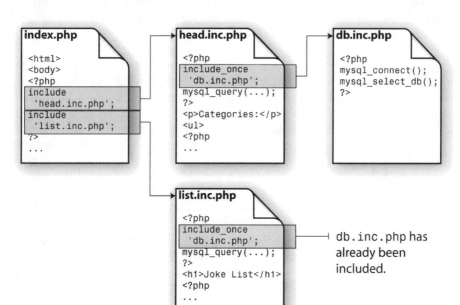

`include_once` and `require_once` are also useful for loading function libraries, as we'll see in the section called "Custom Functions and Function Libraries".

Including HTML Content

The concept of include files came long before PHP. If you're an old codger like me (which, in the Web world, means you're over 25), you may have experimented with Server-Side Includes (SSIs). A feature of just about every Web server out there, SSIs let you put commonly-used snippets of HTML (and JavaScript, and CSS) into include files that you can then use in multiple pages.

In PHP, as we've seen, include files most commonly contain PHP code. But you don't *have* to put PHP code in your include files. If you like, an include file can contain strictly static HTML. This is most useful for sharing common design elements across your site, such as a copyright notice to appear at the bottom of every page.

File: **footer.inc.php**

```
<div id="footer">
  The contents of this webpage are copyright &copy; 1998 - 2005
  SitePoint Pty. Ltd. All Rights Reserved.
</div>
```

File: **staticinclude.php**

```
<!DOCTYPE html PUBLIC "-//W3C//DTD XHTML 1.0 Strict//EN"
  "http://www.w3.org/TR/xhtml1/DTD/xhtml1-strict.dtd">
<html xmlns="http://www.w3.org/1999/xhtml">
<head>
<title>A Sample Page</title>
<meta http-equiv="content-type"
  content="text/html; charset=iso-8859-1" />
</head>
<body>
<p id="main">
  This page uses a static include to display a standard copyright
  notice below.
</p>
<?php include 'footer.inc.php'; ?>
</body>
</html>
```

Figure 12.3 shows what the page looks like in the browser.

Figure 12.3. A static include displays the site's copyright notice.

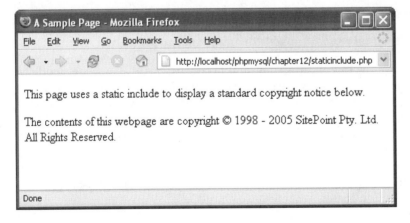

Now, each year (or every few months, if your company gets bought out often!) all you need to do to update your copyright notice is to edit `footer.inc.php`. No more time-consuming and error-prone find-and-replace operations!

Of course, if you *really* want to make your life easy, you can just let PHP do the work for you:

```
<p id="footer">
  The contents of this webpage are copyright &copy; 1998 -
  <?php echo date('Y'); ?> SitePoint Pty. Ltd. All Rights
  Reserved.
</p>
```

Locating Include Files

In all of the examples I've shown you so far, I have assumed that the include file is located in the same directory on your Web server as the file(s) that use it. Often, this is not a valid assumption! On many sites, you'll want to share include files among scripts that span potentially complex directory structures. So the question is, when the include file is *not* in the same directory, how does a PHP script find it?

The most obvious method is to specify the location of the include file as an **absolute path**. Here's how this would look on a Windows server[4]:

```
<?php include 'c:/inetpub/wwwroot/includes/db.inc.php'; ?>
```

And here's the code on a Linux server:

```
<?php include '/usr/local/apache/htdocs/includes/db.inc.php'; ?>
```

While this method will work, it is undesirable because it ties your site's code to your Web server configuration. Ideally, you should be able to drop your PHP-based Website on any PHP-enabled Web server and just watch it run. This is especially important because many developers will build a site on one server, then deploy it publicly on a different server. You can't do that if your code refers to drives and directories that are specific to one particular server. And, even if you *do* have the luxury of working on a single server, you'll be kicking yourself if you ever need to move your Website to another drive/directory on that server.

---

[4] I recommend always using forward slashes in your paths, even when you are working with a Windows server. PHP is smart enough to do the conversion for you, and using forward slashes saves you from having to type double-backslashes (\ \ ) to represent single backslashes in PHP strings.

A better method is to let PHP keep track of the **document root**[5] of your Web server, then specify the path from that location. In any PHP script, you can get the document root of your Web server using $_SERVER['DOCUMENT_ROOT']. Here's an example:

```
<?php include $_SERVER['DOCUMENT_ROOT'] . '/includes/db.inc.php';
?>
```

This will work both on Windows and Linux servers[6] based on Apache and Internet Information Services (IIS). But there's still room for improvement here...

So far, I've assumed that db.inc.php would be placed in a directory called includes located in the document root of your site. Now, if one day you decided to change the name of that directory, or move it to another location on your site, you would yet again be stuck hunting down every mention of the directory in all of your PHP files!

Also, for security reasons[7], you'll often want to put your include files in a directory located *outside* the document root! It doesn't make much sense to specify the location of an include file using the document root if it isn't *in* the document root.

The solution to these final problems is PHP's **include path**, which is a list of directories that PHP will search when it is looking for an include file. The default include path in PHP is .;c:/php/PEAR on Windows and .:/usr/local/php/lib/php on Linux. As you can see, on Windows the directories in the list are separated by semicolons (;), whereas on Linux they are separated by colons (:).

---

[5]The document root is the directory on your server that corresponds to the root directory of your Website. For example, to make index.php available at http://www.example.com/index.php, you would have to place it in the document root directory on the www.example.com Web server.

[6]The one place where you can't count on $_SERVER['DOCUMENT_ROOT'] is on a server running the Common Gateway Interface (CGI) version of PHP. The CGI specification does not require the Web server to inform PHP of the document root directory for the site, so this value will usually be absent on such configurations. Thankfully, CGI installations of PHP are increasingly rare, and should certainly be avoided in production environments.

[7]Include files will often contain sensitive information such as database passwords, which you don't want to become visible as plain text if the PHP support on your Web server should inadvertently become disabled. Placing those files outside the document root of your site ensures that they can never be directly accessed by a browser.

You can set the include path yourself by setting the include_path value in your server's php.ini file, but the value you specify should always begin with the two directories suggested by the default value:

.	The special file name . refers to the current directory. It's this that allows PHP to find include files that are in the current directory, or that you load by specifying a path relative to the current directory.
The PEAR Library	The PHP Extension and Application Repository (PEAR) is a system that automatically extends the capabilities of PHP. For this system to work, the PEAR library directory needs to be in the PHP include path. On Windows, the PEAR library directory is the PEAR subdirectory of your PHP installation. On Linux, it is the lib/php subdirectory of your PHP installation.

So, using a Windows server on which PHP is installed in C:\php, you can tell PHP to look for include files in C:\InetPub\phpinclude by setting the include_path in php.ini as follows:

```
include_path = ".;c:/php/PEAR;c:/InetPub/phpinclude"
```

Using a Linux server on which PHP is installed in /usr/local/php, you can tell PHP to look for include files in /home/www/phpinclude by setting the include_path in php.ini as follows:

```
include_path = ".:/usr/local/php/lib/php:/home/www/phpinclude"
```

With this type of configuration, you can then drop the db.inc.php file from the examples above into the phpinclude directory and use it in any of your site's PHP scripts as follows:

```
<?php include 'db.inc.php'; ?>
```

> **Directory-specific `include_path` settings on Apache**
>
> There are times when it can be inconvenient to specify the `include_path` you need in your Web server's `php.ini` file. You might only need a particular directory to be in PHP's include path for a certain area of your site, for example, or you might host your site with a company that does not allow you to modify `php.ini`.
>
> If you are running PHP on an Apache Web server, you can actually set an include path that will apply only to a given directory and its subdirectories. You do this by creating a file called `.htaccess` in the directory in question. The contents of the file should be as follows:
>
> `php_value include_path ".:/usr/local/php:/…/phpinclude"`
>
> Simply modify the portion shown in bold to specify the include path that will apply to PHP scripts in this directory and its subdirectories.
>
> For more information on directory-specific PHP settings, refer to the Configuration section of the PHP manual[2].

Returning from Includes

In PHP, a `return` statement can be used in include files to jump back into the main file immediately. It's sort of an ejection seat for includes!

In the following example, you can see the code for an include file (options.inc.php) that will display the main menu for a newsletter management system. In a real application, each of the menu items would be a hyperlink, but this will do for our purposes. The menu contains a list of options for all users, as well as a second list of options for administrators only.

File: **options.inc.php**

```
<h2>User Options</h2>
<ul class="menu">
  <li>Subscribe</li>
  <li>Unsubscribe</li>
  <li>View Archives</li>
</ul>
<?php
if (!$administrator) {
  return;
}
```

---

[2] http://www.php.net/configuration.changes

```
?>
<h2>Administrator Options</h2>
<ul class="menu">
  <li>Manage List</li>
  <li>Create an Issue</li>
  <li>Send an Issue</li>
  <li>Edit Template</li>
</ul>
```

Just before the administrator options, there is a fragment of PHP code that checks the value of the $administrator variable. If it's not true, the include file will return, immediately returning control to the main file. Therefore, the administrator options will not be visible unless $administrator is true.

Here's a sample script that lets you set the $administrator variable through the query string:

File: **mainmenu.php**

```
<!DOCTYPE html PUBLIC "-//W3C//DTD XHTML 1.0 Strict//EN"
  "http://www.w3.org/TR/xhtml1/DTD/xhtml1-strict.dtd">
<html xmlns="http://www.w3.org/1999/xhtml">
<head>
<title>A Sample Page</title>
<meta http-equiv="Content-Type"
  content="text/html; charset=iso-8859-1" />
</head>
<body>
<?php
// For demonstration purposes
$administrator = $_GET['administrator'];

include 'options.inc.php';
?>
</body>
</html>
```

Figure 12.4 shows the output of mainmenu.php with and without administrator=1 in the query string.

Figure 12.4. The menu displays with and without administrator options.

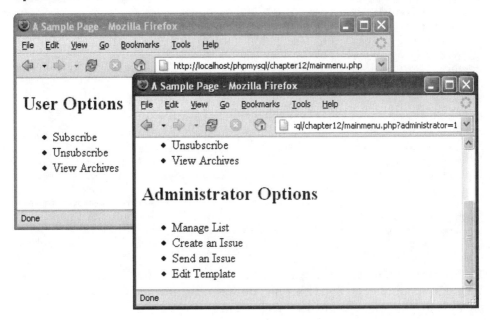

Of course, it would have been just as easy to put the `if` statement around the administrator options in `options.inc.php`, and we could have added more stuff after the administrator options for all users to see. For this reason, the `return` statement is rarely used to bail out of an include file early. Where it *is* useful is in returning a value to the main script.

Previously, I demonstrated that you could share variables between a PHP script and the include files it uses. I showed how this facility could be used to perform a calculation with an include file and then use that calculation in the main file. One problem with this technique is that the include file runs the risk of overwriting a variable (in the example, `$area`) that might already exist in the main PHP file.

The `return` statement provides a neat solution to this problem, as shown in the following code:

File: **show-area-return.php**

```
<!DOCTYPE html PUBLIC "-//W3C//DTD XHTML 1.0 Strict//EN"
  "http://www.w3.org/TR/xhtml1/DTD/xhtml1-strict.dtd">
```

```
<html xmlns="http://www.w3.org/1999/xhtml">
<head>
<title>Area Example</title>
<meta http-equiv="Content-Type"
  content="text/html; charset=iso-8859-1" />
</head>
<body>
<?php
$x = 3;
$y = 5;
$area = include 'calculate-area-return.inc.php';
echo "<p>Area: $area</p>"; // Outputs 15
?>
</body>
</html>
```

File: **calculate-area-return.inc.php**

```
<?php
return $x * $y;
?>
```

In this variation, we are once again calculating an area based on two variables in the main script: $x and $y. This time, however, the include file doesn't create a variable to store the calculated value. Instead, is uses a `return` statement to send it back to the main script.

File: **calculate-area-return.inc.php (excerpt)**

```
return $x * $y;
```

As shown here, a `return` statement can include a value to be sent back to the main script. As you might expect, this value is returned by the `include`, `require`, `include_once`, or `require_once` statement. In our example, we store that value in a variable ($area) so that we can print it out:

File: **show-area-return.php (excerpt)**

```
$area = include 'calculate-area-return.inc.php';
```

While quite subtle, this change means that the include file doesn't need to set a variable that may already be used by the main script in order to give the result of the calculation. The creation of variables is left up to the main script, which is as it should be.

Custom Functions and Function Libraries

By this point, you're probably pretty comfortable with the idea of **functions**. A function is a piece of functionality that you can invoke at will, usually providing one or more **arguments** for it to use, and often getting a **return value** back as a result. You can use PHP's vast library of functions to do just about anything a PHP script could ever be asked to do, from connecting to a database (`mysql_connect`) to generating graphics on the fly (`imagecreatetruecolor`).

But what you may *not* know is that you can create functions of your own! **Custom functions**, once defined, work just like PHP's built-in functions, and they can do anything a normal PHP script can do.

To start you off on familiar ground, let me show you a very simple case. In the previous section, I showed how you could use an include file to calculate a rectangular area based on two variables (`$x` and `$y`) in the main script. Using a `return` statement allowed the include file to pass the calculated value back to the main script for it to use as it pleased. The relevant code in the main script looked like this:

File: **show-area-return.php** (excerpt)

```
$x = 3;
$y = 5;
$area = include 'calculate-area-return.inc.php';
echo "<p>Area: $area</p>"; // Outputs 15
```

Now, although this is pretty convenient, using an include file for this calculation forces us to use the variable names that the include file is expecting (`$x` and `$y` in this case). Not only is this an annoying constraint, but it means that you need superhuman memory (or enough patience to go snooping through the code of your include files) to recall the names of the variables every time you perform the calculation! In even this very straightforward example, I, for one, would have a hard time remembering if the variables had to be named `$x` and `$y` or `$width` and `$height`.

Wouldn't it be simpler if we just had a function called `area` that calculated the area, given any two numbers?

File: **show-area-function.php** (excerpt)

```
$area = area(3, 5);
echo "<p>Area: $area</p>"; // Outputs 15
```

Well, as it happens, PHP *doesn't* have a built-in `area` function, but that needn't stop clever PHP programmers like you and me! We can just roll up our sleeves and write the function ourselves:

File: **show-area-function.php** (excerpt)

```
function area($x, $y) {
  return $x * $y;
}
```

Now, if you think of this as a replacement for our old include file (`calculate-area-return.inc.php`), it shouldn't look *too* intimidating. In fact, the line that does all the work (`return $x * $y;`) is the exact same code that we had in that include file. The first line might have you a bit worried, though:

```
function area($x, $y) {
```

The keyword `function` tells PHP that we wish to define a new function for use in the current script. Then, we supply the function with a name (in this case, `area`). Function names operate under the same rules as variable names—they are case-sensitive, must start with a letter or an underscore (_), and may contain letters, numbers, and underscores—except of course that they aren't prefixed with a dollar sign. Instead, function names are always followed by a set of parentheses (()), which may or may not be empty.

The parentheses that follow a function name enclose the list of parameters that the function will accept. You should already be familiar with this from your experience with PHP's built-in functions; for example, when you use `mysql_connect` to connect to your database, you provide the host name, user name, and password for the connection as parameters within the parentheses.

When declaring a custom function, instead of giving a list of values for the parameters, you give a list of variable names. In this example, we list two variables: `$x` and `$y`. When the function is called, it will therefore expect to be given two parameters. The value of the first parameter will be assigned to `$x`, while the value of the second will be assigned to `$y`. Those variables can then be used to perform the calculation within the function.

Speaking of calculations, the last part of a function definition is the code that performs the calculation—or does whatever else the function is supposed to do. That code must be enclosed in a set of braces ({}). You can think of the code within those braces as a miniature PHP script. That's why the code for this example looks so much like the code for the include file that did the same job!

The following example shows how this all fits together. At the top of the script, I have defined the `area` function as I have just shown. You can actually define a function at any point in the script (even after the code that uses it), but common practice is to define everything you can at the top of the script so that you can find all your definitions in one place. Then, further down in the script, you can see the code that uses the function, just as if it were built into PHP itself.

File: **show-area-function.php**

```php
<?php
function area($x, $y)
{
  return $x * $y;
}
?>
<!DOCTYPE html PUBLIC "-//W3C//DTD XHTML 1.0 Strict//EN"
  "http://www.w3.org/TR/xhtml1/DTD/xhtml1-strict.dtd">
<html xmlns="http://www.w3.org/1999/xhtml">
<head>
<title> Area Example </title>
<meta http-equiv="Content-Type"
  content="text/html; charset=iso-8859-1" />
</head>
<body>
<?php
$area = area(3, 5);
echo "<p>Area: $area</p>"; // Outputs 15
?>
</body>
</html>
```

But, wait—we've lost something here. The main advantage of the include file method we used previously was that if multiple pages needed to calculate the area of a rectangle (don't worry, a less mundane example is on the way!), they wouldn't both need to repeat the code to do so. But, since the above code incorporates the area-calculating code in the script, we've lost that advantage. The solution is to combine both techniques—include files and functions—to create a **function library**.

A function library is simply an include file that only contains function definitions. The following example shows how this works. Instead of defining the function in the main script, we define it in an include file. To demonstrate how an include file can serve as a library of related functions, I've defined a second function that calculates the perimeter of a rectangle, in addition to the by-now-familiar `area`.

File: **rect-geometry.inc.php**

```php
<?php
function area($x, $y) {
  return $x * $y;
}

function perimeter($x, $y)
{
  return ($x + $y) * 2;
}
?>
```

To use any of the functions in this file, a PHP script need only include it with include_once (or require_once if the functions are critical to the script). Do not use include or require; as explained in the section called "Types of Includes", that would risk defining the functions in the library more than once and covering the user's screen with PHP warnings. As shown in the example, where show-area-lib.php uses the area function, it is standard practice (but not required!) to include your function libraries at the top of the script, so you can quickly see which function libraries are used by any particular script.

File: **show-area-lib.php**

```php
<?php
include_once 'rect-geometry.inc.php';
?>
<!DOCTYPE html PUBLIC "-//W3C//DTD XHTML 1.0 Strict//EN"
   "http://www.w3.org/TR/xhtml1/DTD/xhtml1-strict.dtd">
<html xmlns="http://www.w3.org/1999/xhtml">
<head>
<title>Area Example</title>
<meta http-equiv="Content-Type"
   content="text/html; charset=iso-8859-1" />
</head>
<body>
<?php
$area = area(3, 5);
echo "<p>Area: $area</p>"; // Outputs 15
?>
</body>
</html>
```

Variable Scope and Global Access

One big difference between custom functions and include files is the concept of **variable scope**. As I explained in the section called "Include Files", any variable that exists in the main script will be available, and can be changed in the include file. While sometimes this is useful, more often it's a pain in the neck. Unintentionally overwriting one of the main script's variables in an include file is a common cause of error—and one that can take a long time to track down and fix! To avoid such problems, you need to remember not only the variable names in the script you're working on, but also any that exist in the include files your script uses.

Functions protect you from such problems. Variables created inside a function (including any argument variables) exist only within that function, and disappear when the function is complete. In programmer-speak, the **scope** of these variables is the function—they are said to have **function scope**. In contrast, variables created in the main script, outside of any function, are not available inside of functions. The scope of these variables is the main script, and they are said to have **global scope**.

Okay, but beyond the fancy names, what does this really *mean* for us? It means that you can have a variable called, say, $x in your main script, and another variable called $x in your function, and PHP will treat them as two entirely separate variables! Perhaps more usefully, you can have two different functions, each using the same variable names, and they won't interfere with each other because their variables are kept separate by their scope!

Don't believe me? I don't blame you—I was a little suspicious about this when I first learned it, too! But check out this example. We have a function called twice that takes one parameter ($x), multiplies it by two, and then returns its new value. Back in the main script, we create a variable (also $x) with an initial value, then pass it as a parameter to twice. The result is stored in $y; then, both $x and $y are displayed.

File: **scopedemo.php (excerpt)**

```php
<?php
  function twice($x)
  {
    $x = 2 * $x;
    return $x;
  }
```

```
  $x = 5;
  echo "<p>Twice $x ";
  $y = twice($x);
  echo "is not $x, it's $y!";
?>
```

Here's the output:

```
Twice 5 is not 5, it's 10!
```

If the $x in twice were the same variable as the $x in the main script, then, be-cause the function assigned it a new value ($x = 2 * $x;), we would expect its value to be 10 in the second echo statement. As you can see, however, the value of the global-scope $x remains 5, even though the function-scope $x was set to 10. They are indeed two separate variables!

On some occasions you may actually *want* to use a global-scope variable (**global variable** for short) inside one of your functions. For example, if your db.inc.php file creates a database connection for use by your script, you might want to put the connection identifier in a global variable named $dbcnx, which you would then use in any function that needed to access the database. Disregarding variable scope, here's how you might write such a function:

```
function totaljokes()
{
  $result = @mysql_query('SELECT COUNT(*) FROM joke', $dbcnx);
  if (!$result) {
    exit('Database error counting users!');
  }
  return mysql_result($result, 0);
}
```

The problem here is that the global variable $dbcnx, shown in bold, will not be available within the scope of the function. Now, of course you could just add a parameter to the **totaljokes** function and send it the connection identifier that way, but having to pass the identifier to every function that needs database access would be quite tedious.

Instead, let's use the global variable directly within our function. There are two ways to do this. The first is to **import** the global variable into the function's scope:

```
function totaljokes()
{
  global $dbcnx;
```

```
$result = @mysql_query('SELECT COUNT(*) FROM joke', $dbcnx);
if (!$result) {
  exit('Database error counting users!');
}
return mysql_result($result, 0);
}
```

The `global` statement, shown here in bold, lets you give a list of global variables (separated by commas, if you want to import more than one) that you want to make available within the function. Programmers call this importing a variable. This is different from passing the variable as a parameter, because if you modify an imported variable inside the function, the value of the variable changes outside the function, too.

The alternative to importing the variable is to use the `$GLOBALS` array:

```
function totaljokes()
{
  $result = @mysql_query('SELECT COUNT(*) FROM joke',
      $GLOBALS['dbcnx']);
  if (!$result) {
    exit('Database error counting users!');
  }
  return mysql_result($result, 0);
}
```

As you can see, all we've done here is replace `$dbcnx` with `$GLOBALS['dbcnx']`. The special PHP array `$GLOBALS` is available across all scopes (for this reason, it is known as a **super-global**), and contains an entry for every variable in the global scope. You can therefore access any global variable within a function as `$GLOBALS['name']`, where *name* is the name of the global variable (without a dollar sign). The advantage of using `$GLOBALS` is that you can still create a function-scope variable called `$dbcnx` if you want.

Other special PHP arrays that are super-global, and are therefore accessible inside functions, include `$_SERVER`, `$_GET`, `$_POST`, `$_COOKIE`, `$_FILES`, `$_ENV`, `$_REQUEST`, and `$_SESSION`. See the PHP Manual[3] for full details.

One final detail regarding variable scope in PHP remains to be discussed: **static variables**. The purpose of these is best explained with an example:

---

[3] http://www.php.net/manual/en/language.variables.predefined.php

File: **donate-broken.php** (excerpt)

```php
<?php
function donate()
{
  $donations = 0;
  ++$donations;
  echo "You have made $donations donation(s)!<br />";
}

donate();
donate();
donate();
?>
```

Here's the output of this script:

```
You have made 1 donation(s)!
You have made 1 donation(s)!
You have made 1 donation(s)!
```

The intent of the **donate** function in this example is to keep track of the number of donations that had been made in the script. As you can see from the output, however, it doesn't quite work. The problem is that, not only are variables inside a function not visible outside that function, they are destroyed each time the function finishes running! Each time **donate** is run, therefore, $donations starts back at zero.

Static variables are just like normal function variables, except they are not destroyed when the function terminates. That is *not* to say they are available outside the function after it is called, but they *will* still exist the next time the function runs. This tweaked version of the broken example above shows how to make $donations static.

File: **donate.php** (excerpt)

```php
<?php
function donate()
{
  static $donations = 0;
  ++$donations;
  echo "You have made $donations donation(s)!<br />";
}

donate();
donate();
```

```
donate();
?>
```

And the output:

```
You have made 1 donation(s)!
You have made 2 donation(s)!
You have made 3 donation(s)!
```

With this change, `$donations` is only created with a value of 0 the first time the function is called. The second and third times, the previous value of the variable is used, and this is reflected in the output of the script.

Optional and Unlimited Arguments

Some of the built-in PHP functions you have used may have had optional arguments (e.g. `mysql_query` takes an optional connection identifier), while others may have let you give as many arguments as you wanted (e.g. `array` creates an array out of the arguments you pass it, be there zero or hundreds). Both of these features are available for your custom functions.

To make a parameter optional, you need to assign it a default value—that is, the value it should get when one is not specified by the function call. For example, let's look back at our shockingly complex `area` function:

File: **rect-geometry.inc.php (excerpt)**

```
function area($x, $y)
{
  return $x * $y;
}
```

This is great for finding the area of a rectangle, but what if we have a square—both dimensions are equal? Instead of forcing the developer to pass the same value for both arguments, we can just make the second argument optional:

```
function area($x, $y = -1)
{
  if ($y < 0) {
    $y = $x;
  }
  return $x * $y;
}
```

By adding = -1 after the $y argument in the first line of the function definition, we are telling PHP that the second argument is optional. When the developer exercises this option not to give a second argument, $y will be given a value of -1. In this case, -1 is a convenient choice because the side of a rectangle cannot have a negative length (at least, not where I come from!). I've therefore added an if statement to the function that detects when $y is negative and sets it to match $x so that the return statement that follows will correctly calculate the area of the square. Pretty sneaky, huh?

Note that optional argument(s) must come at the end of the argument list for a function. PHP won't complain if you assign default values to arguments that precede required arguments; it will simply ignore those values.

Creating a function that supports an unlimited number of arguments is only slightly more difficult. Let's look at such a function:

File: **sum-for.php (excerpt)**

```php
function sum()
{
  $numargs = func_num_args();
  $sum = 0;
  for ($i = 0; $i < $numargs; $i++) {
    $sum += func_get_arg($i);
  }
  return $sum;
}

echo sum() . '<br />';
echo sum(1, 1) . '<br />';
echo sum(123, 456, 789) . '<br />';
```

Here's the output:

```
0
2
1368
```

This function, sum, calculates the sum of the arguments you give it. As you can see, the function is defined as if it didn't take any arguments, but it uses the two PHP functions func_num_args and func_get_arg to access the list of arguments it was given. func_num_args gives the number of arguments that were passed to the current function, while func_get_arg retrieves the value of a specific argument (func_get_arg(0) returns the first argument, func_get_arg(1) returns the second, and so on).

If you're good with `for` loops, you can probably see exactly how the `sum` function in the above example works. If you're not, you might be happier with a `foreach` loop:

File: **sum-foreach.php** (excerpt)

```php
function sum()
{
  $sum = 0;
  foreach (func_get_args() as $arg) {
    $sum += $arg;
  }
  return $sum;
}
```

This version uses a third PHP function, `func_get_args`. Instead of a single argument, this function returns *all* of the arguments passed to the function, in the form of an array. I've then used a trusty `foreach` loop to breeze through the array with a minimum of syntactic flotsam.

Feel free to choose whichever method you like—they both work.

Constants

Many PHP scripts rely on values that will never change while they are running. **Constants** provide a useful means of organizing those values so that you need not go hunting through your code when you do need to change them.

For example, let's look back at an example we saw earlier in this chapter. This code will display the top ten jokes in the database:

File: **top10.php**

```php
<!DOCTYPE html PUBLIC "-//W3C//DTD XHTML 1.0 Strict//EN"
  "http://www.w3.org/TR/xhtml1/DTD/xhtml1-strict.dtd">
<html xmlns="http://www.w3.org/1999/xhtml">
<head>
<title>Top 10 Jokes</title>
<meta http-equiv="Content-Type"
  content="text/html; charset=iso-8859-1" />
</head>
<body>
<p>The top 10 jokes on our site are:</p>
<?php
include 'db.inc.php';
```

```
$result = @mysql_query(
    "SELECT * FROM joke ORDER BY timesviewed DESC LIMIT 10");
if (!$result) {
  exit('Error fetching jokes from the site database.');
}
while ($joke = mysql_fetch_array($result)) {
  echo '<p>' . $joke['joketext'] . '</p>';
}
?>
</body>
</html>
```

The number 10 in the SQL query is responsible for setting the number of jokes that will appear. While this may be obvious when looking at this isolated fragment of code, finding it in among the complete code of, say, your site's front page is a different matter. If one day you decided you wanted five news items on the front page of your site instead of ten, finding the query and tweaking it could be quite arduous. Furthermore, whenever you changed the number of articles displayed, you would also need to remember to update the heading above the list.

By using a constant for the number of jokes to be displayed, we can alleviate all of these problems:

File: **top10-constant.php**

```
<?php
  define('TOP_JOKES_COUNT', 10);
?>
<!DOCTYPE html PUBLIC "-//W3C//DTD XHTML 1.0 Strict//EN"
  "http://www.w3.org/TR/xhtml1/DTD/xhtml1-strict.dtd">
<html xmlns="http://www.w3.org/1999/xhtml">
<head>
<title>Top <?php echo TOP_JOKES_COUNT; ?> Jokes</title>
<meta http-equiv="Content-Type"
  content="text/html; charset=iso-8859-1" />
</head>
<body>
<p>The top <?php echo TOP_JOKES_COUNT; ?> jokes on our site
    are:</p>
<?php
include 'db.inc.php';

$result = @mysql_query(
    "SELECT * FROM joke ORDER BY timesviewed DESC LIMIT " .
    TOP_JOKES_COUNT);
```

```
if (!$result) {
  exit('Error fetching jokes from the site database.');
}
while ($joke = mysql_fetch_array($result)) {
  echo '<p>' . $joke['joketext'] . '</p>';
}
?>
</body>
</html>
```

At the top of our code[8], we use the built-in PHP function `define` to create a constant named `TOP_JOKES_COUNT` with a value of 10. We then use that constant in the script for the SQL query, the headline, and the title of the page.

Constant names are subject to the same rules as variable names (a letter or underscore followed by a series of letters, underscores, or numbers), except that they don't start with a dollar sign. Convention further dictates that constants should always be in all uppercase.

Constants are super-global, which means they are automatically available in all scopes. So, you can define a constant in your main script, then use it in a function buried in one of the include files it uses.

Perhaps the simplest tool available in PHP to keep your code organized, constants are also the least used. Because constants are simply variables whose values cannot be changed, most developers tend to use variables, with which they are intimately familiar. To effectively structure your code, however, you should distinguish between fixed values that work as configurable parameters in your scripts (constants) and temporary values that are more... well, variable!

Structure In Practice: Access Control

I've shown you a number of tools to help you write structured code—include files, function libraries, and constants—each in isolation. To cap off this discussion, I'd like to stop and show you how everything we've learned so far can fit together in a practical application. The proof is in the pudding, as they say, so consider this a taste test!

One of the most common reasons for building a database-driven Website in PHP is that this approach allows the site owner to update the site from any Web

---

[8]As with functions and includes, it is customary to define constants at the top of the script so they can be found easily when needed.

browser, anywhere! But, in a world where roaming bands of hackers will jubilantly fill your site with viruses and pornography, you need to stop and think about the security of your administration pages.

At the very least, you'll want to require user name and password authentication before a visitor to your site can access the administration area. There are two main ways of doing this:

☐ configure your Web server software to require a valid login for the relevant pages

☐ use PHP to prompt the user and check the login credentials as appropriate

If you have access to your Web server's configuration, the first option is often the easiest to set up, but the second is by far the more flexible. With PHP, you get to design your own login form, and even embed it into the layout of your site if you wish. PHP also makes it easy to change the credentials required to gain access, or manage a database of authorized users, each with their own credentials and privileges.

The following code listing shows how a simple user authentication system may be implemented in PHP. A detailed explanation of this code follows.

File: **admin-unstructured.php**

```
<!DOCTYPE html PUBLIC "-//W3C//DTD XHTML 1.0 Strict//EN"
  "http://www.w3.org/TR/xhtml1/DTD/xhtml1-strict.dtd">
<html xmlns="http://www.w3.org/1999/xhtml">
<head>
<title>Site Administration Area</title>
<meta http-equiv="Content-Type"
  content="text/html; charset=iso-8859-1" />
</head>
<body>
<?php
// Process login
if (isset($_POST['username'])) {
  // Check credentials
  if ($_POST['username'] == 'foxmulder' and
      $_POST['password'] == 'trustno1') {
    $_SESSION['authorized'] = TRUE;
  }
}

// Process logout
```

```
if (isset($_REQUEST['logout'])) {
  unset($_SESSION['authorized']);
}

// Check login
if (isset($_SESSION['authorized'])) {
  // Display secure information
?>
<h1>Administration Options</h1>
<ul>
  <li><a href="news.php">News items</a></li>
  <li><a href="jobs.php">Job advertisements</a></li>
  <li><a href="comps.php">Competitions</a></li>
  <li><a href="events.php">Special events</a></li>
</ul>
<p><a href="<?php echo $_SERVER['PHP_SELF']; ?>?logout=1">Log
  Out</a></p>
<?php
} else {
  // Display login form
?>
<h1>Please log in for access</h1>
<div>
  <form action="<?php echo $_SERVER['PHP_SELF']; ?>"
      method="post">
    <label>User name:
      <input type="text" name="username" /></label><br />
    <label>Password:
      <input type="password" name="password" /></label>
    <input type="submit" value="Log In" />
  </form>
</div>
<?php
}
?>
</body>
</html>
```

Having a little trouble seeing how the example works at first glance? I don't blame you! The lack of structure means that the code that prompts the user for login details, the code that processes that login, the code that processes the user logging out, and the code that displays the secure information is all mixed together! And if you think *this* code is hard to follow, imagine if it used a database to store authorized user credentials instead of using a fixed user name and password!

As a favor from me to you (you owe me one!), let me break down this horribly unstructured code into manageable chunks to explain how it works.

When the user submits the form to log in, this is the code that processes that submission:

File: **admin-unstructured.php** (excerpt)

```php
// Process login
if (isset($_POST['username'])) {
  // Check credentials
  if ($_POST['username'] == 'foxmulder' and
      $_POST['password'] == 'trustno1') {
    $_SESSION['authorized'] = TRUE;
  }
}
```

The code identifies that a login attempt as been made by looking for the $_POST['username'] variable, which will be created by the first field in the form. If a login attempt is detected, the code proceeds to check the submitted credentials ($_POST['username'] and $_POST['password']) for validity. In this example, the login is considered valid if the user name is foxmulder and the password is trustno1. Finally, if the credentials are found to be valid, the script sets a variable in the user's session ($_SESSION['authorized']) to indicate that he or she is logged in.

When the user logs out, the code removes the session variable:

File: **admin-unstructured.php** (excerpt)

```php
// Process logout
if (isset($_REQUEST['logout'])) {
  unset($_SESSION['authorized']);
}
```

The script then checks for the existence of that session variable to decide whether to show the list of administration options:

File: **admin-unstructured.php** (excerpt)

```php
// Check login
if (isset($_SESSION['authorized'])) {
  // Display secure information
?>
<h1>Administration Options</h1>
<ul>
  <li><a href="news.php">News items</a></li>
```

```
<li><a href="jobs.php">Job advertisements</a></li>
<li><a href="comps.php">Competitions</a></li>
<li><a href="events.php">Special events</a></li>
</ul>
<p><a href="<?php echo $_SERVER['PHP_SELF']; ?>?logout=1">Log
  Out</a></p>
```

Notice the link at the end of the administration options that lets the user log out by passing a `logout` value in the query string.

If, on the other hand, the session variable *doesn't* exist, the script displays a login form, which submits back to the current script:

File: **admin-unstructured.php (excerpt)**

```
<?php
} else {
  // Display login form
?>
<h1>Please log in for access</h1>
<div>
  <form action="<?php echo $_SERVER['PHP_SELF']; ?>"
      method="post">
    <label>User name:
      <input type="text" name="username" /></label><br />
    <label>Password:
      <input type="password" name="password" /></label>
    <input type="submit" value="Log In" />
  </form>
</div>
<?php
}
?>
```

Now, in addition to making a tangled mess, the unstructured code in this example has several other weaknesses, which should by now be familiar to you:

❏ Each page on your site that needs password protection will have to include a copy of the login form.

❏ To check if the user is logged in, a script must explicitly check the session variable, which can be a pain to remember.

❏ Changing the user name and password required for login means updating every protected page on the site.

We can fix each of these problems using one of the techniques introduced earlier in this chapter.

Figure 12.5. Structure the files as a secure application.

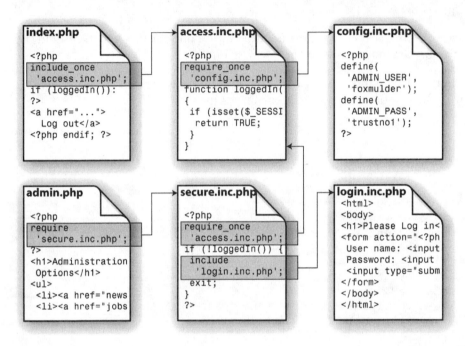

Figure 12.5 illustrates one way that this application can be structured. The files represented therein are as follows:

index.php

This is a non-secure page of the site. This particular page will display a Log out link when the user is logged in. In order to check if the user is logged in, it uses the loggedIn function defined in access.inc.php.

access.inc.php

This include file is responsible for logging the user in and out, and keeping track of the user's state. It will detect and process submissions of the HTML form in login.inc.php, as well as links with logout=1 in the query string. In order to validate login attempts, it uses the ADMIN_USER and ADMIN_PASS constants defined in config.inc.php.

This file also defines a function called `loggedIn` that returns true if the user is logged in, and false if not.

config.inc.php
This file is responsible for defining constants that control the configuration of the entire site. For the purposes of this example, those constants are the user name and password required to log into the site as an administrator, `ADMIN_USER` and `ADMIN_PASS` respectively.

admin.php
This is a secure page of the site, which requires the user to log in before it can be viewed. To make this page secure, the script includes `secure.inc.php` with `require`, to guard against users seeing the page when the include fails.

secure.inc.php
This script checks if the user is logged in before allowing control to return to the main script (e.g. `admin.php`). It uses the `loggedIn` function defined in `access.inc.php` to do this. If the user is not logged in, it includes `login.inc.php` to display the login form and then exits, preventing the user from seeing the contents of the main script.

login.inc.php
A near-static include, this file displays the login form for the site. The only use of PHP in this file is for the `action` attribute of the form, which uses `$_SERVER['PHP_SELF']` to point back at the secure page that the user wants to see (e.g. `admin.php`). Assuming the correct user name and password are submitted, `access.inc.php` will validate the login and return true when `secure.inc.php` checks if the user is logged in.

Here's the complete code for this structured application. Uses of include files, functions, and constants are shown in bold.

File: **index.php**

```php
<?php include_once 'access.inc.php'; ?>
<!DOCTYPE html PUBLIC "-//W3C//DTD XHTML 1.0 Strict//EN"
  "http://www.w3.org/TR/xhtml1/DTD/xhtml1-strict.dtd">
<html xmlns="http://www.w3.org/1999/xhtml">
<head>
```

```
<title>An Unprotected Page</title>
<meta http-equiv="Content-Type"
  content="text/html; charset=iso-8859-1" />
</head>
<body>
<p>This is an unprotected page. Anyone can view it.</p>
<?php if (loggedIn()): ?>
  <p>You are currently logged in!
    <a href="<?php echo $_SERVER['PHP_SELF']; ?>?logout=1"
    >Logout</a></p>
<?php endif; ?>
</body>
</html>
```

File: **access.inc.php**

```
<?php
require_once 'config.inc.php';

function loggedIn()
{
  return isset($_SESSION['authorized']);
}

// Process login attempt
if (isset($_POST['login'])) {
  if ($_POST['username'] == ADMIN_USER and
      $_POST['password'] == ADMIN_PASS) {
    $_SESSION['authorized'] = TRUE;
  }
}

// Process logout
if (isset($_REQUEST['logout'])) {
  unset($_SESSION['authorized']);
}
?>
```

File: **config.inc.php**

```
<?php
define('ADMIN_USER', 'foxmulder');
define('ADMIN_PASS', 'trustno1');
?>
```

File: **admin.php**

```
<?php require 'secure.inc.php'; ?>
<!DOCTYPE html PUBLIC "-//W3C//DTD XHTML 1.0 Strict//EN"
```

```
    "http://www.w3.org/TR/xhtml1/DTD/xhtml1-strict.dtd">
<html xmlns="http://www.w3.org/1999/xhtml">
<head>
<title>Site Administration Area</title>
<meta http-equiv="Content-Type"
  content="text/html; charset=iso-8859-1" />
</head>
<body>
<h1>Administrative Options</h1>
<ul>
  <li><a href="news.php">News items</a></li>
  <li><a href="jobs.php">Job advertisements</a></li>
  <li><a href="comps.php">Competitions</a></li>
  <li><a href="events.php">Special events</a></li>
</ul>
<p><a href="<?php echo $_SERVER['PHP_SELF']; ?>?logout=1"
  >Logout</a></p>
</body>
</html>
```

File: **secure.inc.php**

```php
<?php
require_once 'access.inc.php';
if (!loggedIn()) {
  include 'login.inc.php';
  exit;
}
?>
```

File: **login.inc.php**

```
<!DOCTYPE html PUBLIC "-//W3C//DTD XHTML 1.0 Strict//EN"
  "http://www.w3.org/TR/xhtml1/DTD/xhtml1-strict.dtd">
<html xmlns="http://www.w3.org/1999/xhtml">
<head>
<title>Login Required for Access</title>
<meta http-equiv="Content-Type"
  content="text/html; charset=iso-8859-1" />
</head>
<body>
<h1>Please log in for access</h1>
<div>
  <form action="<?php echo $_SERVER['PHP_SELF']; ?>"
      method="post">
    <label>User name:
      <input type="text" name="username" /></label><br />
    <label>Password:
```

```
      <input type="password" name="password" /></label>
    <input type="submit" value="Log In" />
  </form>
</div>
</body>
</html>
```

Is this more complex than the unstructured version we saw above? Of course! But just look what we've gained:

☐ You can password-protect any page on your site by adding one line of PHP at the top:

```
<?php require 'secure.inc.php'; ?>
```

☐ Unprotected pages can use the loggedIn function in access.inc.php to display special content for logged-in users.

☐ You can change the user name and password required to log into the site at any time simply by editing config.inc.php.

☐ You only need to maintain a single login form, in login.inc.php, for the entire site.

☐ PHP code and HTML code are generally stored in separate files, simplifying the lives of both designers and developers, who will rarely need to work on the same file.

Summary

In this final chapter, I have helped you to rise above the basic questions of what PHP can do for you, and begin to look for the *best way* of doing something. Sure, you can approach many simple scripts as lists of things you want PHP to do for you, but when you tackle site-wide issues such as database connections, shared navigation elements, visitor statistics, and access control systems, it really pays off to structure your code in an intelligent way.

We explored a number of simple but effective devices for writing structured PHP code in this chapter. Include files let you reuse a single piece of code across multiple pages of your site, greatly reducing the burden when you need to make changes. Writing your own functions to put in these include files lets you build powerful libraries of functions that can perform tasks as needed and return values to the scripts that call them. Finally, constants let you reliably set fixed values in your scripts at a single location, making for more general code that can be reused in future projects.

If you want to take the next step into structuring your PHP code, you'll want to explore PHP's object oriented programming (OOP) features. Already powerful in PHP 4, this is where most of the improvements in PHP 5 were concentrated. The PHP Manual[4] has some useful reading on the subject, but for a more complete guide you'll want to check out *The PHP Anthology: Object Oriented PHP Solutions*[5] by Harry Fuecks.

[4] http://www.php.net/oop5
[5] http://www.sitepoint.com/books/phpant1/

Appendix A: MySQL Syntax

This appendix describes the syntax of the majority of SQL statements implemented in MySQL, as of version 4.0.20 (current as of this writing).

The following conventions are used in this reference:

- Queries are listed in alphabetical order for easy reference.

- Optional components are surrounded by square brackets ([ ]), while mutually exclusive alternatives appear in braces ({}) separated by vertical bars (|).

- Lists of elements from which one element must be chosen are surrounded by braces ({}).

- An ellipsis (...) means that the preceding element may be repeated.

The query syntax documented in this appendix has been simplified in several places by the omission of the alternative syntax, and of keywords that didn't actually perform any function, but which were originally included for compatibility with more advanced database systems. Query features having to do with some advanced features such as transactions have also been omitted. For a complete, up-to-date reference to supported MySQL syntax, see the MySQL Reference Manual[1].

ALTER TABLE

```
ALTER [IGNORE] TABLE tbl_name action[, action ...]
```

In this code, *action* refers to an action as defined below.

ALTER TABLE queries may be used to change the definition of a table without losing any of the information in that table (except in obvious cases, such as the deletion of a column). Here are the main actions that are possible:

ADD [COLUMN] *create_definition* [FIRST | AFTER column_name]
    This action adds a new column to the table. The syntax for *create_definition* is as described for the section called "CREATE TABLE". By default, the column will be added to the end of the table, but by specifying FIRST or

---

[1] http://www.mysql.com/doc/en/Reference.html

AFTER `column_name`, you can place the column wherever you like. The optional word `COLUMN` does not actually do anything—leave it off unless you particularly like to see it there.

ADD INDEX [index_name] (index_col_name, ...)

This action creates a new index to speed up searches based on the column(s) specified. It's usually a good idea to assign a name to your indices by specifying the `index_name`, otherwise, a default name based on the first column in the index will be used. When creating an index based on `CHAR` and/or `VARCHAR` columns, you can specify a number of characters to index as part of `index_col_name` (e.g. `myColumn(5)` will index the first 5 characters of `myColumn`). This number must be specified when indexing `BLOB` and `TEXT` columns. For detailed information on indexes, see the MySQL Reference Manual[2], or Mike Sullivan's excellent article "Optimizing your MySQL Application[3]" on SitePoint.

ADD FULLTEXT [index_name] (index_col_name, ...)

This action creates a full-text index on the column(s) specified. This special type of index allows you to perform complex searches for text in `CHAR`, `VARCHAR`, or `TEXT` columns using the `MATCH` MySQL function. For full details, see the MySQL Reference Manual[4].

ADD PRIMARY KEY (index_col_name, ...)

This action creates an index for the specified row(s) with the name `PRIMARY`, identifying it as the primary key for the table. All values (or combinations of values) must be unique, as described for the `ADD UNIQUE` action below. This action will cause an error if a primary key already exists for this table. `index_col_name` is defined as it is for the `ADD INDEX` action above.

ADD UNIQUE [index_name] (index_col_name, ...)

This action creates an index on the specified columns, but with a twist: all values in the designated column, or all combinations of values, if more than one column is included in the index, must be unique. The parameters `index_name` and `index_col_name` are defined as they are for the `ADD INDEX` action above.

---

[2] http://dev.mysql.com/doc/mysql/en/Indexes.html
[3] http://www.sitepoint.com/article/optimizing-mysql-application
[4] http://dev.mysql.com/doc/mysql/en/Fulltext_Search.html

ALTER [COLUMN] col_name {SET DEFAULT value | DROP DEFAULT}

This action assigns a new default value to a column (SET DEFAULT), or removes the existing default value (DROP DEFAULT). Again, the word COLUMN is completely optional, and has no effect.

CHANGE [COLUMN] col_name *create_definition*

This action replaces an existing column (col_name) with a new column, as defined by *create_definition* (the syntax of which is as specified for the section called "CREATE TABLE"). The data in the existing column is converted, if necessary, and placed in the new column. Note that *create_definition* includes a new column name, so this action may be used to rename a column. If you want to leave the name of the column unchanged, however, don't forget to include it twice (once for col_name and once for *create_definition*), or use the MODIFY action below.

DISABLE KEYS
ENABLE KEYS

When you insert a large number of records into a table, MySQL can spend a lot of time updating the index(es) of the table to reflect the new entries. Executing ALTER TABLE ... DISABLE KEYS before you perform the inserts will instruct MySQL to postpone those index updates. Once the inserts are complete, execute ALTER TABLE ... ENABLE KEYS to update the indexes for all the new entries at once. This will usually save time over performing the updates one at a time.

DROP [COLUMN] col_name

Fairly self-explanatory, this action completely removes a column from the table. The data in that column is irretrievable after this query completes, so be sure of the column name you specify. COLUMN, as usual, can be left off—it doesn't do anything but make the query sound better when read aloud.

DROP PRIMARY KEY
DROP INDEX index_name

These actions are quite self-explanatory: they remove from the table the primary key, and a specific index, respectively.

MODIFY [COLUMN] *create_definition*

Nearly identical to the CHANGE action above, this action lets you specify a new declaration for a column in the table, but assumes you will not be changing its name. Thus, you simply have to re-declare the column with the same name in the *create_definition* parameter (as defined for the section called "CREATE TABLE"). As before, COLUMN is completely optional and does nothing. Although convenient, this action is not standard SQL syntax, and was added for compatibility with an identical extension in Oracle database servers.

ORDER BY col_name

This action lets you sort a table's entries by a particular column. However, this is not a persistent state; as soon as new entries are added to the table, or existing entries modified, the ordering can no longer be guaranteed. The only practical use of this action would be to increase performance of a table that you sorted regularly in a certain way in your application's SELECT queries. Under some circumstances, arranging the rows in (almost) the right order to begin with will make sorting quicker.

RENAME [TO | AS] new_tbl_name

This action renames the table. The words TO and AS are completely optional, and don't do anything. Use 'em if you like 'em.

table_options

Using the same syntax as in the CREATE TABLE query, this action allows you to set and change advanced table options. These options are fully documented in the MySQL Reference Manual[5].

ANALYZE TABLE

```
ANALYZE TABLE tbl_name[, tbl_name, ...]
```

This function updates the information used by the SELECT query in the optimization of queries that take advantage of table indices. It pays in performance to run this query periodically on tables whose contents change a lot over time. The table(s) in question are locked "read-only" while the analysis runs.

CREATE DATABASE

```
CREATE DATABASE [IF NOT EXISTS] db_name
```

This action simply creates a new database with the given name (db_name). This query will fail if the database already exists (unless IF NOT EXISTS is specified), or if you don't have the required privileges.

---

[5] http://www.mysql.com/doc/en/CREATE_TABLE.html

CREATE INDEX

```
CREATE [UNIQUE | FULLTEXT] INDEX index_name ON tbl_name
(col_name[(length)], …)
```

This query creates a new index on an existing table. It works identically to ALTER TABLE ADD {INDEX | UNIQUE | FULLTEXT}, described in the section called "ALTER TABLE".

CREATE TABLE

```
CREATE [TEMPORARY] TABLE [IF NOT EXISTS] [db_name.]tbl_name
{   [(create_definition, …)]
    [table_options] [[IGNORE | REPLACE] select_statement]

  | LIKE [db_name.]old_tbl_name }
```

Where *create_definition* is:

```
{   col_name type [NOT NULL] [DEFAULT default_value]
      [AUTO_INCREMENT] [PRIMARY KEY]

  | PRIMARY KEY (index_col_name, …)

  | INDEX [index_name] (index_col_name, …)

  | FULLTEXT [index_name] (index_col_name, …)

  | UNIQUE [INDEX] [index_name] (index_col_name, …) }
```

In this code, *type* is a MySQL column type (see Appendix C), and *index_col_name* is as described for ALTER TABLE ADD INDEX in the section called "ALTER TABLE".

CREATE TABLE is used to create a new table called tbl_name in the current database (or in a specific database if db_name.tbl_name is specified). If TEMPORARY is specified, the table disappears upon termination of the connection by which it was created. Creating a temporary table with the same name as an existing table will hide the existing table from the current client session until the temporary table is deleted or the session ends; however, other clients will continue to see the original table.

Assuming TEMPORARY is not specified, this query will fail if a table with the given name already exists, unless IF NOT EXISTS is specified. A CREATE TABLE query will also fail if you don't have the required privileges.

Most of the time, the name of the table will be followed by a series of column declarations (*create_definition* above). Each column definition includes the name and data type for the column, and any of the following options:

❏ NOT NULL

This specifies that the column may not be left empty (NULL). Note that NULL is a special "no value" value, which is quite different from, say, an empty string (' '). A column of type VARCHAR, for instance, which is set NOT NULL may be set to ' ' but will not be NULL. Likewise, a NOT NULL column of type INT may contain zero (0), which is a value, but it may not contain NULL, as this is not a value.

❏ DEFAULT default_value

DEFAULT lets you specify a value to be given to a column when no value is assigned in an INSERT statement. When this option is not specified, NULL columns (columns for which the NOT NULL option is not set) will be assigned a value of NULL when they are not given a value in an INSERT statement. NOT NULL columns will instead be assigned a "default default value" (an empty string (' '), or zero (0), '0000-00-00', or a current timestamp, depending on the data type of the column.

❏ AUTO_INCREMENT

As described in Chapter 2, an AUTO_INCREMENT column will automatically insert a number that is one greater than the current highest number in that column, when NULL is inserted. AUTO_INCREMENT columns must also be NOT NULL, and be either a PRIMARY KEY or UNIQUE.

❏ PRIMARY KEY

This option specifies that the column in question should be the primary key for the table; that is, the values in the column must identify uniquely each of the rows in the table. This forces the values in this column to be unique, and speeds up searches for items based on this column by creating an index of the values it contains.

❏ UNIQUE

Very similar to PRIMARY KEY, this option requires all values in the column to be unique, and indexes the values for high speed searches.

In addition to column definitions, you can list additional indexes you wish to create on the table using the PRIMARY KEY, INDEX, FULLTEXT, and FULLTEXT forms of *create_definition*. See the descriptions of the equivalent forms of ALTER TABLE in the section called "ALTER TABLE" for details.

The *table_options* portion of the CREATE TABLE query is used to specify advanced properties of the table, and is described in detail in the MySQL Reference Manual[6].

The *select_statement* portion of the CREATE TABLE query allows you to create a table from the results of a SELECT query (see the section called "SELECT"). When you create this table, you don't have to declare separately the columns that correspond to those results. This type of query is useful if you want to obtain the result of a SELECT query, store it in a temporary table, and then perform a second SELECT query upon it. To some extent, this may be used to make up for MySQL's lack of support for **sub-selects**[1], which allow you to perform the same type of operation in a single query.

Instead of defining a table from scratch, you can instead instruct MySQL to create the new table using the same structure as some other table. Instead of a list of *create_definition*s and the *table_options*, simply end the CREATE TABLE query with LIKE, followed by the name of the existing table.

DELETE

```
DELETE [LOW_PRIORITY] [QUICK] [IGNORE]
{   FROM tbl_name
        [WHERE where_clause]
        [ORDER BY order_by_expr]
        [LIMIT rows]

    | tbl_name[, tbl_name …]
        FROM table_references
        [WHERE where_clause]

    | FROM tbl_name[, tbl_name …]
```

---

[6] http://dev.mysql.com/doc/mysql/en/CREATE_TABLE.html
[1] Support for sub-selects is planned for inclusion in MySQL 4.1.

```
        USING table_references
        [WHERE where_clause] }
```

The first form of this query deletes all rows from the specified table, unless the optional (but desirable!) WHERE or LIMIT clauses are specified. The WHERE clause works the same way as its twin in the SELECT query (see the section called "SE-LECT"). The LIMIT clause simply lets you specify the maximum number of rows to be deleted. The ORDER BY clause lets you specify the order in which the entries are deleted, which, in combination with the LIMIT clause, allows you to do things like delete the ten oldest entries from the table.

The second and third forms are equivalent, and enable you to delete rows from multiple tables in a single operation, in much the same way as you can retrieve entries from multiple tables using a join in a SELECT query (see the section called "SELECT"). The table_references work the same way as they do for SELECT queries (you can create simple joins or outer joins), while the WHERE clause lets you narrow down the rows that are considered for deletion. The first list of tables (tbl_name[, tbl_name, …]), however, identifies from the table_references the tables from which rows will actually be deleted. In this way, you can use a complex join involving a number of tables to isolate a set of results, then delete the rows from only one of those tables.

The LOW_PRIORITY option causes the query to wait until there are no clients reading from the table before performing the operation. The QUICK option attempts to speed up lengthy delete operations by changing the way it updates the table's index(es). The IGNORE option instructs MySQL not to report any errors that occur while the delete is performed.

DESCRIBE

```
{DESCRIBE | DESC} tbl_name [col_name | wild]
```

This command supplies information about the columns, a specific column (col_name), or any columns that match a pattern containing wild cards '%' and '_' (wild), that make up the specified table. The information returned includes the column name, its type, whether it accepts NULL as a value, whether the column has an index, the default value for the column, and any extra features it has (e.g. AUTO_INCREMENT).

DROP DATABASE

```
DROP DATABASE [IF EXISTS] db_name
```

This is a dangerous command. It will immediately delete a database, along with all of its tables. This query will fail if the database does not exist (unless IF EXISTS is specified), or if you don't have the required privileges.

DROP INDEX

```
DROP INDEX index_name ON tbl_name
```

DROP INDEX has exactly the same effect as ALTER TABLE DROP INDEX, described in the section called "ALTER TABLE".

DROP TABLE

```
DROP TABLE [IF EXISTS] tbl_name [, tbl_name, ...]
```

This query completely deletes one or more tables. *This is a dangerous query*, since the data cannot be retrieved once this action is executed. Be very careful with it!

This query will fail with an error if the table doesn't exist (unless IF EXISTS is specified) or if you don't have the required privileges.

EXPLAIN

The explain query has two very different forms. The first,

```
EXPLAIN tbl_name
```

is equivalent to DESCRIBE tbl_name or SHOW COLUMNS FROM tbl_name.

The second format,

```
EXPLAIN select_satement
```

where *select_statement* can be any valid SELECT query, will produce an explanation of how MySQL would determine the results of the SELECT statement. This query is useful for finding out where indexes will help speed up your SELECT queries, and also for determining if MySQL is performing multi-table queries in optimal order. See the STRAIGHT_JOIN option of the SELECT query in the section called "SELECT" for information on how to override the MySQL optimizer, and control this order manually. See the MySQL Reference Manual[7] for complete information on how to interpret the results of an EXPLAIN query.

GRANT

```
GRANT priv_type [(column_list)], …
  ON {tbl_name | * | *.* | db_name.*}
  TO user_name [IDENTIFIED BY 'password'], …
  [WITH GRANT OPTION]
```

GRANT adds new access privileges to a user account, and creates a new account if the specified user_name does not yet exist, or changes the password if IDENTIFIED BY 'password' is used on an account that already has a password.

See the section called "MySQL Access Control" in Chapter 8 for a complete description of this query.

INSERT

```
INSERT [LOW_PRIORITY | DELAYED] [IGNORE] [INTO] tbl_name

{   [(col_name, …)] VALUES (expression, …), …

  | SET col_name=expression, col_name=expression, …

  | [(col_name, …)] SELECT … }
```

The INSERT query is used to add new entries to a table. It supports three general options:

LOW_PRIORITY

The query will wait until there are no clients reading from the table before it proceeds.

DELAYED

The query completes immediately from the client's point of view, and the INSERT operation is performed in the background. This option is useful when you wish to insert a large number of rows without waiting for the operation

---

[7] http://dev.mysql.com/doc/mysql/en/EXPLAIN.html

to complete. Be aware that the client will not know the last inserted ID on an AUTO_INCREMENT column when a DELAYED insert is performed (e.g. mysql_insert_id in PHP will not work correctly).

IGNORE

Normally, when an inserted operation causes a clash in a PRIMARY KEY or UNIQUE column, the insert fails and produces an error message. This option allows the insert to fail silently—the new row is not inserted, but no error message is displayed.

The word INTO is entirely optional, and has no effect on the operation of the query.

As you can see above, INSERT queries may take three forms. The first form lets you insert one or more rows by specifying the values for the table columns in parentheses. If the optional list of column names is omitted, then the list(s) of column values must include a value for every column in the table, in the order in which they appear in the table.

The second form of INSERT can be used only to insert a single row, but, very intuitively, it allows you to assign values to the columns in that row by giving them in col_name=value format.

In the third and final form of INSERT, the rows to be inserted result from a SELECT query. Again, if the list of column names is omitted, the result set of the SELECT must contain values for each and every column in the table, in the correct order. A SELECT query that makes up part of an insert statement may not contain an ORDER BY clause, and you cannot use the table into which you are inserting in the FROM clause.

Columns to which you assign no value (e.g. if you leave them out of the column list) are assigned their default. By default, inserting a NULL value into a NOT NULL field will also cause that field to be set to its default value; however, if MySQL is configured with the DONT_USE_DEFAULT_FIELDS option enabled, such an INSERT operation will cause an error. For this reason, it's best to avoid them.

LOAD DATA INFILE

```
LOAD DATA [LOW_PRIORITY | CONCURRENT] [LOCAL] INFILE
  'file_name.txt' [REPLACE | IGNORE] INTO TABLE tbl_name
  [FIELDS
    [TERMINATED BY 'string']
```

```
    [[OPTIONALLY] ENCLOSED BY 'char']
    [ESCAPED BY 'char'] ]
  [LINES [STARTING BY ''] [TERMINATED BY 'string']]
  [IGNORE number LINES]
  [(col_name, …)]
```

The LOAD DATA INFILE query is used to import data from a text file either on the MySQL server, or on the LOCAL (client) system (for example, a text file created with a SELECT INTO OUTFILE query). The syntax of this command is given above; however, I refer you to the MySQL Reference Manual[8] for a complete explanation of this query and the issues that surround its use.

LOCK/UNLOCK TABLES

```
LOCK TABLES
  tbl_name [AS alias] {READ [LOCAL] | [LOW_PRIORITY] WRITE},
  tbl_name …
```

```
UNLOCK TABLES
```

LOCK TABLES locks the specified table(s) so that the current connection has exclusive access to them, while other connections will have to wait until the lock is released with UNLOCK TABLES, with another LOCK TABLES query, or with the closure of the current connection.

A READ lock prevents the specified table(s) from being written by this, or any other connection. This allows you to make certain that the contents of a table (or set of tables) are not changed for a certain period of time. READ LOCAL allows INSERT statements to continue to be processed on the table while the lock is held, but UPDATEs and DELETEs are blocked as usual.

A WRITE lock prevents all other connections from reading or writing the specified table(s). It's useful when a series of INSERT or UPDATE queries must be performed together to maintain the integrity of the data model in the database. New support for **transactions** in MySQL provides more robust support for these types of "grouped queries" (see the sidebar in the section called "LOCKing TABLES" in Chapter 9 for details).

By default, a WRITE lock that is waiting for access to a table will take priority over any READ locks that may also be waiting. To specify that a WRITE lock should yield to all other READ lock requests, you can use the LOW_PRIORITY option. Be

[8] http://dev.mysql.com/doc/mysql/en/LOAD_DATA.html

aware, however, that if there are always READ lock requests pending, a LOW_PRIORITY WRITE lock will never be allowed to proceed.

When locking tables, you must list the same aliases that you're going to use in the queries you'll be performing. If, for example, you are going to refer to the same table with two different aliases in one of your queries, you will need to obtain a lock for each of those aliases beforehand.

For more information on locking tables, see the section called "LOCKing TABLES" in Chapter 9.

OPTIMIZE TABLE

```
OPTIMIZE TABLE tbl_name[, tbl_name, …]
```

Much like a hard disk partition becomes fragmented if existing files are deleted or resized, MySQL tables become fragmented over time as you delete rows and modify variable-length columns (such as VARCHAR or BLOB). This query performs the database equivalent of a "defrag" on the table, reorganizing the data it contains to eliminate wasted space.

It's important to note that a table is *locked* while an optimize operation occurs, so if your application relies on a large table being constantly available, that application will grind to a halt while the optimization takes place. In such cases, it's better to copy the table, optimize the copy, and then replace the old table with the newly optimized version using a RENAME query. Changes made to the original table in the interim will be lost, so this technique is not appropriate for all applications.

RENAME TABLE

```
RENAME TABLE tbl_name TO new_table_name[, tbl_name2 TO …, …]
```

This query quickly and conveniently renames one or more tables. This differs from ALTER TABLE tbl_name RENAME in that all the tables being renamed in the query are locked for the duration of the query, so that no other connected clients may access them. As the MySQL Reference Manual explains[9], this assurance of atomicity lets you replace a table with an empty equivalent, for example, if

---

[9] http://dev.mysql.com/doc/mysql/en/RENAME_TABLE.html

you wanted safely to start a new table once a certain number of entries was reached:

```
CREATE TABLE new_table (…)
RENAME TABLE old_table TO backup_table, new_table TO old_table;
```

You can also move a table from one database to another by specifying the table name as db_name.tbl_name, as long as both tables are stored on the same physical disk, which is usually the case.

You must have ALTER and DROP privileges on the original table, as well as CREATE and INSERT privileges on the new table, in order to perform this query. A RENAME TABLE query that fails to complete halfway through will automatically be reversed, so that the original state is restored.

REPLACE

```
REPLACE [LOW_PRIORITY | DELAYED] [INTO] tbl_name

{   [(col_name, …)] VALUES (expression, …), …

  | [(col_name, …)] SELECT …

  | SET col_name=expression, col_name=expression, … }
```

REPLACE is identical to INSERT, except that if an inserted row clashes with an existing row in a PRIMARY KEY or UNIQUE column, the old entry is replaced with the new.

REVOKE

```
REVOKE priv_type [(column_list)], …
  ON {tbl_name | * | *.* | db_name.*}
  FROM user, …
```

This function removes access privileges from a user account. If all privileges are removed from an account, the user will still be able to log in, though he or she won't be able to access any information.

See the section called "MySQL Access Control" in Chapter 8 for a complete description of this query.

SELECT

```
SELECT [select_options]
  select_expression, …
  [INTO {OUTFILE | DUMPFILE} 'file_name' export_options]
  [FROM table_references
    [WHERE where_definition]
    [GROUP BY {col_name | col_pos } [ASC | DESC], …]
    [HAVING where_definition]
    [ORDER BY {col_name | col_pos } [ASC | DESC], …]
    [LIMIT [offset,] rows]]
```

SELECT is the most complex query in SQL, and is used to perform all data retrieval operations. This query supports the following *select_options*, which may be specified in any sensible combination simply by listing them separated by spaces:

ALL | DISTINCT | DISCTINCTROW

Any one of these options may be used to specify the treatment of duplicate rows in the result set. ALL (the default) specifies that all duplicate rows appear in the result set, while DISTINCT and DISTINCTROW (they have the same effect) specify that duplicate rows should be eliminated from the result set.

HIGH_PRIORITY

This option does exactly what it says—it assigns a high priority to the SELECT query. Normally, if a query is waiting to update a table, all read-only queries (such as SELECT) must yield to it. A SELECT HIGH_PRIORITY, however, will go first.

STRAIGHT_JOIN

Forces MySQL to join multiple tables specified in the *table_references* argument in the order specified there. If you think MySQL's query optimizer is doing it the "slow way," this argument lets you override it. For more information on joins, see the section called "Joins" below.

SQL_SMALL_RESULT

This option shouldn't be needed in MySQL 3.23 or later; however, it remains available for compatibility. This option informs MySQL that you are expecting a relatively small result set from a query that uses the DISTINCT option or the GROUP BY clause, so it uses the faster, but more memory-intensive method of generating a temporary table in memory to hold the result set as it is created.

SQL_BIG_RESULT

Along the same lines as SQL_SMALL_RESULT, this option informs MySQL that you are expecting a large number of results from a query that makes use of DISTINCT or GROUP BY. When it creates the result set, MySQL will create on disk, as needed, a temporary table in which the results are sorted. This is a quicker solution than generating an index on the temporary table, which would take longer to update for each result row in a large result set.

SQL_BUFFER_RESULT

This option forces MySQL to store the result set in a temporary table. This frees up the tables that were used in the query for use by other processes, while the result set is transmitted to the client.

SQL_CACHE

This option instructs MySQL to store the result of this query in the **query cache**, an area of memory set aside by the server to store the results of frequently-run queries so that they don't need to be recalculated from scratch if the contents of the relevant tables have not changed. MySQL can be configured so that only queries with the SQL_CACHE option are cached. If the query cache is disabled, this option will have no effect.

SQL_NO_CACHE

This option instructs MySQL not to store the result of this query in the query cache (see the previous option). MySQL can be configured so that every query is cached unless it has the SQL_NO_CACHE option. If the query cache is disabled, this option will have no effect.

SQL_CALC_FOUND_ROWS

For use in conjunction with a LIMIT clause, this option calculates and sets aside the total number of rows that would be returned from the query if no LIMIT clause were present. You can then retrieve this number using SELECT FOUND_ROWS() (see Appendix B).

select_expression defines a column of the result set to be returned by the query. Typically, this is a table column name, and may be specified as col_name, tbl_name.col_name, or db_name.tbl_name.col_name, depending on how specific you need to be for MySQL to identify the column to which you are referring. *select_expression*s need not refer to a database column—a simple mathematical formula such as 1 + 1 or a complex expression calculated with MySQL functions may also be used. Here's an example of the latter, which will give the date one month from now in the form "January 1, 2002":

```
SELECT DATE_FORMAT(
  DATE_ADD(CURDATE(), INTERVAL 1 MONTH), '%M %D, %Y')
```

*select_expression*s may also contain an alias, or assigned name for the result column, if the expression is followed with [AS] `alias` (the AS is entirely optional). This expression must be used when referring to that column elsewhere in the query (e.g. in WHERE and ORDER BY clauses), as follows:

```
SELECT jokedate AS jd FROM joke ORDER BY jd ASC
```

MySQL lets you use an INTO clause to output the results of a query into a file instead of returning them to the client. The most typical use of this clause is to export the contents of a table into a text file containing comma-separated values (CSV). Here's an example:

```
SELECT * INTO OUTFILE '/home/user/myTable.txt'
FIELDS TERMINATED BY ',' OPTIONALY ENCLOSED BY '"'
LINES TERMINATED BY '\n'
FROM myTable
```

The file to which the results are dumped must not exist beforehand, or this query will fail. This restriction prevents an SQL query from being used to overwrite critical operating system files. The created file will also be world-readable on systems that support file security, so consider this before you export sensitive data to a text file that anyone on the system can read.

DUMPFILE may be used instead of OUTFILE to write to the file only a single row, without row or column delimiters. It can be used, for example, to dump a BLOB stored in the table to a file (SELECT blobCol INTO DUMPFILE …). For complete information on the INTO clause, see the MySQL Reference Manual[10]. For information on reading data back from a text file, see the section called "LOAD DATA INFILE".

The FROM clause contains a list of tables from which the rows composing the result set should be formed. At its most basic, *table_references* is a comma-separated list of one or more tables, which may be assigned aliases with or without using AS as described above for *select_expression*. If you specify more than one table name, you are performing a **join**. These are discussed in the section called "Joins" below.

The *where_definition* in the WHERE clause sets the condition for a row to be included in the table of results sent in response to the SELECT query. This may

---

[10] http://dev.mysql.com/doc/mysql/en/SELECT.html

be a simple condition (e.g. id=5), or a complex expression that makes use of MySQL functions and combines multiple conditions using Boolean operators (AND, OR, NOT).

The GROUP BY clause lets you specify one or more columns (by name, alias, or column position, where 1 is the first column in the result set) for which rows with equal values should be collapsed into single rows in the result set. This clause should usually be used in combination with the MySQL grouping functions such as COUNT, MAX, and AVG, described in Appendix B, to produce result rows that give summary information about the groups produced. By default, the grouped results are sorted in ascending order of the grouped column(s); however, the ASC or DESC argument may be added following each column reference to explicitly sort that column's results in ascending or descending order, respectively. Results are sorted by the first column listed, then tying sets of rows are sorted by the second, and so on.

Note that the WHERE clause is processed before GROUP BY grouping occurs, so conditions in the WHERE clause may not refer to columns produced by the grouping operation. To impose conditions on the post-grouping result set, you should use the HAVING clause instead. This clause's syntax is identical to that of the WHERE clause, except the conditions specified here are processed just prior to returning the set of results, and are not optimized. For this reason, you should use the WHERE clause whenever possible. For more information on GROUP BY and the HAVING clause, see Chapter 9.

The ORDER BY clause lets you sort results according the values in one or more rows before they are returned. As for the GROUP BY clause, each column may be identified by a column name, alias, or position (where 1 is the first column in the result set), and each column may have an ASC or DESC argument to specify that sorting occurs in ascending or descending order, respectively (ascending is the default). Rows initially are sorted by the first column listed, then tying sets of rows are sorted by the second, and so on.

The LIMIT clause instructs the query to return only a portion of the results it would normally generate. In the simple case, LIMIT n returns only the first n rows of the complete result set. You can also specify an offset by using the form LIMIT x, n. In this case, up to n rows will be returned, beginning from the xth row of the complete result set. The first row corresponds to $x = 0$, the second to $x = 1$ and so on.

Joins

As described above, the FROM clause of a SELECT query lets you specify the tables that are combined to create the result set. When multiple tables are combined in this way, it is called a **join**. MySQL supports several types of joins, as defined by the following supported syntaxes for the *table_references* component of the FROM clause above:

```
table_ref
table_references, table_ref
table_references [CROSS] JOIN table_ref
table_references INNER JOIN table_ref join_condition
table_references STRAIGHT_JOIN table_ref
table_references LEFT [OUTER] JOIN table_ref join_condition
{ oj table_ref LEFT OUTER JOIN table_ref ON cond_expr }
table_references NATURAL [LEFT [OUTER]] JOIN table_ref
table_references RIGHT [OUTER] JOIN table_ref join_condition
table_references NATURAL [RIGHT [OUTER]] JOIN table_ref
```

Where *table_ref* is defined as:

```
table_name [[AS] alias] [USE INDEX (key_list)]
  [IGNORE INDEX (key_list)]
```

and *join_condition* is defined as one of the following:

```
ON cond_expr
USING (column_list)
```

Don't be disheartened by the sheer variety of join types; I'll explain how each of them works below.

The most basic type of join, an **inner join**, produces rows made up of all possible pairings of the rows from the first table with the second. You can perform an inner join in MySQL either by separating the table names with a comma (,) or with the words JOIN, CROSS JOIN, or INNER JOIN (these are all equivalent).

Normally, the WHERE clause of the SELECT query is used to specify a condition to narrow down which of the combined rows are actually returned (e.g. to match up a primary key in the first table with a column in the second); however, when the INNER JOIN syntax is used, the ON form of the *join_condition* can play this role as well. As a final alternative, the USING (*column_list*) form of *join_condition* lets you specify columns that must match between the two tables. For example:

```
SELECT * FROM t1 INNER JOIN t2 USING (tid)
```

The above is equivalent to:

```
SELECT * FROM t1 INNER JOIN t2 ON t1.tid = t2.tid
```

It's also equivalent to:

```
SELECT * FROM t1, t2 WHERE t1.aid = t2.aid
```

STRAIGHT_JOIN works in the same way as an inner join, except that the tables are processed in the order listed (left first, then right). Normally, MySQL selects the order that will produce the shortest processing time, but if you think you know better, you can use a STRAIGHT_JOIN.

The second type of join is an **outer join**, which is accomplished in MySQL with LEFT/RIGHT [OUTER] JOIN (OUTER is completely optional, and has no effect). In a LEFT outer join, any row in the left-hand table that has no matching rows in the right-hand table (as defined by the *join_condition*), will be listed as a single row in the result set. NULL values will appear in all the columns that come from the right-hand table.

The { oj ... } syntax is equivalent to a standard left outer join; it is included for compatibility with other ODBC databases.

RIGHT outer joins work in the same way as LEFT outer joins, except in this case, it is the table on the right whose entries are always included, even if they do not have matching entries in the left-hand table. Since RIGHT outer joins are nonstandard, it is usually best to stick to LEFT outer joins for cross-database compatibility.

For some practical examples of outer joins and their uses, see Chapter 9.

Natural joins are somewhat "automatic" in that they automatically will match up rows based on column names that are found to match between the two tables. Thus, if a table called joke has an authorid column that refers to entries in an author table whose primary key is another authorid column, you can perform a join of these two tables on that column very simply (assuming there are no other columns with identical names in the two tables):

```
SELECT * FROM joke NATURAL JOIN author
```

Unions

A union combines the results from a number of SELECT queries to produce a single result set. Each of the queries must produce the same number of columns, and these columns must be of the same types. The column names produced by the first query are used for the union's result set.

```
SELECT …
UNION [ALL | DISTINCT]
SELECT …
  [UNION [ALL | DISTINCT]
   SELECT …] …
```

By default, duplicate result rows in the union will be eliminated such that each row in the result set is unique. The DISTINCT option can be used to make this clear, but it has no actual effect. The ALL option, on the other hand, allows duplicate results through to the final result set.

SET

```
SET option = value, …
```

The SET query allows you to set a number of options both on your client and on the server.

There are two common uses of the SET OPTION query; the first is to change your password:

```
SET PASSWORD = PASSWORD('new_password')
```

The second is to change another user's password (if you have appropriate access privileges):

```
SET PASSWORD FOR user = PASSWORD('new_password')
```

For a complete list of the options that may be SET, refer to the MySQL Reference Manual[11].

---

[11] http://dev.mysql.com/doc/mysql/en/SET_OPTION.html

SHOW

The SHOW query may be used in a number of forms to get information about the MySQL server, the databases, and the tables it contains. Many of these forms have an optional LIKE *wild* component, where *wild* is a string that may contain wild card characters ('%' for multiple characters, '_' for just one) to filter the list of results. Each of the forms of the SHOW query are described below:

SHOW DATABASES [LIKE *wild*]

This query lists the databases that are available on the MySQL server.

SHOW [OPEN] TABLES [FROM db_name] [LIKE *wild*]

This query lists the tables (or, optionally, the currently OPEN tables) in the default or specified database.

SHOW [FULL] COLUMNS FROM tbl_name [FROM db_name] [LIKE *wild*]

When FULL is not used, this query provides the same information as a DE-SCRIBE query (see the section called "DESCRIBE"). The FULL option adds to this information a listing of the privileges you have on each column. SHOW FIELDS is equivalent to SHOW COLUMNS.

SHOW INDEX FROM tbl_name [FROM db_name]

This query provides detailed information about the indexes that are defined on the specified table. See the MySQL Reference manual[12] for a guide to the results produced by this query. SHOW KEYS is equivalent to SHOW INDEX.

SHOW TABLE STATUS [FROM db_name] [LIKE *wild*]

This query displays detailed information about the tables in the default or specified database.

SHOW STATUS [LIKE *wild*]

This query displays detailed statistics for the server. See the MySQL Reference Manual[13] for details on the meaning of each of the figures.

SHOW VARIABLES [LIKE *wild*]

This query lists the MySQL configuration variables and their settings. See the MySQL Reference Manual[14] for a complete description of these options.

---

[12] http://www.mysql.com/doc/en/SHOW_DATABASE_INFO.html
[13] http://www.mysql.com/doc/en/SHOW_STATUS.html
[14] http://www.mysql.com/doc/en/SHOW_VARIABLES.html

SHOW [FULL] PROCESSLIST

This query displays all threads running on the MySQL server, and the queries being executed by each. If you don't have the 'process' privilege, you will only see threads executing your own queries. The FULL option causes the complete queries to be displayed, rather than only the first 100 characters of each (the default).

SHOW GRANTS FOR *user*

This query lists the GRANT queries that would be required to recreate the privileges of the specified user.

SHOW CREATE TABLE table_name

This query displays the CREATE TABLE query that would be required to reproduce the specified table.

UNLOCK TABLES

See the section called "LOCK/UNLOCK TABLES".

UPDATE

```
UPDATE [LOW_PRIORITY] [IGNORE] tbl_name
  SET col_name=expr, …
  [WHERE where_definition]
  [ORDER BY …]
  [LIMIT #]
```

The UPDATE query updates existing table entries by assigning new values to the specified columns. Columns that are not listed are left alone, with the exception of the TIMESTAMP column (see Appendix C). The WHERE clause lets you specify a condition (*where_definiton*) that rows must satisfy if they are to be updated, while the LIMIT clause lets you specify a maximum number of rows to be updated.

IMPORTANT

If WHERE and LIMIT are not specified, then every row in the table will be updated!

The ORDER BY clause lets you specify the order in which entries are updated. This is most useful in combination with the LIMIT clause—together they let you create queries like "update the ten most recent rows."

An UPDATE operation will fail with an error if the new value assigned to a row clashes with an existing value in a PRIMARY KEY or UNIQUE column, unless the IGNORE option is specified, in which case the query will simply have no effect on that particular row.

The LOW_PRIORITY option instructs MySQL to wait until there are no other clients reading the table before it performs the update.

Like the DELETE query (see the section called "DELETE"), UPDATE has an alternate form that can affect multiple tables in a single operation:

```
UPDATE [LOW_PRIORITY] [IGNORE] tbl_name[, tbl_name …]
  SET col_name=expr, …
  [WHERE where_definition]
```

USE

```
USE db_name
```

This simple query sets the default database for MySQL queries in the current session. Tables in other databases may still be accessed as db_name.tbl_name.

Appendix B: MySQL Functions

MySQL provides a sizeable library of functions to format and combine data within SQL queries in order to produce the desired results in the desired format. This appendix provides a reference to the most useful of these functions, as implemented in MySQL as of version 4.0.20 (current as of this writing).

For a complete, up-to-date reference to supported SQL functions, see the MySQL Reference Manual[1].

Control Flow Functions

IFNULL(*expr1*, *expr2*)
: This function returns *expr1* unless it is NULL, in which case it returns *expr2*.

NULLIF(*expr1*, *expr2*)
: This function returns *expr1* unless it equals *expr2*, in which case it returns NULL.

IF(*expr1*, *expr2*, *expr3*)
: If *expr1* is TRUE (that is, not NULL or 0), this function returns *expr2*; otherwise, it returns *expr3*.

CASE *value* WHEN [*compare-value1*] THEN *result1* [WHEN …] [ELSE *else-result*] END
: This function returns *result1* when *value=compare-value1* (note that several compare-value/result pairs can be defined); otherwise, it returns *else-result*, or NULL if none is defined.

CASE WHEN [*condition1*] THEN *result1* [WHEN …] [ELSE *else-result*] END
: This function returns *result1* when *condition1* is TRUE (note that several condition/result pairs can be defined); otherwise, it returns *else-result*, or NULL if none is defined.

Mathematical Functions

ABS(*expr*)
: This function returns the absolute (positive) value of *expr*.

---

[1] http://dev.mysql.com/doc/mysql/en/Functions.html

SIGN(*expr*)

This function returns -1, 0, or 1 depending on whether *expr* is negative, zero, or positive, respectively.

MOD(*expr1*, *expr2*)
expr1 % expr2

This function returns the remainder of dividing *expr1* by *expr2*.

FLOOR(*expr*)

This function rounds down *expr* (i.e. returns the largest integer value that is less than or equal to *expr*).

CEILING(*expr*)
CEIL(*expr*)

This function rounds up *expr* (i.e. returns the smallest integer value that is greater than or equal to *expr*).

ROUND(*expr*)

This function returns *expr* rounded to the nearest integer. Note that this function's behavior when the value is exactly an integer plus 0.5 is system-dependant. Thus, you should not rely on any particular outcome when migrating to a new system.

ROUND(*expr*, *num*)

This function rounds *expr* to a number with *num* decimal places, leaving trailing zeroes in place. Use a *num* of 2, for example, to format a number as dollars and cents. Note that the same uncertainty about the rounding of 0.5 applies as discussed for ROUND() above.

EXP(*expr*)

This function returns e^{expr}, the base of natural logarithms raised to the power of *expr*.

LOG(*expr*)

This function returns ln(*expr*), or $\log_e$(*expr*), the natural logarithm of *expr*.

LOG(*B*, *expr*)

This function returns the logarithm of *expr* with the arbitrary base *B*.

```
LOG(B, expr) = LOG(expr) / LOG(B)
```

LOG10(*expr*)

This function returns the base-10 logarithm of *expr*.

POW(*expr1*, *expr2*)
POWER(*expr1*, *expr2*)

This function returns *expr1* raised to the power of *expr2*.

SQRT(*expr*)

This function returns the square root of *expr*.

PI()

This function returns the value of (pi).

COS(*expr*)

This function returns the cosine of *expr* in radians (e.g. COS(PI()) = -1).

SIN(*expr*)

This function returns the sine of *expr* in radians (e.g. SIN(PI()) = 0).

TAN(*expr*)

This function returns the tangent of *expr* in radians (e.g. TAN(PI()) = 0).

ACOS(*expr*)

This function returns the arc cosine ($\cos^{-1}$ or inverse cosine) of *expr* (e.g. ACOS(-1) = 3.141593).

ASIN(*expr*)

This function returns the arc sine ($\sin^{-1}$ or inverse sine) of *expr* (e.g. ASIN(0) = 3.141593).

ATAN(*expr*)

This function returns the arc tangent ($\tan^{-1}$ or inverse tangent) of *expr* (e.g. ATAN(0) = 3.141593).

ATAN(*y*, *x*)
ATAN2(*y*, *x*)

This function returns the angle (in radians) made at the origin between the positive x axis and the point (x,y) (e.g. ATAN(1, 0) = 1.570796).

COT(*expr*)

This function returns the cotangent of *expr* (e.g. COT(PI() / 2) = 0).

RAND()
RAND(*expr*)
> This function returns a random, floating point number between 0.0 and 1.0. If *expr* is specified, a random number will be generated based on that value, which will always be the same.

LEAST(*expr1*, *expr2*, …)
> This function returns the smallest of the values specified.

GREATEST(*expr1*, *expr2*, …)
> This function returns the largest of the values specified.

DEGREES(*expr*)
> This function returns the value of *expr* (in radians) in degrees.

RADIANS(*expr*)
> This function returns the value of *expr* (in degrees) in radians.

TRUNCATE(*expr*, *num*)
> This function returns the value of floating point number *expr* truncated to *num* decimal places (i.e. rounded down).

BIN(*expr*)
> This function converts decimal *expr* to binary, equivalent to CONV(expr, 10, 2).

OCT(*expr*)
> This function converts decimal *expr* to octal, equivalent to CONV(expr, 10, 8).

HEX(*expr*)
> This function converts decimal *expr* to hexadecimal, equivalent to CONV(expr, 10, 16).

CONV(*expr*, *from_base*, *to_base*)
> This function converts a number (*expr*) in base *from_base* to a number in base *to_base*. Returns NULL if any of the arguments are NULL.

String Functions

ASCII(*str*)
This function returns the ASCII code value of the left-most character in *str*, 0 if *str* is an empty string, or NULL if *str* is NULL.

ORD(*str*)
This function returns the ASCII code of the left-most character in *str*, taking into account the possibility that it might be a multi-byte character.

CHAR(*expr*, ...)
This function creates a string composed of characters, the ASCII code values of which are given by the expressions passed as arguments.

CONCAT(*str1*, *str2*, ...)
This function returns a string made up of the strings passed as arguments joined end-to-end. If any of the arguments are NULL, NULL is returned instead.

CONCAT_WS(*separator*, *str1*, *str2*, ...)
CONCAT "with Separator" (WS). This function is the same as CONCAT, except that the first argument is placed between each of the additional arguments when they are combined.

LENGTH(*str*)
OCTET_LENGTH(*str*)
CHAR_LENGTH(*str*)
CHARACTER_LENGTH(*str*)
All of these return the length in characters of *str*. CHAR_LENGTH and CHARACTER_LENGTH, however, take multi-byte characters into consideration when performing the count.

BIT_LENGTH(*str*)
This function returns the length (in bits) of *str* (i.e. BIT_LENGTH(*str*) = 8 * LENGTH(*str*)).

LOCATE(*substr*, *str*)
POSITION(*substr* IN *str*)
This function returns the position of the first occurrence of *substr* in *str* (1 if it occurs at the beginning, 2 if it starts after one character, and so on). It returns 0 if *substr* does not occur in *str*.

LOCATE(*substr, str, pos*)

Same as LOCATE(*substr, str*), but begins searching from character number *pos*.

INSTR(*str, substr*)

This function is the same as LOCATE(*substr, str*), but with argument order swapped.

LPAD(*str, len, padstr*)

This function shortens or lengthens *str* so that it is of length *len*. Lengthening is accomplished by inserting *padstr* to the left of the characters of *str* (e.g. LPAD('!', '5', '.') = '....!').

RPAD(*str, len, padstr*)

This function shortens or lengthens *str* so that it is of length *len*. Lengthening is accomplished by inserting *padstr* to the right of the characters of *str* (e.g. RPAD('!','5','.') = '!....').

LEFT(*str, len*)

This function returns the left-most *len* characters of *str*. If *str* is shorter than *len* characters, *str* is returned with no extra padding.

RIGHT(*str, len*)

This function returns the right-most *len* characters of *str*. If *str* is shorter than *len* characters, *str* is returned with no extra padding.

SUBSTRING(*str, pos, len*)
SUBSTRING(*str* FROM *pos* FOR *len*)
MID(*str, pos, len*)

This function returns a string up to *len* characters long taken from *str* beginning at position *pos* (where 1 is the first character). The second form of SUBSTRING is the ANSI standard.

SUBSTRING(*str, pos*)
SUBSTRING(*str* FROM *pos*)

This function returns the string beginning from position *pos* in *str* (where 1 is the first character) and going to the end of *str*.

SUBSTRING_INDEX(*str, delim, count*)

MySQL counts *count* occurrences of *delim* in *str*, then takes the substring from that point. If *count* is positive, MySQL counts to the right from the start of the string, then takes the substring up to but not including that delimiter. If *count* is negative, MySQL counts to the left from the end of the string, then takes the substring that starts right after that delimiter, and runs to the end of *str*.

LTRIM(*str*)

This function returns *str* with any leading white space trimmed off.

RTRIM(*str*)

This function returns *str* with any trailing white space trimmed off.

TRIM([[BOTH | LEADING | TRAILING] [*remstr*] FROM] *str*)

This function returns *str* with either white space (by default) or occurrences of the string *remstr* removed from the start of the string (LEADING), end of the string (TRAILING), or both (BOTH, the default).

SOUNDEX(*str*)

This function produces a string that represents how *str* sounds when read aloud. Words that sound similar should have the same "soundex string."

E.g.:

```
SOUNDEX("tire") = "T600"
SOUNDEX("tyre") = "T600"
SOUNDEX("terror") = "T600"
SOUNDEX("tyrannosaur") = "T6526"
```

SPACE(*num*)

This function returns a string of *num* space characters.

REPLACE(*str*, *from_str*, *to_str*)

This function returns *str* after replacing all occurrences of *from_str* to *to_str*.

REPEAT(*str*, *count*)

This function returns a string made up of *str* repeated *count* times, an empty string if *count* <= 0, or NULL if either argument is NULL.

REVERSE(*str*)

This function returns *str* spelled backwards.

INSERT(*str*, *pos*, *len*, *newstr*)

This function takes *str*, and removes the substring beginning at *pos* (where 1 is the first character in the string) with length *len*, then inserts *newstr* at that position. If *len* = 0, the function simply inserts *newstr* at position *pos*.

ELT(*N*, *str1*, *str2*, *str3*, …)

This function returns the *N*th string argument (*str1* if *N*=1, *str2* if *N*=2 and so on), or NULL if there is no argument for the given *N*.

FIELD(*str*, *str1*, *str2*, *str3*, …)

This function returns the position of *str* in the subsequent list of arguments (1 if *str* = *str1*, 2 if *str* = *str2*, and so on).

FIND_IN_SET(*str*, *strlist*)

When *strlist* is a list of strings of the form 'string1,string2,string3,…' this function returns the index of *str* in that list, or 0 if *str* is not in the list. This function is ideally suited (and optimized) for determining if *str* is selected in a column of type SET (see Appendix C).

MAKE_SET(*bits*, *str1*, *str2*, …)

This function returns a list of strings of the form 'string1,string2,string3,…' using the string parameters (*str1*, *str2*, etc.) that correspond to the bits that are set in the number *bits*. For example, if *bits* = 10 (binary 1010) then bits 2 and 4 are set, so the output of MAKE_SET will be 'str2,str4'.

EXPORT_SET(*bits*, *on_str*, *off_str*[, *separator*[, *number_of_bits*]])

This function returns a string representation of which bits are, and are not set in *bits*. Set bits are represented by the *on_str* string, while unset bits are represented by the *off_str* string. By default, these bit representations are comma-separated, but the optional *separator* string lets you define your own. By default, up to 64 bits of bits are read; however, *number_of_bits* lets you specify that a smaller number be read.

E.g.:

```
EXPORT_SET(10, 'Y', 'N', ',', 6) = 'N,Y,N,Y,N,N'
```

LCASE(*str*)
LOWER(*str*)

This function returns *str* with all letters in lowercase.

UCASE(*str*)
UPPER(*str*)

This function returns *str* with all letters in uppercase.

LOAD_FILE(*filename*)

This function returns the contents of the file specified by *filename* (an absolute path to a file readable by MySQL). Your MySQL user should also have file privileges.

QUOTE(*str*)

This function returns *str* surrounded by single quotes, and with any special characters escaped with backslashes. If *str* is NULL, the function returns the string NULL (without surrounding quotes).

Date and Time Functions

DAYOFWEEK(*date*)

This function returns the weekday of *date* in the form of an integer, according to the ODBC standard (1 = Sunday, 2 = Monday, 3 = Tuesday ... 7 = Saturday).

WEEKDAY(*date*)

This function returns the weekday of *date* in the form of an integer (0 = Monday, 1 = Tuesday, 2 = Wednesday ... 6 = Sunday).

DAYOFMONTH(*date*)

This function returns the day of the month for *date* (from 1 to 31).

DAYOFYEAR(*date*)

This function returns the day of the year for *date* (from 1 to 366—remember leap years!).

MONTH(*date*)

This function returns the month for *date* (from 1, January, to 12, December).

DAYNAME(*date*)

Returns the name of the day of the week for *date* (e.g. Tuesday).

MONTHNAME(*date*)

This function returns the name of the month for *date* (e.g. "April").

QUARTER(*date*)

This function returns the quarter of the year for *date* (e.g.: QUARTER('2005-04-12') = 2).

WEEK(date[, mode])

This function returns the week of the year for *date*, by default in the range 0-53 (where week 1 is the first week that starts in this year), assuming that the first day of the week is Sunday.

By specifying one of the *mode* values in Table B.1, you can alter the way this value is calculated.

Table B.1. Modes for Week Calculations

mode	Week Starts On	Return Value Range	Week 1
0	Sunday	0 to 53	first week that starts in this year
1	Monday	0 to 53	first week that has more than 3 days in this year
2	Sunday	1 to 53	first week that starts in this year
3	Monday	1 to 53	first week that has more than 3 days in this year
4	Sunday	0 to 53	first week that starts in this year
5	Monday	0 to 53	first week that has more than 3 days in this year
6	Sunday	1 to 53	first week that starts in this year
7	Monday	1 to 53	first week that has more than 3 days in this year

YEAR(date)

This function returns the year for *date* (from 1000 to 9999).

YEARWEEK(date)
YEARWEEK(date, first)

This function returns the year and week for *date* in the form *YYYYWW*. Note that the first or last day or two of the year may often belong to a week of the year before or after, respectively.

E.g.:

```
YEARWEEK("2006-12-31") = 200701
```

HOUR(*time*)

This function returns the hour for *time* (from 0 to 23).

MINUTE(*time*)

This function returns the minute for *time* (from 0 to 59).

SECOND(*time*)

This function returns the second for *time* (from 0 to 59).

PERIOD_ADD(*period, num_months*)

This function adds *num_months* months to period (specified as *YYMM* or *YYYYMM*) and returns the value in the form *YYYYMM*.

PERIOD_DIFF(*period1, period2*)

This function returns the number of months between *period1* and *period2* (each of which should be specified as *YYMM* or *YYYYMM*).

DATE_ADD(*date,* INTERVAL *expr type*)
DATE_SUB(*date,* INTERVAL *expr type*)
ADDDATE(*date,* INTERVAL *expr type*)
SUBDATE(*date,* INTERVAL *expr type*)

This function returns the result of either adding or subtracting the specified interval of time to or from *date* (a DATE or DATETIME value). DATE_ADD and ADDDATE are identical, as are DATE_SUB and SUBDATE. *expr* specifies the interval to be added or subtracted and may be negative if you wish to specify a negative interval, and *type* specifies the format of *expr*, as shown in Table B.2.

If *date* and *expr* involve only date values, the result will be a DATE value; otherwise, this function will return a DATETIME value.

Here are a few examples to help you see how this family of functions works.

The following both return the date six months from now:

```
ADDDATE(CURDATE(), INTERVAL 6 MONTH)
DATE_ADD(CURDATE(), INTERVAL '0-6' YEAR_MONTH)
```

The following all return this time tomorrow:

```
ADDDATE(NOW(), INTERVAL 1 DAY)
SUBDATE(NOW(), INTERVAL -1 DAY)
DATE_ADD(NOW(), INTERVAL '24:0:0' HOUR_SECOND)
DATE_ADD(NOW(), INTERVAL '1 0:0' DAY_MINUTE)
```

Table B.2. Interval Types for Date Addition/Subtraction Functions

type	Format for expr
SECOND	number of seconds
MINUTE	number of minutes
HOUR	number of hours
DAY	number of days
MONTH	number of months
YEAR	number of years
MINUTE_SECOND	`'minutes:seconds'`
HOUR_MINUTE	`'hours:minutes'`
DAY_HOUR	`'days hours'`
YEAR_MONTH	`'years-months'`
HOUR_SECOND	`'hours:minutes:seconds'`
DAY_MINUTE	`'days hours:minutes'`
DAY_SECOND	`'days hours:minutes:seconds'`

TO_DAYS(*date*)

This function converts date to a number of days since year 0. Allows you to calculate differences in dates (i.e. TO_DAYS(*date1*) - TO_DAYS(*date2*) = *days_in_between*).

FROM_DAYS(*days*)

Given the number of *days* since year 0 (as produced by TO_DAYS), this function returns a date.

DATE_FORMAT(*date, format*)

This function takes the date or time value date and returns it formatted according to the formatting string *format*, which may contain as placeholders any of the symbols shown in Table B.3.

TIME_FORMAT(*time, format*)

This function is the same as DATE_FORMAT, except the *format* string may only contain symbols referring to hours, minutes, and seconds.

Table B.3. DATE_FORMAT Symbols (2004-01-01 01:00:00)

Symbol	Displays	Example
%M	Month name	January
%W	Weekday name	Thursday
%D	Day of the month with English suffix	1st
%Y	Year, numeric, 4 digits	2004
%y	Year, numeric, 2 digits	03
%a	Abbreviated weekday name	Thu
%d	Day of the month	01
%e	Day of the month	1
%m	Month of the year, numeric	01
%c	Month of the year, numeric	1
%b	Abbreviated month name	Jan
%j	Day of the year	001
%H	Hour of the day (24 hour format, 00-23)	01
%k	Hour of the day (24 hour format, 0-23)	1
%h	Hour of the day (12 hour format, 01-12)	01
%I	Hour of the day (12 hour format, 01-12)	01
%l	Hour of the day (12 hour format, 1-12)	1
%i	Minutes	00
%r	Time, 12 hour (hh:mm:ss AM/PM)	01:00:00 AM
%T	Time, 24 hour (hh:mm:ss)	01:00:00
%S	Seconds	00
%s	Seconds	00
%p	AM or PM	AM
%w	Day of the week, numeric (0=Sunday)	4
%U	Week (00-53), Sunday first day of the week	00
%u	Week (00-53), Monday first day of the week	01
%X	Year of the week where Sunday is the first day of the week, 4 digits (use with %V)	2003

Symbol	Displays	Example
%V	Week (01-53), Sunday first day of week (%X)	53
%X	Like %X, Monday first day of week (use with %v)	2004
%v	Week (01-53), Monday first day of week (%x)	01
%%	An actual percent sign	%

CURDATE()
CURRENT_DATE

This function returns the current system date in the SQL date format `'YYYY-MM-DD'` (if used as a date) or as *YYYYMMDD* (if used as a number).

CURTIME()
CURRENT_TIME
CURRENT_TIME()

This function returns the current system time in the SQL time format `'HH:MM:SS'` (if used as a time) or as *HHMMSS* (if used as a number).

NOW()
SYSDATE()
CURRENT_TIMESTAMP
CURRENT_TIMESTAMP()
LOCALTIME
LOCALTIME()
LOCALTIMESTAMP
LOCALTIMESTAMP()

This function returns the current system date and time in SQL date/time format `'YYYY-MM-DD HH:MM:SS'` (if used as a date/time) or as *YYYYMMDDHHMMSS* (if used as a number).

UNIX_TIMESTAMP()
UNIX_TIMESTAMP(date)

This function returns either the current system date and time, or the specified date/time as the number of seconds since 1970-01-01 00:00:00 GMT.

FROM_UNIXTIME(unix_timestamp)

The opposite of UNIX_TIMESTAMP, this function converts a number of seconds from 1970-01-01 00:00:00 GMT to `'YYYY-MM-DD HH:MM:SS'` (if used as a date/time) or *YYYYMMDDHHMMSS* (if used as a number), local time.

FROM_UNIXTIME(*unix_timestamp*, *format*)
 This function formats a UNIX timestamp according to the *format* string, which may contain any of the symbols listed in Table B.3.

SEC_TO_TIME(*seconds*)
 This function converts some number of *seconds* to the format *'HH:MM:SS'* (if used as a time) or *HHMMSS* (if used as a number).

TIME_TO_SEC(*time*)
 This function converts a *time* in the format *'HH:MM:SS'* to a number of seconds.

Miscellaneous Functions

DATABASE()
 This function returns the currently selected database name, or an empty string if no database is currently selected.

USER()
SYSTEM_USER()
SESSION_USER()
 This function returns the current MySQL user name, including the client host name (e.g. `'kevin@localhost'`). The SUBSTRING_INDEX function may be used to obtain the user name alone:

```
SUBSTRING_INDEX(USER(), "@", 1) = 'kevin'
```

CURRENT_USER()
 This function returns the user entry in the MySQL access control system that was used to authenticate the current connection, and which controls its privileges, in the form *'user@host'*. In many cases, this will be the same as the value returned by USER(), but when entries in the access control system contain wild cards, this value may be less specific (e.g. `'@%.mycompany.com'`).

PASSWORD(*str*)
 This is a one-way password encryption function, which converts any string (typically a plain text password) into an encrypted format precisely 16 characters in length. A particular plain text string always will yield the same encrypted string of 16 characters; thus, values encoded in this way can be used to verify the correctness of a password without actually storing the password in the database.

This function does not use the same encryption mechanism as UNIX passwords; use ENCRYPT for that type of encryption.

ENCRYPT(*str*[, *salt*])

This function uses standard UNIX encryption (via the crypt() system call) to encrypt *str*. The *salt* argument is optional, and lets you control the seed that is used for the generation of the password. If you want the encryption to match a UNIX password file entry, the salt should be the two first characters of the encrypted value you're trying to match. Depending on the implementation of crypt() on your system, the encrypted value may only depend on the first eight characters of the plain text value.

On systems where crypt() is not available, this function returns NULL.

ENCODE(*str*, *pass_str*)

This function encrypts *str* using a two-way password-based encryption algorithm, with password *pass_str*. To subsequently decrypt the value, use DECODE.

DECODE(*crypt_str*, *pass_str*)

This function decrypts the encrypted *crypt_str* using two-way password-based encryption, with password *pass_str*. If the same password is given that was provided to ENCODE the value originally, the original string will be restored.

MD5(*string*)

This function calculates an MD5 hash based on string. The resulting value is a 32-digit hexadecimal number. A particular string will always produce the same MD5 hash; however, MD5(NOW()) may be used, for instance, to obtain a semi-random string when one is needed (as a default password, for instance).

LAST_INSERT_ID()

This function returns the last number that was automatically generated for an AUTO_INSERT column in the current connection.

FOUND_ROWS()

When you execute a SELECT query with a LIMIT clause, you may sometimes want to know how many rows would have been returned if you didn't have a LIMIT clause. To do this, use the SQL_CALC_FOUND_ROWS option for the SELECT query (see Appendix A), then call this function in a second SELECT query.

Calling this function is considerably quicker than repeating the query without a LIMIT clause, since the full result set does not need to be sent to the client.

FORMAT(*expr*, *num*)

This function formats a number expr with commas as "thousands separators" and num decimal places (rounded to the nearest value, and padded with zeroes).

VERSION()

This function returns the MySQL server version (e.g. '4.0.20a-nt').

CONNECTION_ID()

This function returns the thread ID for the current connection.

GET_LOCK(*str*, *timeout*)

If two or more clients must synchronize tasks beyond what table locking can offer, named locks may be used instead. GET_LOCK attempts to obtain a lock with a given name (*str*). If the named lock is already in use by another client, this client will wait up to *timeout* seconds before giving up waiting for the lock to become free.

Once a client has obtained a lock, it can be released either using RELEASE_LOCK or by using GET_LOCK again to obtain a new lock.

GET_LOCK returns 1 if the lock was successfully retrieved, 0 if the time specified by *timeout* elapsed, or NULL if some error occurred.

GET_LOCK is not a MySQL command in and of itself—it must appear as part of another query.

E.g.:

```
SELECT GET_LOCK("mylock", 10)
```

RELEASE_LOCK(*str*)

This function releases the named lock that was obtained by GET_LOCK. It returns 1 if the lock was released, 0 if the lock wasn't locked by this thread, or NULL if the lock doesn't exist.

IS_FREE_LOCK(*str*)

This function checks if the named lock is free to be locked. It returns 1 if the lock was free, 0 if the lock was in use, or NULL if an error occurred.

BENCHMARK(*count, expr*)

> This function repeatedly evaluates *expr count* times, for the purposes of speed testing. The MySQL command line client allows the operation to be timed.

INET_NTOA(*expr*)

> This function returns the IP address represented by the integer *expr*. See INET_ATON to create such integers.

INET_ATON(*expr*)

> This function converts an IP address *expr* to a single integer representation.

> E.g.:

```
INET_ATON('64.39.28.1') = 64 * 2553 + 39 * 2552 + 28 * 255 + 1
                        = 1063751116
```

Functions for Use with GROUP BY Clauses

Also known as **summary functions**, the following are intended for use with GROUP BY clauses, where they will produce values based on the set of records making up each row of the final result set.

If used without a GROUP BY clause, these functions will cause the result set to be displayed as a single row, with a value calculated based on all of the rows of the complete result set. Without a GROUP BY clause, mixing these functions with columns that do not contain summary functions will cause an error, because you cannot collapse those columns into a single row and get a sensible value.

COUNT(*expr*)

> This function returns a count of the number of times in the ungrouped result set that *expr* had a non-NULL value. If COUNT(*) is used, it will simply provide a count of the number of rows in the group, irrespective of NULL values.

COUNT(DISTINCT *expr*[, *expr* ...])

> This function returns a count of the number of different non-NULL values (or sets of values, if multiple expressions are provided).

AVG(*expr*)

> This function calculates the arithmetic mean (average) of the values appearing in the rows of the group.

MIN(*expr*)
MAX(*expr*)

This function returns the smallest or largest value of *expr* in the rows of the group.

SUM(*expr*)

This function returns the sum of the values for *expr* in the rows of the group.

STD(*expr*)
STDDEV(*expr*)

This function returns the standard deviation of the values for *expr* in the rows of the group (either of the two function names may be used).

BIT_OR(*expr*)
BIT_AND(*expr*)

This function calculates the bit-wise OR and the bit-wise AND of the values for *expr* in the rows of the group, respectively.

Appendix C: MySQL Column Types

When you create a table in MySQL, you must specify the data type for each column. This appendix documents all of the column types that MySQL provides as of version 4.0.20 (current as of this writing).

In this reference, many column types can accept **optional parameters** to further customize how data for the column is stored or displayed. First, there are the M and D parameters, which are indicated (in square brackets when optional) immediately following the column type name.

The parameter M is used to specify the display size (i.e. maximum number of characters) to be used by values in the column. In most cases, this will limit the range of values that may be specified in the column. M may be any integer between 1 and 255. Note that for numerical types (e.g. INT), this parameter does not actually restrict the range of values that may be stored. Instead, it causes spaces (or zeroes in the case of a ZEROFILL column—see below for details) to be added to the values so that they reach the desired display width when they're displayed. Note also that the storage of values longer than the specified display width can cause problems when the values are used in complex joins, and thus should be avoided whenever possible.

The parameter D lets you specify how many decimal places will be stored for a floating-point value. This parameter may be set to a maximum of 30, but M should always allow for these places (i.e. D should always be less than or equal to M-2 to allow room for a zero and a decimal point).

The second type of parameter is an optional **column attribute**. The attributes supported by the different column types are listed for each; to enable them, simply type them after the column type, separated by spaces. Here are the available column attributes and their meanings:

ZEROFILL
: Values for the column always occupy their maximum display length, as the actual value is padded with zeroes. The option automatically sets the UNSIGNED option as well.

UNSIGNED
: The column may accept only positive numerical values (or zero). This restriction frees up more storage space for positive numbers, effectively doubling the range of positive values that may be stored in the column,

and should always be set if you know that you won't need to store negative values.

BINARY By default, comparisons of character values in MySQL (including sorting) are case-insensitive. However, comparisons for BINARY columns are case-sensitive.

For a complete, up-to-date reference to supported SQL column types, see the MySQL Reference Manual[1].

Numerical Types

TINYINT[(*M*)]
Description: A tiny integer value

Attributes allowed: UNSIGNED, ZEROFILL

Range: -128 to 127 (0 to 255 if UNSIGNED)

Storage space: 1 byte (8 bits)

SMALLINT[(*M*)]
Description: A small integer value

Attributes allowed: UNSIGNED, ZEROFILL

Range: -32768 to 32767 (0 to 65535 if UNSIGNED)

Storage space: 2 bytes (16 bits)

MEDIUMINT[(*M*)]
Description: A medium integer value

Attributes allowed: UNSIGNED, ZEROFILL

Range: -8588608 to 8388607 (0 to 16777215 if UNSIGNED)

Storage space: 3 bytes (24 bits)

INT[(*M*)]
Description: A regular integer value

---

[1] http://dev.mysql.com/doc/mysql/en/Column_types.html

Attributes allowed: UNSIGNED, ZEROFILL

Range: -2147483648 to 2147483647 (0 to 4294967295 if UNSIGNED)

Storage space: 4 bytes (32 bits)

Alternative syntax: INTEGER[(*M*)]

BIGINT[(*M*)]

Description: A large integer value

Attributes allowed: UNSIGNED, ZEROFILL

Range: -9223372036854775808 to 9223372036854775807 (0 to 18446744073709551615 if UNSIGNED)

Storage space: 8 bytes (64 bits)

Notes: MySQL performs all integer arithmetic functions in signed BIGINT format; thus, BIGINT UNSIGNED values over 9223372036854775807 (63 bits) will only work properly with bit functions (e.g. bit-wise AND, OR, and NOT). Attempting integer arithmetic with larger values may produce inaccurate results due to rounding errors.

FLOAT[(*M*, *D*)]
FLOAT(*precision*)

Description: A floating point number

Attributes allowed: ZEROFILL

Range: 0 and $\pm 1.175494351E\text{-}38$ to $\pm 3.402823466E\text{+}38$

Storage space: 4 bytes (32 bits)

Notes: precision (in bits), if specified, must be less than or equal to 24, or else a DOUBLE column will be created instead (see below).

DOUBLE[(*M*, *D*)]
DOUBLE(*precision*)

Description: A high-precision floating point number

Attributes allowed: ZEROFILL

Range: 0 and $\pm 2.2250738585072014\text{-}308$ to $\pm 1.7976931348623157E\text{+}308$

Storage space: 8 bytes (64 bits)

Notes: precision (in bits), if specified, must be greater than or equal to 25, or else a FLOAT column will be created instead (see above). precision may not be greater than 53.

Alternative syntax: DOUBLE PRECISION[(*M*,*D*)] or REAL([*M*,*D*])

DECIMAL[(*M*[, *D*])]

   Description: A floating point number stored as a character string

   Attributes allowed: ZEROFILL

   Range: As for DOUBLE, but constrained by M and D (see Notes)

   Storage space: M+2 bytes (8M+16 bits) (see Notes, prior to MySQL 3.23)

   Notes: If D is not specified, it defaults to 0 and numbers in this column will have no decimal point or fractional part. If M is not specified, it defaults to 10. In versions of MySQL prior to 3.23, M had to include space for the negative sign and the decimal point, so the storage space required was M bytes (8M bits). The newer format in MySQL 3.23 or later is ANSI SQL compliant.

   Alternative syntax: NUMERIC([*M*[,*D*]])

Character Types

CHAR(*M*)

   Description: A fixed-length character string

   Attributes allowed: BINARY

   Maximum Length: M characters

   Storage space: M bytes (8M bits)

   Notes: CHAR values are stored as strings of length M, even though the assigned value may be shorter. When the string does not occupy the full length of the field, spaces are added to the end of the string to bring it exactly to M characters. Trailing spaces are stripped off when the value is retrieved.

CHAR columns are quicker to search than variable-length character column types such as VARCHAR, since their fixed-length nature makes the underlying database file format more regular.

M may take any integer value from 0 to 255, with a CHAR(0) column able to store only two values: NULL and ' ' (the empty string), which occupy a single bit.

Alternative syntax: CHARACTER(M)

VARCHAR(M)

Description: A variable-length character string

Attributes allowed: BINARY

Maximum Length: M characters

Storage space: Length of stored value, plus 1 byte to store length

Notes: As VARCHAR values occupy only the space they require, there usually is no point to specifying a maximum field length M of anything less than 255 (the maximum). Values anywhere from 1 to 255 are acceptable, however, and will cause strings longer than the specified limit to be chopped to the maximum length when inserted. Trailing spaces are stripped from values before they are stored.

Alternative syntax: CHARACTER VARYING(M)

TINYBLOB
TINYTEXT

Description: A short, variable-length character string

Maximum Length: 255 characters

Storage space: Length of stored value, plus 1 byte to store length

Notes: These types are basically equivalent to VARCHAR(255) BINARY and VARCHAR(255), respectively. However, these column types do not trim trailing spaces from inserted values. The only difference between TINYBLOB and TINYTEXT is that the former performs case-sensitive comparisons and sorts, while the latter does not.

BLOB
TEXT

Description: A variable-length character string

Maximum Length: 65535 characters (65KB)

Storage space: Length of stored value, plus 2 bytes to store length

Notes: The only difference between BLOB and TEXT is that the former performs case-sensitive comparisons and sorts, while the latter does not.

MEDIUMBLOB
MEDIUMTEXT

Description: A medium, variable-length character string

Maximum Length: 16777215 characters (16.8MB)

Storage space: Length of stored value, plus 3 bytes to store length

Notes: The only difference between MEDIUMBLOB and MEDIUMTEXT is that the former performs case-sensitive comparisons and sorts, while the latter does not.

LONGBLOB
LONGTEXT

Description: A long, variable-length character string

Maximum Length: 4294967295 characters (4.3GB)

Storage space: Length of stored value, plus 4 bytes to store length

Notes: The only difference between LONGBLOB and LONGTEXT is that the former performs case-sensitive comparisons and sorts, while the latter does not.

ENUM(*value1*, *value2*, ...)

Description: A set of values from which a single value must be chosen for each row

Maximum Length: One value chosen from up to 65535 possibilities

Storage space:

❑ 1 to 255 values: 1 byte (8 bits)

☐ 256 to 65535 values: 2 bytes (16 bits)

Notes: Values in this type of field are stored as integers that represent the element selected. 1 represents the first element, 2 the second, and so on. The special value 0 represents the empty string ' ', which is stored if a value that does not appear in column declaration is assigned.

NOT NULL columns of this type default to the first value in the column declaration if no particular default is assigned.

SET(*value1*, *value2*, ...)
Description: A set of values, each of which may be set or not set

Maximum Length: Up to 64 values in a given SET column

Storage space:

☐ 1 to 8 values: 1 byte (8 bits)

☐ 9 to 16 values: 2 bytes (16 bits)

☐ 17 to 24 values: 3 bytes (24 bits)

☐ 25 to 32 values: 4 bytes (32 bits)

☐ 33 to 64 values: 8 bytes (64 bits)

Notes: Values in this type of field are stored as integers representing the pattern of bits for set and unset values. For example, if a set contains eight values, and in a particular row the odd values are set, then the binary representation 01010101 becomes the decimal value 85. Values may therefore be assigned either as integers, or as a string of set values, separated by commas (e.g. 'value1,value3,value5,value7' = 85). Searches should be performed either with the LIKE operator, or the FIND_IN_SET function.

Date/Time Types

DATE
Description: A date

Range: '1000-01-01' to '9999-12-31', and '0000-00-00'

Storage space: 3 bytes (24 bits)

TIME

Description: A time

Range: '-838:59:59' to '838:59:59'

Storage space: 3 bytes (24 bits)

DATETIME

Description: A date and time

Range: '1000-01-01 00:00:00' to '9999-12-31 23:59:59'

Storage space: 8 bytes (64 bits)

YEAR

Description: A year

Range: 1901 to 2155, and 0000

Storage space: 1 byte (8 bits)

Notes: You can specify a year value with a four-digit number (1901 to 2155, or 0000), a four-digit string ('1901' to '2155', or '0000'), a two-digit number (70 to 99 for 1970 to 1999, 1 to 69 for 2001 to 2069, or 0 for 0000), or a two-digit string ('70' to '99' for 1970 to 1999, '00' to '69' for 2000 to 2069). Note that you cannot specify the year 2000 with a two-digit number, and you can't specify the year 0000 with a two-digit string. Invalid year values are always converted to 0000.

TIMESTAMP[(*M*)]

Description: A timestamp (date/time), in YYYYMMDDHHMMSS format

Range: 19700101000000 to sometime in 2037 on current systems

Storage space: 4 bytes (32 bits)

Notes: An INSERT or UPDATE operation on a row that contains one or more TIMESTAMP columns automatically will update the first TIMESTAMP column in the row with the current date/time. This lets you use such a column as the "last modified date/time" for the row. Assigning a value of NULL to the column will have the same effect, thereby providing a means of "touching" the date/time. You can also assign actual values as you would for any other column.

Allowable values for M are 14, 12, 10, 8, 6, 4, and 2, and correspond to the display formats YYYYMMDDHHMMSS, YYMMDDHHMMSS, YYMMDDHHMM, YYYYMMDD, YYMMDD, YYMM, and YY respectively. Odd values from 1 to 13 automatically will be bumped up to the next even number, while values of 0 or greater than 14 are changed to 14.

Appendix D: PHP Functions for Working with MySQL

PHP provides a vast library of built-in functions that let you perform all sorts of tasks without having to look to third-party software vendors for a solution. The online reference[1] to these functions provided by the PHP Official Website is second to none. Obtaining detailed information about a function is as simple as opening your browser and typing:

```
http://www.php.net/functionname
```

As a result of the convenience of this facility, we have judged that a complete PHP function reference is beyond the scope of this book. All the same, this appendix contains a reference to those PHP functions specifically designed to interact with MySQL databases, so that if you use this book as your primary reference while building a database-driven Website, you won't have to look elsewhere for the information you need.

This list of functions and their definitions are current as of PHP 5.0.1.

mysql_affected_rows

```
mysql_affected_rows([link_id])
```

This function returns the number of affected rows in the previous MySQL INSERT, UPDATE, DELETE, or REPLACE operation performed with the specified link_id. If the link is not specified, then the last-opened link is assumed. It returns -1 if the previous operation failed.

mysql_client_encoding

```
mysql_client_encoding([link_id])
```

This function returns the name of the default character set in use by the current or specified connection (e.g. latin1).

---

[1] http://www.php.net/mysql

mysql_close

```
mysql_close([link_id])
```

This function closes the current or specified (`link_id`) MySQL connection. If the link is a persistent link opened by `mysql_pconnect` (see below), this function call is ignored. As non-persistent connections automatically are closed by PHP at the end of a script, this function is usually not needed.

This function returns `true` on success, `false` on failure.

mysql_connect

```
mysql_connect([hostname[:port|:/socket/path][, username[,
    password[, new_link[, client_flags]]]]])
```

This function opens a connection to a MySQL server and returns a connection ID (which evaluates to true) that may be used in other MySQL-related functions. The following default values are assumed if they are not specified:

hostname:port	`'localhost:3306'`
username	server process name
password	`' '`

If true, the `new_link` parameter forces a new connection to be made, even if the other parameters correspond to an existing connection that could be reused.

The `client_flags` parameter lets you switch on advanced options for the connection with the constants `MYSQL_CLIENT_COMPRESS`, `MYSQL_CLIENT_IGNORE_SPACE`, and `MYSQL_CLIENT_INTERACTIVE`. To use more than one of these, specify them in a list separated by the bitwise OR operator (`|`).

If the connection attempt is unsuccessful, an error message will be displayed by default and the function will return `false`. To bypass display of the error message (e.g. to display your own by checking the return value), put "@" at the start of the function name (i.e. `@mysql_connect(…)`).

mysql_create_db

`mysql_create_db(db_name[, link_id])`

This function creates a new MySQL database with the specified name, using the default or specified (`link_id`) MySQL connection. It returns `true` on success, or `false` on error. The function name `mysql_createdb` may also be used, but is deprecated.

 `mysql_create_db` is deprecated. Use `mysql_query` to issue a `CREATE DATABASE` command to MySQL, instead.

mysql_data_seek

`mysql_data_seek(result_id, row_number)`

This function moves the internal result pointer of the result set identified by `result_id` to row number `row_number`, so that the next call to a `mysql_fetch_*` function will retrieve the specified row. It returns `true` on success, and `false` on failure. The first row in a result set is number 0.

mysql_db_name

`mysql_db_name(result_id, row_number)`

`result_id` should refer to a result set produced by a call to `mysql_list_dbs` (see below), and will retrieve the name of the database listed on the row specified by `row_number`. The first row in a result set is row 0. The function name `mysql_dbname` may also be used, but is deprecated.

mysql_db_query

`mysql_db_query(db_name, sql_query[, link_id])`

This function selects the MySQL database identified by `db_name` as if with `mysql_select_db`, then executes the specified MySQL query (`sql_query`). If the MySQL connection identifier (`link_id`) is not specified, PHP will use the currently active connection. If no such connection exists, PHP will attempt to open a connection by implicitly calling `mysql_connect` with default parameters.

If the query fails, an error message to that effect will be displayed unless "@" is added to the beginning of the function name, and the function will return `false` instead of a result identifier (which evaluates to `true`). If the error occurred due to an error in the SQL query, the error number and message can be obtained using `mysq_errno` and `mysql_error`, respectively.

The function name `mysql` may also be used, but is deprecated.

As of PHP 4.0.6, this function is deprecated. Use `mysql_select_db`, and then `mysql_query`, or use only `mysql_query` and fully specify the table names in your query as *dbname.tblname*.

mysql_drop_db

`mysql_drop_db(db_name[, link_id])`

This function drops (deletes) the specified database and all the tables it contains, using the default or specified (`link_id`) MySQL connection. It returns `true` on success and `false` on failure.

The function name `mysql_dropdb` may also be used, but is deprecated.

mysql_errno

`mysql_errno([link_id])`

This function returns the numerical value of the error message from the last MySQL operation on the default or specified (`link_id`) MySQL connection.

mysql_error

`mysql_error([link_id])`

This function returns the text of the error message from the last MySQL operation on the default or specified (`link_id`) MySQL connection.

mysql_escape_string

`mysql_escape_string(string)`

This function returns an escaped version of a string (with backslashes before special characters such as quotes) for use in a MySQL query. This function is a little more thorough than addslashes or PHP's Magic Quotes feature, but those methods generally are sufficient (and in the case of Magic Quotes, automatic), so this function is rarely used.

As of PHP 4.3.0, this function is deprecated. Use mysql_real_escape_string instead.

mysql_fetch_array

`mysql_fetch_array(result_id[, array_type])`

This function fetches the next row of a MySQL result set, then advances the internal row pointer of the result set to the next row. It returns the row as an associative array, a numeric array, or both, depending on the value of array_type.

When array_type is not specified, or is set to MYSQL_BOTH, each field in the row will be given a numerical index ($row[0]) as well as a string index ($row['col_name']) in the returned array. MYSQL_NUM causes only numerical indices to be assigned, while MYSQL_ASSOC assigns only string indices.

This function returns false if there are no rows left in the specified result set.

mysql_fetch_assoc

`mysql_fetch_assoc(result_id)`

This function fetches a result row as an associative array. It's identical to mysql_fetch_array called with the MYSQL_ASSOC parameter.

mysql_fetch_field

`mysql_fetch_field(result_id[, field_position])`

This function returns an object that contains information about a particular column in the supplied result set (result_id). If the field_position (the first column is position 0) is not specified, then repeated calls to mysql_fetch_field will retrieve each of the columns one at a time, from left to right. Assuming the result of this function is stored in `$field`, then the properties of the retrieved field are accessible as shown in Table D.1.

Table D.1. Object Fields for `mysql_fetch_field`

Object Property	Information Contained
`$field->name`	Column name
`$field->table`	Name of table to which the column belongs
`$field->max_length`	Maximum length of the column
`$field->not_null`	1 if the column is set `NOT NULL`
`$field->primary_key`	1 if the column is set `PRIMARY KEY`
`$field->unique_key`	1 if the column is set `UNIQUE`
`$field->multiple_key`	1 if the column is a non-unique key
`$field->numeric`	1 if the column is numeric
`$field->blob`	1 if the column is a `BLOB`
`$field->type`	The data type of the column
`$field->unsigned`	1 if the column is `UNSIGNED`
`$field->zerofill`	1 if the column is set `ZEROFILL`

mysql_fetch_lengths

`mysql_fetch_lengths(result_id)`

This function returns an array containing the lengths of each of the fields in the last-fetched row of the specified result set.

mysql_fetch_object

`mysql_fetch_object(result_id)`

This function returns the next result row from `result_id` in the form of an object, and advances the internal row pointer of the result set to the next row. Column values for the row become accessible as named properties of the object (e.g. `$row->user` for the value of the `user` field in the `$row` object).

mysql_fetch_row

`mysql_fetch_row(result_id)`

This function fetches a result row as a numerical array. It is identical to `mysql_fetch_array` called with the `MYSQL_NUM` parameter.

mysql_field_flags

`mysql_field_flags(result_id, field_position)`

This function returns a string containing the flags associated with the specified field (`field_position`) in the specified result set (`result_id`). The flags are separated by spaces in the returned string. Possible flags are: `not_null`, `primary_key`, `unique_key`, `multiple_key`, `blob`, `unsigned`, `zerofill`, `binary`, `enum`, `auto_increment`, and `timestamp`.

The function name `mysql_fieldflags` may also be used, but is deprecated.

mysql_field_len

`mysql_field_len(result_id, field_position)`

This function returns the length of the specified field (`field_position`) in a result set (`result_id`).

The function name `mysql_fieldlen` may also be used, but is deprecated.

mysql_field_name

`mysql_field_name(result_id, field_position)`

This function returns the name of the specified field (`field_position`) in a result set (`result_id`).

The function name `mysql_fieldname` may also be used, but is deprecated.

mysql_field_seek

`mysql_field_seek(result_id, field_position)`

This function sets the default field position for the next call to `mysql_fetch_field`.

mysql_field_table

`mysql_field_table(result_id, field_position)`

This function returns the name of the table containing the specified field (`field_position`) of the specified result set (`result_id`).

The function name `mysql_fieldtable` may also be used, but is deprecated.

mysql_field_type

`mysql_field_type(result_id, field_position)`

This function returns the type of the specified field (`field_position`) in the specified result set (`result_id`).

The function name `mysql_fieldtype` may also be used, but is deprecated.

mysql_free_result

`mysql_free_result(result_id)`

This function destroys the specified result set (`result_id`), freeing all memory associated with it. As all memory is freed automatically at the end of a PHP script, this function is only really useful when working with multiple very large result sets in a single script.

The function name `mysql_freeresult` may also be used, but is deprecated.

mysql_get_client_info

`mysql_get_client_info()`

This function returns a string indicating the version of the MySQL client library that PHP is using (e.g. `'4.0.20a'`).

mysql_get_host_info

```
mysql_get_host_info([link_id])
```

This function returns a string describing the type of connection and server host name for the specified (link_id) or last-opened MySQL connection (e.g. 'Localhost via UNIX socket').

mysql_get_proto_info

```
mysql_get_proto_info([link_id])
```

This function returns an integer indicating the MySQL protocol version in use for the specified (link_id) or last-opened MySQL connection (e.g. 10).

mysql_get_server_info

```
mysql_get_server_info([link_id])
```

This function returns a string indicating the version of MySQL server in use on the specified (link_id) or last-opened MySQL connection (e.g. '4.0.20a-nt').

mysql_info

```
mysql_info([link_id])
```

This function returns detailed information about the last query executed on the current or specified connection.

mysql_insert_id

```
mysql_insert_id([link_id])
```

This function returns the value that was automatically assigned to an AUTO_INCREMENT column in the previous INSERT query for the default or specified (link_id) MySQL connection. If no AUTO_INCREMENT value was assigned in the previous query, 0 is returned instead.

mysql_list_dbs

```
mysql_list_dbs([link_id])
```

This function returns a result set containing a list of the databases available from the current or specified (link_id) MySQL connection. Use mysql_db_name to retrieve the individual database names from this result set.

The function name mysql_listdbs may also be used, but is deprecated.

mysql_list_fields

```
mysql_list_fields(db_name, table_name[, link_id])
```

This function returns a result set with information about all the fields in the specified table (table_name) in the specified database (db_name) using the default or specified (link_id) MySQL connection. The result set produced may be used with mysql_field_flags, mysql_field_len, mysql_field_name, and mysql_field_type.

The function name mysql_listfields may also be used, but is deprecated.

mysql_list_processes

```
mysql_list_processes([link_id])
```

This function returns a result set with information about all of the threads running on the MySQL server and what they are doing, using the default or specified (link_id) MySQL connection. The fields in the result set are the thread ID (Id), the client hostname (Host), the selected database name (db), the command being run (Command), and the server time used (Time).

mysql_list_tables

```
mysql_list_tables(db_name[, link_id])
```

This function returns a result set containing a list of the tables in the specified database (db_name) from the current or specified (link_id) MySQL connection. Use mysql_tablename to retrieve the individual table names from this result set.

The function name `mysql_listtables` may also be used, but is deprecated.

This function is deprecated. Use `mysql_query` to perform a SHOW TABLES query instead (see Appendix A).

mysql_num_fields

`mysql_num_fields(result_id)`

This function returns the number of fields in a MySQL result set (`result_id`).

The function name `mysql_numfields` may also be used, but is deprecated.

mysql_num_rows

`mysql_num_rows(result_id)`

This function returns the number of rows in a MySQL result set (`result_id`). This method is not compatible with result sets created by `mysql_unbuffered_query`.

mysql_pconnect

`mysql_pconnect([hostname[:port|:/socket/path][, username[, password[, client_flags]]]])`

This function opens a persistent connection to a MySQL Server. It works the same as `mysql_connect`, except that the connection is not closed by `mysql_close` or at the end of the script. If a persistent connection is already found to exist with the specified parameters, then this is used, avoiding the creation of a new one.

mysql_ping

`mysql_ping([link_id])`

When a PHP script runs for a long time, it's possible that an open MySQL connection may be closed or disconnected at the server end. If you suspect this possibility, call this function before using the suspect connection to confirm that it is active, and to reconnect if the connection did indeed go down.

mysql_query

```
mysql_query(sql_query[, link_id])
```

This function executes the specified MySQL query (`sql_query`) on the currently selected database.

If the MySQL connection identifier (`link_id`) is not specified, PHP will use the currently active connection. If no such connection exists, PHP will attempt to open a connection by implicitly calling `mysql_connect` with default parameters.

If the query fails, an error message to that effect will be displayed unless "@" is added to the beginning of the function name, and the function will return `false` instead of a result identifier (which evaluates to `true`). If the error occurred due to an error in the SQL query, the error number and message can be obtained using `mysq_errno` and `mysql_error` respectively.

mysql_real_escape_string

```
mysql_real_escape_string(string[, link_id])
```

This function returns an escaped version of a `string` (with backslashes before special characters such as quotes) for use in a MySQL query. This function is a little more thorough than `addslashes` or PHP's Magic Quotes feature.

Unlike the now-deprecated `mysql_escape_string`, this function takes into account the character set of the current or specified MySQL connection when determining which characters need to be escaped.

mysql_result

```
mysql_result(result_id, row[, field])
```

This function returns the value of a particular field of the specified row (`row`) of the specified result set (`result_id`). The `field` argument may be the name of the field (either `fieldname` or `dbname.fieldname`), or its numerical position, where the first field in a row is at position 0. If field is not specified, then 0 is assumed.

mysql_select_db

mysql_select_db(*db_name*[, *link_id*])

This function selects the default database (db_name) for the current or specified (link_id) MySQL connection.

The function name mysql_selectdb may also be used, but is deprecated.

mysql_stat

This function returns a string describing the current status of the MySQL server. The string is identical in format to that produced by the mysqladmin utility:

```
Uptime: 28298  Threads: 1  Questions: 56894  Slow queries: 0
Opens: 16 Flush tables: 1  Open tables: 8 Queries per second avg:
36.846
```

mysql_tablename

mysql_tablename(*result_id*, *row_number*)

result_id should refer to a result set produced by a call to mysql_list_tables, and will retrieve the name of the table listed on the row specified by row_number. The first row in a result set is row 0.

mysql_thread_id

mysql_thread_id(*link_id*)

This function returns the ID of the server thread responsible for handling the current or specified connection.

mysql_unbuffered_query

mysql_unbuffered_query(*query*[, *link_id*[, *result_mode*]])

This function sends an SQL query to MySQL, without fetching or buffering the result rows automatically, as mysql_query and mysql_db_query do. This method has two advantages: PHP does not need to allocate a large memory buffer to store the entire result set, and you can begin to process the results as soon as PHP receives the first row, instead of having to wait for the full result set to be received.

The downside is that functions that require information about the full result set (such as `mysql_num_rows`) are not available for result sets produced by `mysql_unbuffered_query`, and you must use `mysql_fetch_*` functions to retrieve all of the rows in the result set before you can send another query using that MySQL connection.

Index

Symbols

!, negation operator, PHP, 65, 70

!=, inequality operator, PHP, 61

$

    (*see also* variables, PHP)

    prefix identifying PHP variables, 47

    use in regular expressions, 146

%

    modulus operator, MySQL, 302

    wild card for LIKE operator, 40

    wild card in hostnames, 172–173

&&, and operator, PHP, 58

&, query string variable separator, 52

()

    calling PHP functions, 47

    in regular expressions, 148

*

    in regular expressions, 147

    multiplication operator, PHP, 48

    wild card in myisamchk, 179

+

    addition operator, PHP, 47

    in regular expressions, 147

++, signifying increment by one, 60

.

    concatenation operator, PHP, 48

    in regular expressions, 148

    referring to the current directory, 248

.=, append operator, PHP, 127

/

    division operator, PHP, 48

    file path separator, 208

// and /* */, comment indicators, PHP, 48

;

    on the MySQL command prompt, 33

terminating PHP statements, 45

<, less than, PHP, 61

<=, less than or equal to, PHP, 61

<?php ?> code delimiters, 44, 63

=, assignment operator, PHP, 47

==, equality operator, PHP, 58

>(=), greater than (or equal to), PHP, 61

?

    in regular expressions, 147

    introducing a query string, 50

@, error suppression operator, PHP, 70, 202

\ (*see* backslashes)

\c, on the MySQL command prompt, 33

\n, line feed character, PHP, 124

\r, carriage return character, PHP, 125

\t, tab character, PHP, 125

^, in regular expressions, 146

| in regular expressions, 148

||, or operator, PHP, 58

A

absolute paths, include file location, 246

access control example, 265

    structured version, 270–271

    unstructured version, 266

access control, MySQL, 170

    anonymous user problem, 175

    further resource, 170

    tips, 174

    unrestricted access, 177

access privileges

    GRANT command and, 171

    level of application, 172

    REVOKE command and, 174

addition operator, PHP, 47

addslashes function, PHP, 115
   mysql_escape_string and, 335, 342
administration area security, 266
administration interface
   content management systems as, 101
   managing authors example, 107
administrator options example, 249
airline booking system example, 189
aliasing
   columns and tables, 189–192
   summary function results, 193
ALL privilege, GRANT command, 172
ALTER TABLE command, 86, 277–280
   adding indexes using, 185
   dropping columns, 89
ampersand, query string variable separator, 52
ANALYZE TABLE command, 280
and operator, PHP, 58
anonymous users, MySQL access control, 175
Apache Web server
   Apache 2.0 compatibility with PHP, 10, 18
   building by hand, 12
   built into Mac OS X, 20
   directory-specific include paths, 249
   installing PHP as a loadable module, 17
   root document folder, 27
   Windows PHP installation, 7, 9
append operator, PHP, 127
apxs program, 18
areas of rectangles, example calculation, 241
   using a custom function, 253
   using a return statement, 252
   using optional arguments, 261
arguments
   (see also parameters)
   calculate sum example, 262
   optional and unlimited, 261

arithmetic operators, 48
array function, PHP, 49, 134, 229
array_map function, PHP, 117
arrays, 48
   (see also variables, PHP)
   associative, 49, 74
   empty arrays, 134
   looping through elements, 134–136, 230, 263
   processing when submitted, 132
   split function and, 155
   submitting in a form, 130
   super-global arrays, 259
   use with checkboxes, 130
AS keyword, SELECT queries, 191
   use with summary functions, 193
assignment operator, PHP, 47
associative arrays, 49
   rows in result sets, 74
asterisk wild card in myisamchk, 179
authentication, access control example, 266
AUTO_INCREMENT columns, 35
   obtaining last assigned value, 133
automatic content submission, 162
automatic link adjustment, 231

B

backslashes
   avoiding in path notation, 3, 208, 246
   escaping special characters, 116, 147, 149–150
backups, MySQL
   importance of, 165
   inadequacy of standard file backups, 166
   update logs and incremental backups, 168
   using mysqldump, 167
BINARY attribute, MySQL, 322

binary data files, 199–220
  MySQL column types tabulated, 210
BLOB (Binary Large Object) column
    types, 208–209, 326
boldface text, 149, 152
bookmarking queries, 55
braces, use in custom functions, 254
brackets (*see* parentheses; square
    brackets)
browsers
  identification, with HT-
      TP_USER_AGENT, 214
  limits on cookies, 225
  views of PHP files, 27
bug database, PHP, 10
built-in functions, PHP, 46, 253, 331–
    344
  (*see also* custom functions)
  array function, 49
  array_map, 117
  define, 265
  get_magic_quotes_gpc, 117
  mysql_connect, 69
  number_format, 230
  str_ireplace, 154–155
  strlen, 212
  strpos, 214

C

cancelling a query, 33
caret, use in regular expressions, 146
carriage returns, platform-specific is-
    sues, 150
case-sensitivity
  eregi function and, 146
  eregi_replace function and, 149
  function names, 254
  in SQL queries, 36
  TEXT and BLOB column types, 209

categories
  assigning to CMS items with PHP,
    123
  database design and, 97
  managing with PHP, 117
CGI (Common Gateway Interface), 247
character column types, MySQL, 324–
    327
character entities, HTML, 112
characters, escaping (*see* special charac-
    ters)
checkboxes
  passing values to variables, 133
  selecting multiple categories, 130
checking and repairing files, 178
CMS (*see* content management systems)
.cnf files, 4
  (*see also* my.cnf file)
code archive, downloading, xiii
code delimiters, PHP, 44, 63
code maintainability (*see* structured
    programming)
column attributes, MySQL column
    tyes, 321
column types, MySQL
  binary data storage, 208–209
  character types, 324
  date/time types, 327
  ENUM, 163
  full listing, 321–329
  INT, 35
  numerical types, 322
  TEXT, 35
  TEXT vs. BLOB types, 209
columns, 30
  (*see also* fields)
  access privileges on, 173
  adding, 86
  renaming, using aliases, 189
  setting data types, 36
command line utilities, Linux, 13

command prompt, Windows, 5
commands, MySQL (*see* queries)
comments, PHP, 48
   structured code and, 237
Common Gateway Interface (CGI), 247
commonhttpd.conf file, 19
concatenation operators, 48
concurrent operations, locking tables,
   187
conditional structures, PHP (*see* control
   structures)
configuration files, creating update logs,
   169
connecting to MySQL, 69
   using global variables, 258
   using include files, 238, 240
   using include_once, 243
connection identifiers, 69
constants, 263
   access control example, 271
constraints
   checking, search engine example, 127
   foreign key constraints, 108
   NOT NULL constraints, 35
content formatting, 143
   index page, 159
content management system example
   adding authors, 110
   deleting authors, 107
   editing authors, 112
   formatting stage, 144
   index page, 102
   managing authors, 105
   managing categories, 117
   managing jokes, 123–141
   update semi-dynamic pages link, 203
content management systems, 101–142
content submission by visitors, 162
content-disposition header, HTTP,
   213–214
content-length header, HTTP, 212

content-type header, HTTP, 212
control flow functions, MySQL, 301
control structures, PHP, 56
   for loops, 61
   if-else statements, 56, 63
   looping through arrays, 135
   short-circuit evaluation, 208
   while loops, 59
cookies, 221–225
   browser-enforced limits, 225
   session alternative to, 226, 231
   setting and deleting, 223
copy function, 201, 208
copyright notices, 244
corrupted data recovery, 178, 180
COUNT function, MySQL, 39, 192,
   318
   omitting NULLs, 196
count function, PHP, 134, 230
   links to next page, 156
CREATE DATABASE command, 34,
   280
   alternative to mysql_create_db, 333
CREATE INDEX command, 185, 281
CREATE TABLE command, 35, 281
   binary file details, 209
   nondestructive alternative, 89
cron utility
   managing update logs, 169
   updating semi-dynamic pages, 203
CURDATE function, MySQL, 77
currency information display, 230
custom functions, 253–263
   accessing global variables, 258
   difference from include files, 257
   function libraries and, 255
   naming, 254
   optional and unlimited arguments,
     261
   unlimited arguments, 262
   variable scope, 257
custom markup languages, 149

D

data relationships (*see* relationships)
data types
   (*see also* column types, MySQL)
   PHP as a loosely-typed language, 47
database administration, 165–180
database design, 85–100
   delete anomalies, 87
   further resources on, 85
   relationships, 94
   update anomalies, 87
database servers, 29
database-driven Websites
   role of content management systems, 101
   role of scripting languages, 68
   semi-dynamic pages and performance, 199
databases, 29, 69
   (*see also* MySQL)
   adding items with PHP, 110
   binary data storage, 208
   creating, 34
   inserting data using PHP, 75
   listing available, 32
   management using a CMS, 101
   mysql and test databases, 33
   selection, in PHP, 70
   storing Website content in, 29, 67
   using, 34
date and time functions, MySQL, 309–315
   CURDATE function, 77, 314
   DATE_FORMAT symbols, 314
   interval types for date addition/subtraction, 312
   modes for week calculation, 310
date function, PHP, 46
date/time column types, MySQL, 327–329
default values, optional arguments, 261

define function, PHP, 265
delete anomalies, 87
DELETE command, 41, 283
   challenge exercise, 80
DELETE queries
   confirmation page, 109
   deleteauthor.php example, 109
   deletecat.php example, 119
   rows affected by, 41, 72
deleting items with PHP, 80, 107
DESCRIBE command, 36, 86, 284
directory listing in include paths, 247
directory-specific include paths, 249
DISTINCT keyword, 87
division operator, PHP, 48
"do nothing" WHERE clauses, 126
document root tracking, include files, 247
documentation and structured code, 237
dollar sign
   PHP variable prefix, 47
   use in regular expressions, 146
double equals sign, 58
DROP DATABASE command, 33, 285
DROP INDEX command, 285
DROP TABLE command, 37, 285
   recovering from unintentional, 168
drop-down lists and checkboxes, 130
duplication
   avoiding, by refreshing pages, 215
   avoiding, using DISTINCT, 87
   avoiding, using include files, 238
   avoiding, using structured programming, 236

E

echo statement, PHP, 45
   example, 46
   exit function compared to, 71
   parentheses and, 241

editing items with PHP, 112
else clause (*see* if-else statements)
empty arrays, 134
enctype attribute, form tag, 204
ENUM column type, 163, 326
equality operator, PHP, 58
equals sign, as PHP assignment operator, 47
ereg function, PHP, 146
ereg_replace function, PHP, 148, 150
  str_replace and, 153
eregi function, 146
eregi_replace function, 148, 150
  example using, 149
error checking
  include files and, 238
  using myisamchk, 179
error messages
  require statement and, 243
  simple join example, 92
error suppression operator, PHP, 70, 202
escaping special characters (*see* special characters)
exclamation mark, as PHP negation operator, 65
exit command, MySQL, 34
exit function, PHP, 70
  calling with a parameter, 71
  include file example, 238
expiry time, cookies, 223
EXPLAIN command, 285
explode function, PHP, 155

F
fclose function, 200, 202
fcopy function, 203
fields
  (*see also* columns)
  as database components, 30

inadvisability of multiple values, 94, 97
file extensions
  potential problems with Notepad, 3
  potential problems with Notepad and TextEdit, 26
  Windows .cnf files, 4
file sizes
  problems with large files, 220
  uploading files and, 206
files
  assigning unique names, 206
  downloading stored files, 213
  file access functions in PHP, 200
  storing in MySQL, 210
  uploading, 204–209
  viewing stored files, 212
flow of control (*see* control structures)
fopen function, 200, 202
for loops, 61
  argument sum example, 263
  creating tables, 230
  looping through arrays, 135
forced rows, 195
foreach loops, 136
  argument sum example, 263
foreign key constraints, 108
form tags and file uploads, 204
formatting content, 143
forms submission methods, 54
forward slash path separator, 3, 208, 246
fread function, 200, 202
front pages (*see* index pages)
func_get_arg function, 262
func_get_args function, 263
func_num_args function, 262
function calls used as conditions, 71
function keyword, PHP, 254
function libraries, PHP, 255
function scoped variables, 257

static variables and, 260
functions, MySQL
    COUNT function, 39, 192, 318
    LEFT function, 39
    listed by type, 301–319
functions, PHP
    (*see also* built-in functions)
    custom functions, 253–263
    parameters, 47
    return values, 69
    session management functions, 227
    working with MySQL, reference,
        331–344
fwrite function, 201, 203

G

global variables, 257–258
GRANT command, 171, 286
    examples of use, 173
"greedy" special characters, 153
GROUP BY clause, SELECT queries,
    193, 294
group-by functions (*see* summary func-
    tions)

H

HAVING clause, SELECT command,
    197, 294
header function, PHP, 212, 215
hidden form fields, 112
    MAX_FILE_SIZE, 206
.htaccess file
    protecting directories with, 102
    setting include paths, 249
HTML
    embedding in PHP output text, 45
    embedding PHP code in markup, 62
    forms, user interaction with, 53
    include files containing, 244
    PHP code conversion to, 44
    static pages from URL requests, 202

stripping out of content, 144
    tags, PHP code to match, 152
"HTML Safe" content, 144
htmlspecialchars function, PHP, 112,
    144
    authors.php example, 106
    search engine example, 125
HTTP headers
    cookie, 222
    header function and, 215
    sending file details, 212
    set-cookie, 222
HTTP methods (*see* variables, $_GET;
    variables, $_POST)
httpd.conf file, 11, 13, 19
hyperlinks within content, 150

I

ID columns, 30, 35
    (*see also* primary keys)
if statements, error handling, 70–71
if-else statements, 56
    alternative form, 63
IGNORE keyword, 136
IIS (Internet Information Services), 7–
    8, 27
importing global variables, 258
include files, 238–252, 255
    (*see also* function libraries)
    access control example, 270–271
    access to variables, 241
    containing HTML, 244
    custom functions, 271
    database connection example, 240
    difference from custom functions,
        257
    locating, 246
    naming, 240
    PHP statements usable with, 242
    return statement and, 251
    returning from includes, 249

include paths, 247
　directory-specific, 249
include statement, PHP, 241
　require statement and, 243
include_once statement, PHP, 243, 256
incrementing values by one, 60, 186
index pages
　as semi-dynamic pages, 200
　configuring as default pages, 9, 11,
　　19
indexes
　adding and removing, 185
　further resources on, 186
　regenerating after corruption, 180
　sorting and, 185
InnoDB tables, 108, 189
INSERT command, 286
　IGNORE keyword, 136
　REPLACE command compared to,
　　290
　TIMESTAMP columns and, 328
　two forms of, 37
INSERT function, MySQL, 307
INSERT queries, 77
　newauthor.php example, 110
　newcat.php example, 120
　rows affected by, 72
　storing uploaded files, 211
INT MySQL column type, 35, 322
INTO clause, SELECT queries, 293
is_uploaded_file function, 207, 211
isset function, 65
italic text, 149, 152

J

JavaScript and server-side languages,
　43
joins, 91–93, 295–296
　airline booking system example, 190
　inner joins, 295
　left joins, 194–197, 296

MySQL supported types, 295–296
natural joins, 296
outer joins, 296
self joins, 191

K

killing servers, 177

L

LEFT function, MySQL, 39, 306
left joins, 194–197
LIKE operator, SQL, 40, 127
LIMIT clause, SELECT queries, 186
line breaks as platform-specific issues,
　150
line feed character, PHP, 124
links within content, 150
Linux
　installation of MySQL, 14
　installation of MySQL and PHP, 12
　installation of PHP, 17
　Mac OS X similarity, 22
LOAD DATA INFILE command, 287
localhost access privileges, 174–176
location header, HTTP, 215
LOCK TABLES command, 188, 288
locking functions, MySQL, 317
login credentials, access control ex-
　ample, 266
lookup tables, 97
　queries using, 99
loops (*see* control structures)

M

Mac OS X
　installation, 20
　MySQL installation, 20
　PHP installation, 22
　TextEdit and .php files, 26
　treatment as Unix/Linux, 22
magic quotes feature, 115–117

mysql_escape_string and, 335, 342
  security and, 24
many-to-many relationships, 96
many-to-one relationships, 94
markup languages
  (*see also* HTML)
  custom markup languages, 149
mathematical functions, MySQL, 301–304
max_allowed_packet option,
  my.cnf/my.ini, 220
MAX_FILE_SIZE field, 206
MEDIUMTEXT and MEDIUMBLOB
  column types, 209
menu options, include file example, 249
method attribute, form tag, 54
MIME type checking, uploadable files, 205
modifying data (*see* UPDATE command)
multiplication operator, PHP, 48
multipurpose pages, 61
  delete confirmation prompt, 109
  deleting data, 80
  example, 62
  inserting data, 77
my.cnf file, 169
  Linux installation, 16
  max_allowed_packet option, 220
  Windows installation and, 2
my.ini file, 169
  max_allowed_packet option, 220
  renaming my.cnf as, 3
MyISAM table format, 108
myisamchk utility, 178
MySQL
  administration, 165–180
  as RDBMS, 1
  assigning a root password, 22
  backing up data, 166, 168

command-line client, mysql.exe, 31, 170
connecting to, from PHP, 69
  using global variables, 258
  using include files, 238, 240
  using include_once, 243
controlling access to, 170
data directory structure, 178
getting started with, 29–41
killing server process, 177
logging on to, 31
lost password recovery, 177
mysql and test databases, 33
password prompts, 23, 32
repairing corrupt data files, 178, 180
restoring backed up data, 167, 170
running automatically at start-up, 6, 15
syntax, 277–300
transaction support, 189
user names, 32
MySQL client programs, 25
MySQL column types (*see* column types, MySQL)
MySQL Control Center, 25
mysql database
  access control and, 170
  assigning root passwords, 23
  function in MySQL, 33
MySQL functions (*see* functions, MySQL)
MySQL installation
  in Linux, 14
  in Windows, 2
  on Mac OS X, 20
  post-installation setup, 22
  removing packaged versions, 13
  server versions, 4
  servers provided by Web hosts, 25
  as a system service, 6

MySQL queries (*see* queries, MySQL)
MySQL syntax, 277–300
mysql.exe program, 31
    restoring the database using, 170
mysql.server script, 16
mysql_* functions, PHP, listed, 331–344
mysql_affected_rows function, 72, 331
mysql_connect function, 69, 332
mysql_error function, 72, 334
mysql_fetch_array function, 73, 335
mysql_insert_id function, 133, 287, 339
mysql_install_db script, 14
mysql_num_rows function, 145, 341
mysql_query function, 71, 342
    insert queries, 77
    using result sets from, 72
mysql_select_db function, 70, 343
mysqld.exe file and server versions, 4
mysqld_safe script, 15
mysqldump utility, 167

N

naming conventions
    custom functions, 254
    include files, 240
negation operator, PHP, 65, 70
nested tags, 153
new line characters
    in PHP, 124
    platform-specific issues, 150
NOT NULL column constraint, 35, 163
not operator, PHP, 65
Notepad editor
    treatment of file extensions, 3, 26
NULL values and LEFT JOINs, 195
number_format function, PHP, 230
numerical column types, MySQL, 322–324

O

ON keyword, 195
one-to-many relationships, 94
one-to-one relationships, 94
OOP (object oriented programming), 235, 275
operators, PHP, 47–48
    append operator, 127
    comparative and inequality operators, 61
    equality and logical operators, 58
    error suppression operator, 70, 202
    negation operator, 65, 70
OPTIMIZE TABLE command, 289
optional arguments, PHP functions, 261
optional parameters, MySQL column types, 321
or operator, PHP, 58
ORDER BY clause, SELECT queries, 184, 294

P

packaged distributions, 12
    removing, 13
packet size, MySQL, 220
paging result sets, 155, 187
paragraph tags, custom markup language, 149
parameters
    (*see also* arguments)
    in PHP functions, 47, 254
    MySQL column types, 321
parentheses
    in PHP functions, 47, 254
    in PHP statements, 241
    in regular expressions, 148, 150
passwords
    changing, using GRANT, 173
    instructing MySQL to prompt for, 23, 32

MySQL root passwords, 22
page protection in access control example, 274
recovery from losing, 177
specifying using GRANT, 172
PEAR (PHP Extension and Application Repository), 248
perimeters of rectangles, calculation, 255
period
concatenation operator, PHP, 48
in regular expressions, 148
referring to the current directory, 248
Perl Compatible Regular Expressions (PCRE), 145, 153
personalized welcome messages, 51, 53
with special messages, 57
without query strings, 55
PHP
(see also functions, PHP; PHP installation)
as Web server plug-in, 1
basic syntax, 45
code delimiters, 44, 63
editors for .php files, 26
getting started with, 43–66
object oriented features, 235, 275
PHP 5 new features
object orientation, 275
str_ireplace function, 154–155
PHP Extension and Application Repository (PEAR), 248
PHP functions (see functions, PHP)
PHP installation
in Linux, 17
in Windows, 6
in Windows with Apache , 9
on Mac OS X, 22
PHP provided by Web hosts, 25
post-installation setup, 24

removing packaged versions, 13
with IIS, 8
php.exe file, 203
php.ini file
configuring PHP, 24
effects of disabling errors, 243
installing PHP in Windows, 7
php.ini-dist and, 19
post_max_size setting, 206
session setup, 226
setting include_path, 248
upload_max_filesize setting, 206
upload_tmp_dir setting, 205
php4apache(2).dll and php5apache(2).dll files, 11
php4apache2.dll file, 10
php4isapi.dll and php5isapi.dll files, 8
php4ts.dll and php5ts.dll files, 7
phpMyAdmin script, 31
pipe character, in regular expressions, 148
POSIX regular expressions, 145, 153
post_max_size setting, php.ini file, 206
primary keys, 98
product catalogue, shopping cart example, 229

Q

queries, MySQL, 34
advanced SQL, 183
cancelling, 33
case sensitivity, 36
depending on lookup tables, 99
search engine example, 128
semicolon terminator, 33
sending, using PHP, 71
query strings, 50
passing variables in, 62, 80, 250
question marks, introducing query strings, 50
quit command, MySQL, 34

quotes
    double, as PHP string delimiter, 48
    replacing with character entities, 112
    single, around PHP strings, 47
    single, around strings in PHP, 48
    single, escaping, 152

R
read locks, 188
readability of structured code, 237
rectangles
    calculate area example, 241
        using a custom function, 253
        using a return statement, 252
        using optional arguments, 261
    calculate perimeter example, 255
redirection to the same page, 215
referential integrity, 108
refreshing pages and duplicating ac-
        tions, 215
register_globals setting, 52
regular expressions, 145–162
    capturing matched text, 150
    matching hyperinks, 151
    matching paired tags, 152
    string replacement with, 148
    tutorial on, 146
    two forms of, 145
    validating MIME types, 205
relationships
    example, 88
    many-to-many relationships, 96
    preserving referential integrity, 108
    relationship types, 94
RENAME TABLE command, 289
REPLACE command, 290
require statement, PHP
    access control example, 271
    include statement and, 243
require_once statement, PHP, 243, 256

required columns (see NOT NULL)
restoring MySQL databases
    from mysqldump backups, 167
    using update logs, 170
result sets, 73
    paging, 155, 187
    processing order in MySQL, 197
    restricting the size of, 186, 197
    sorting, 183
return statement, PHP, 249, 251
return values, PHP functions, 69
REVOKE command, 174, 290
root document folder, 27
root passwords, 22
rows, 30
    affected by deetes and updates, 72
    counting, in MySQL, 39
    deleting, 41
    updating, 40

S
safe_mysqld script, 15
script timeouts, PHP, 220
scripting languages, role, 68
scripts, UNIX, for managing update
        logs, 169
search engine example, 123
security
    access control example, 266
    creating a special MySQL user in
        Linux, 14
    escaping special characters and, 117
    include file location and, 247
    MySQL root passwords, 22
    register_globals setting and, 52
    upload_max_filesize setting, 206
    using is_uploaded_file, 207
SELECT command, 38, 72, 291–297
    (see also SELECT queries)
    DISTINCT keyword, 87
    GROUP BY clause, 294

HAVING clause, 294
INTO clause, 293
LIKE operator, 40, 127
ORDER BY clause, 294
WHERE clauses, 39, 293
   "do nothing" WHERE clauses,
      126
select multiple tag, 131
SELECT queries
   aliases in, 191
   authors.php example, 106
   building dynamically with PHP, 126
   cats.php example, 118
   from multiple tables, 93
   grouping results, 192–194
   limiting number of results, 186, 197
   search engine example, 125
   sorting results, 183
   sub-selects, 283
   table joins and, 91
   using LEFT JOINs, 195
   using result sets from, 72
   with multiple tables, 90
self-closing tags, 53
semicolon
   PHP statement terminator, 45
semicolon, on the MySQL command
      prompt, 33
semi-dynamic pages, 199–204
server restarts
   update log flushing, 168
   with unrestricted access, 177
server-side languages, 43
   advantages, 45
session management functions, PHP,
      227
session_destroy function, PHP, 227
session_start function, PHP, 227, 230
sessions, 225–227
   shopping cart example, 228–234
SET command, 297
set_time_limit function, PHP, 220

setcookie function, PHP, 222–223
   position, 224
shopping cart example, 228–234
   buy link, 230
   product catalog, 229
   viewing link, 231
short-circuit evaluation, 208
SHOW DATABASES command, 32
SHOW queries, 298–299
SHOW TABLES command, 36
sorting result sets, 183
special characters, 112
   escaping single quotes, 152
   escaping, in regular expressions,
      147, 149, 151
   escaping, with addslashes, 116
   PHP codes, 125
split and spliti functions, PHP, 155
SQL
   advanced queries, 183
   MySQL and, 34
   MySQL command syntax, 277–300
SQL injection, 24
square brackets
   array indices, 49
   use in regular expressions, 147
SSIs (Server-Side Includes), 244
state preservation (see cookies)
statements, PHP, 45
static includes, 244
static or semi-dynamic pages, 200
static variables, 259
str_ireplace function, 154–155
str_replace function, PHP, 153
string functions, MySQL, 305–309
stripslashes function, PHP, 116
strlen function, PHP, 212
strpos function, PHP, 214
structured programming, 235–274
   access control example, 265, 270–
      271
   book about, 236

problems avoided by using, 236
Structured Query Language (*see* SQL)
sub-selects, 283
subtraction operator, PHP, 47
sum of arguments example, 262
summary functions, MySQL, 192, 318–319
super-global variables
    constants as, 265
    super-global arrays, 259

T

table formats, 108
table joins (*see* joins)
tables
    as database components, 30
    checking with myisamchk, 179
    counting number of entries, 39
    creating, 35
    deleting, 37
    deleting entries, 41
    inserting data, 37
    listing, 36
    locking, 188
    recovery after corruption, 178, 180
    relationships between (*see* relationships)
    renaming, using aliases, 189
    repairing damaged tables, 179
    separating data with, 87
    structural overview, 30
    temporary, 281
    updating entries, 40
    viewing entries, 38
Task Scheduler, Windows, 203
    managing update logs, 169
    updating semi-dynamic pages, 203
test database, in MySQL, 33
text formatting, 143, 155
    (*see also* paging result sets)

string replacement with regular expressions, 148
stripping out HTML, 144
TEXT MySQL column types, 326
    TEXT type, 35
TextEdit, problems with .php files, 26
time function, PHP
    constructing unique names, 207
    cookie expiry and, 223
time functions, MySQL (*see* date and time functions)
top ten jokes, using constants, 263
transactions, 189

U

underscore character, 242
unions, 297
unique file names, 206
UNIX
    (*see also* Linux)
    update log script, 169
unlimited arguments, 262
unlink function, 201, 203
UNLOCK TABLES command, 188, 288
unset function, PHP, 227, 233
UNSIGNED attribute, MySQL, 321
update anomalies, 87
UPDATE command, 40, 299
    TIMESTAMP columns and, 328
    WHERE clause, 41
update logs, 168
    managing, 169
UPDATE queries
    editauthor.php example, 112
    editcat.php example, 121
    rows affected by, 72, 299
upload_max_filesize setting, php.ini file, 206
upload_tmp_dir setting, php.ini file, 205

uploading files, 204–209
  unique file names, 206
urlencode function, 62
USAGE privilege, GRANT command, 172–173
USE command, 34, 300
user accounts, restricting access, 170
user interaction in PHP, 50
  prompting only once, 66
user names, MySQL, 32
user privileges
  granting, 171
  revoking, 174
users
  removing, 174
  specifying in GRANT commands, 172, 174
utility programs, MySQL, 167

V

variable interpolation, 48
variable scope, 257
  static variables, 259
variables, PHP, 47–48, 265
  (see also arrays; constants)
  $_COOKIE, 222
  $_FILES array, 204, 210
  $_GET and query strings, 51
  $_POST array, 55, 268
  $_REQUEST array, 56
  $_SERVER array, 65
    access control example, 271
    DOCUMENT_ROOT, 247
    HTTP_USER_AGENT, 214
    PHP_SELF, 215
  $_SESSION array, 227, 230–231, 233, 268
  $GLOBALS array, 259
  created outside include files, 252
  custom function declarations, 254
  embedding in text strings, 48

identifying as local, 242
include file access, 241–242
incrementing by one, 60
passing in query strings, 62
returning from include files, 251
super-global arrays, 259

W

Web servers
  (see also Apache Web server; IIS)
  restricting access to administration pages, 102
  supporting PHP, 6
Web-based management consoles, 26
welcome pages, personalizing, 50
WHERE clauses
  "do nothing" WHERE clauses, 126
  SELECT command, 39, 293
  simple joins, 91
  UPDATE command, 41
while loops, 59
  looping through arrays, 135
  processing result sets, 73
wild cards
  control problems from, 175
  for LIKE operator, 40
  in hostnames, 172–173
  myisamchk utility, 179
Windows
  MySQL installation, 2
  PHP installation, 6
Windows Task Scheduler, 169, 203
WITH GRANT OPTION clause, 172
write locks, 188

X

XHTML (Extensible HTML), 53

Z

ZEROFILL attribute, MySQL, 321

Books for Web Developers from SitePoint

Visit http://www.sitepoint.com/books/
for sample chapters or to order!

sitepoint

Build Your Own

Database Driven Website

Using PHP & MySQL

By Kevin Yank

A Practical Step-by-Step Guide

HTML Utopia:

Designing Without Tables

Using CSS

By Dan Shafer

A Practical Step-by-Step Guide

The PHP Anthology

Object Oriented PHP Solutions

Volume I

By Harry Fuecks

Practical Solutions to Common Problems

The PHP Anthology

Object Oriented PHP Solutions

Volume II

By Harry Fuecks

Practical Solutions to Common Problems

Build Your Own

ASP.NET Website

Using C# & VB.NET

By Zak Ruvalcaba

A Practical Step-by-Step Guide

Flash
MX 2004

The Flash Anthology

Cool Effects &
Practical ActionScript

By Steven Grosvenor

Practical Solutions to Common Problems

Kits for Web Professionals
from SitePoint

Available exclusively from
http://www.sitepoint.com/

The Web Design Business Kit

By Brendon Sinclair

Manual